HISTORY OF MODERN ORISSA

HISTORY OF MODERN ORISSA

(1936-2000)

Dr. Kartik Chandra Rout

ANMOL PUBLICATIONS PVT. LTD.
NEW DELHI - 110 002 (INDIA)

ANMOL PUBLICATIONS PVT. LTD.
4374/4B, Ansari Road, Daryaganj
New Delhi - 110 002
Ph.: 23261597, 23278000
Visit us at: www.anmolpublications.com

History of Modern Orissa (1936-2000)

First Published, 2004

ISBN 81-261-2006-1

PRINTED IN INDIA

Published by J.L. Kumar for Anmol Publications Pvt. Ltd., New Delhi - 110 002 and Printed at Mehra Offset Press, Delhi.

Dedicated
to
My Mother
Late Annapurna Rout
and Motherland - Orissa

Contents

PREFACE

It is a stupendous task to write down the atom of every details of all the events, personalities, institutions, culture, organisations, finance and administration of Orissa since the 1st April, 1936. Out of the widest diversity of events and facts, much care has been taken to sort out the guiding events and to present before you a graphic scenario of Orissa state.

Countless books on Orissa History have been written down by different foreign, Indian and Orissan authors. During the last quarter of 20th Century, many scholars have worked for their doctoral research on Orissa history and culture from different angles. Besides this, some edited books on Orissa History like "Sidelights on History and Culture of Orissa" (1978) edited by Dr. M.N. Das and "Comprehensive History and Culture of Orissa" (1998) edited by Dr. P.K. Misra and Dr. J.K. Samal, "Reference Orissa" edited by A.N. Tiwari and Dr. A.P. Padhi and others have thrown a flood light on the History and Culture of Orissa from the time immemorial in the last decade.

Many important events, facts and personalities have deliberately been omitted because it is increasingly difficult to accommodate all the events of long 64 years in a single volume. The economic history of Orissa is one of the chapters, which I have intentionally left out and the education too.

This book is not the product of strenuous research works but I have put my enormous energy, rapt attention and severe sincerity to articulate and assimilate the divergent events and facts of modern Orissa for last two years and I have tried my best to present before the innumerable anxious readers of the world about the glittering image and a comprehensive history of modern Orissa, which was in dire need from the last decade.

I have also sought help from the Orissa Review, Utkal Prasanga, District Gazetters of the Orissa Govt. publication, Reference Orissa by A.N. Tiwari and Dr. A.P. Padhi, Orissa (Oriya), and Odissa Rajanitira Gopan Katha (Oriya) by the eminent journalist Sri Basant Das to fill up some of the gaps during the preparation of the script. I express my deep gratitude to all of them.

I am just like a florist who has arranged the flowers of different colours into a spectrum of grand garland of modern Orissan History.

I beg excuse for the omission of facts and unintentional errors on the other hand, I am happy that I have unfolded the history of modern Orissa before the readers.

My daughter Miss Devayani, M.Sc., B.Ed. and Debalina B.E. have computerised some of the chapters of the entire book and especially Devayani took utmost care and pain to bring out the print outs, without which the work of the book would have been awfully delayed. Affectionately I thank them.

No less is the cooperation and inspiration of my wife Smt. Urmila Misra, Reader in English and my son, Sri Debasish Rout, M.Sc.(Ag.) towards the preparation of my script. I thank them.

I am also thankful to the dual brothers, Mr. Durga Prasad Panda and Mr. Kali Prasad Panda of Genius Computer Centre, Berhampur, who have immensely helped to bring out the prints of the chapters.

I express my deep sense of gratitude to Mr. J.L. Kumar, Managing Director and Mr. Kripal Joshi, Editor, Anmol Publications Pvt. Ltd., New Delhi for their unequivocal cooperation and readiness to bring out this book to the light.

Dr. Kartik Chandra Rout

1

Reminiscence of the Past

Orissa in the present form is situated between the 17°49″ N to 22°34" N latitude and 81° 29" E to 87° 29"E longitude in the middle eastern part of India.

Orissa as a full-fledged state of India is completed on 1st January, 1949 after the merger of Mayur Bhanj estate with Orissa. Although the Government of India reorganised all the states of India on the basis of regional languages in 1956, many of the oriya speaking territories of Midnapur, Bahadaguda, Sareikala, Kharsuan, Jagadalpur, Manjusa, Tekkali and Jalanthara were tagged with the West Bengal, Bihar, Madhya Pradesh and Andhra Pradesh. The Oriyas spend their lives there in the teeth of adversities of the local people and local Government.

Orissa is flanked by the Bay of (Kalinga Sagar) Bengal in the east; West Bengal and Bihar in the north; Madhya Pradesh in the west and Andhra Pradesh in the south.

The retrospective study of Orissa history reveals that Orissa was a peculiar mixture of the Aryans, Dravidians and the Tribal populations. So there is a diversion of population, behaviour, food habits, clothings and the way of life among the people of Orissa. During the mythological years of Mahabharat, the Kalinga Adhipati fought against the Pandavas in the Kurukshetra battles for eighteen days.

During the historical period, the Kalinga soldiers waged the bloodiest Kalinga war in 261 B.C. against the organised and well-equipped Magadhan soldiers of Ashok Maurya. The horrors and halocaust of Kalinga war were indescribable. One lakh of soldiers lay dead in the battlefield and one lakh and fifty thousand soldiers were taken as the captives. Kalinga was subdued with Magadha by Ashok. The invincible conqueror Ashok was turned into a Buddhist monk. The gospels of Buddhism guided Ashok throughout his reign in religion and administration. As H.G. Wells estimated Ashok "Ashok was the only military monarch on record who abandoned warfare after victory". Ahimsa or non-violence became the creed of his life—the essence of his Government and the guiding spirit of his administration. His life was a selfless dedication to the noble cause of the common welfare that had been singled out with a title—"Devanam Priyadarshi"—the beloved of Gods.

Kharavela, the scion of the Chedi dynasty, smashed the false vanity of the countless kings of India and spread the net of Kalinga imperialism from Mathura in the northern India down to Pithunda in the south—the citadel of the Tamil League. He ruled Kalinga for a brief period of 13 years only from the capital—Kalinga Nagar between the Khandagiri Hills and Tosali. During this short span of administration, Kharavela proved himself as the greatest conqueror of ancient India—a successful administrator and a great patron of Jainism. The Hathigumpha Inscriptions bear the living testimony of his spectacular achievements. The Hathigumpha, Ranigumpha, Baghagumpha and Ganeshgumpha were the rare specimen of the ancient Kalinga architecture. Kharavela laid the foundation of the ancient Kalinga culture.

During the military campaign of 12 Kingdoms of the South India, the valiant soldiers of Kosala, Mahendragiri, Mantraraja of Korala (Sonepur district), Swamidutta of Kottura (Mahendragiri of Ganjam) fought against the Gupta soldiers of Samudragupta. Although Samudragupta overran all the twelve Kingdoms with the ferocity of a strong imperialist and inflicted a crushing defeat, he did not like to annex them with the Gupta Empire.

In 643 AD Harshavardhana, the king of the Pushyabhuti dynasty of Thaneswar led his military expedition upto Kangada or Ganjam—the Southern part of present Orissa and annexed it with his empire. The Ganjam plate inscriptions testified to the annexation of Kangada territory with Thaneswar. Harshavardhana held a Mahajana Conference in Orissa where a number of Buddhist scholars from Nalanda had participated.

Through the Corridor of Time in the early medieval period of Orissa during the glorious reign of the Keshari Kings and Ganga kings (9th century to 13th century) had presented a panorama of artistic elegance and beauty in the body of the countless temples in Orissa. Bhubaneswar, Konark and Puri—the triangular shape of territorial zone were dotted with the innumerable beautiful temples of the Sun-God, Siva, Vishnu and Lakshmi etc. The Lingaraj Temple, Mukteswar temple, Rajarani Temple, Jagannath Temple, the Konark Temple are the imperishable—undying specimen of the Kalinga architecture and sculpture. The iconography of Konark temple is so exquisitely elegant and attractive that the British lover of Art Mr. Farguesson commented, "One must visit Konark in his lifetime at least once and he can go by aeroplane or by a vehicle — if not he should visit Konark by a bullock-cart, but he must visit it". The chiseled and finest art engraved in the rock pieces of the body of the temples mesmerised the tourists and artists.

It was the golden period of the Kalinga sculpture.

But the longest reign of the Suryavamsi—Gajapati Kings of Kapilendra Deva (1435-1468), Purasottam Deva (1468-1497) and Prataprudra Deva (1497-1538) presented the climax of the undaunted valour of the Kalinga soldiers. Kapilendra

Deva by his imperial army overran Bengal, Raj Mahendry, Vijaynagar, Bahamani Kingdoms and Belama and established his hegemony. Raja Purusottam Deva also defeated Saluva Narsingh of Kanchi and brought his beloved daughter, Padmavati to Puri. May it be a legend or mythological truth, that Lord Jagannath and Balabhadra sided with Purusottam to defeat Saluva Narasingh in the battlefield. Purusottam Deva ordered the minister to get married Padmavati with a sweeper. But the minister took Padmavati to his residence and kept her till the next Car festival. On the auspicious day of Car festival, when the king Purusottam Deva began to sweep the chariots, the minister was present with Padmavati and requested the His Majesty to accept Padmavati as his wife because the King was now a sweeper. Raja Purusottam Deva was struck with wonder and appreciated the wit of the minister. He ultimately accepted Padmavati as his queen.

Prataprudra Deva defeated the soldiers of Bengal and occupied it. He also annexed Simanchalam with his empire. But he was defeated by Krishnadeva Ray of Vijaynagar empire and lost most of his territories in the south including the Kondavidu fort.

The boundary of the Kalinga empire during this period was extended from Bengal to the river Krishna and Kondavidu fort of the south—a vast and gigantic empire the India has never seen in the past.

All this military expeditions evinced the truth that the Oriyas were a historic race—a race of the valiant warriors.

The disintegration of the Gajapati Kingdom of Orissa rapidly started after the death of Prataprudra Deva in 1538. There was a series of regicide one after another. Govind Vidyadhar murdered the two sons of Prataprudra Deva. After the death of Govind Vidyadhar, his son Chakrapratap became the king of Orissa who too was murdered by his son, Narasingh Jena. Narasingh Jena was murdered by Mukunda

Harichandan—the Governor of Cuttack and installed the son of Raghuram Jena—the youngest son of Narsingh Jena. After some months, Mukunda Harichandan killed Raghuram Jena and himself became the King in 1558. Within a period of 18 years several political murders of the Kings were accomplished for throne and the powers. This period was the darkest period in the entire history of Orissa.

Mukunda Deva out of fear made alliance with Akbar—which made Sulaiman Kirrani—the Governor of Bengal, hostile to Mukunda Deva. When Sulaiman Kirrani invaded Orissa in 1567. Simultaneously the Sarangaraja Rama Chandra Bhanja also declared war on Mukunda Deva. Mukunda Deva made friendship with Sulaiman Kirrani and advanced with army to punish Rama Chandra Bhanja. A battle was fought between Mukunda Deva and Rama Chandra Bhanja in 1568 at Gohiratikiri where Mukunda Deva was killed.

The Bengal General Kala Pahad invaded Orissa in 1568 and marched up to Puri. Kala Pahad himself was known as Kalachand Roy—working as the General of Sulaiman Kirrani—the Governor of Bengal. He fell in love with the daughter of Kirrani and got married. There after he became a converted muslim. But repentance came who wanted to come back to Hinduism. For this he came to Puri to convert himself again to Hinduism—but the orthodox pandas of Puri Jagannath temple refused him to accept as Hindu. Kala Pahad became a renegade and destroyed many valuable temples and deities of Bhubaneswar, Puri and Jajpur. The conservative Hindu society excommunicated him. As a result he started vandalism in Orissa.

The Afghans occupied Cuttack in 1568 and ruled up to 1592. Raja Akbar despatched a military contigent under Mansingh to punish Daud—the son of Sulaiman Kirrani who took shelter in Cuttack. Raja Mansingh defeated Daud and the Afghans of Orissa and annexed Orissa with the Mughal Empire in 1592. Raja Todar Mal assessed the land revenue of

Orissa and 1/3rd was collected as the land revenue from the people of Orissa.

Akbar died in 1605. During Jahangir's reign. Hakim Khan was appointed as the Governor of Orissa in 1606. Hakim Khan was an anti-Hindu Governor who interfered in the affairs of Lord Jagannath. Kesho Das, the Rajput General got hold of Puri temple. The ruling chief of Khurda, Purusottam fought with Kesho Das but was defeated. Purusottam was forced to offer his daughter in marriage to Jahangir and his sister to Kesho Das with heavy dowry. Purusottam was also obliged to pay tributes to Jahangir.

The Mughal Governors, Raja Kalyan Malla (1611), Mukaram Khan (1617) and Hussain Ali Khan (1620) have exploited and tortured the King and people of Orissa. They destroyed many Hindu temples of Orissa. Raja Purusottam died in 1621 at Karnat village near Banapur.

The condition of Orissa became miserable during the reign of Shah Jahan and Aurangzeb. Shah Jahan's Governor Md. Baker Khan imprisoned many Zamindars of Orissa and tortured them. Once due to his carelessness, 700 Zamindars were killed. The reign of Shah Jahan opened the gates of trade and commerce to the British traders in Orissa. He permitted the British traders to establish different factories in Hariharpur (1633) in the delta of Suvarnarekha (1634) and in Balasore (1642).

In a terrific fratricidal war among the four brothers of Aurangzeb, Aurangzeb was treacherously successful. He eliminated all his brothers—Dara Shuko, Murad and Shuja and ascended the throne of Delhi in 1658. Shah Jahan was detained in the Agra fort as a prisoner.

The governors of Aurangzeb also exploited the people. Aurangzeb ordered the subedar and the Mughal soldiers to destroy the Hindu Temples of Orissa and to build Mosques.

In 1692, Aurangzeb ordered to demolish the Jagannath temple of Puri—but the order was not carried out.

Aurangzeb died in 1707. But his Governors began to rule as an independent rulers of different subas. The history of Orissa from 1707 to 1751 was a period of absolute chaos and confusion. Taking the advantage of weak position of the subedar of Bengal, Ali Vardhi Khan, the Marathas who have already established their supremacy in Bihar and Bengal invaded Orissa. Ali Vardhi Khan ceded Orissa to Raghuji Bhonsle—the King of Nagpur. Thus the Maratha rule was established in Orissa in 1751.

The controversy centered round the nature of the Maratha administration in Orissa. The British Historian—Andrew Sterling expressed his opinion that the Maratha administration in Orissa was fatal to the welfare of the people. Their rule was marked by the anarchy, weakness and violence. It was a type of tyrannical rule in Orissa. The Marathas collected taxes by force from the Zamindars and people.

Historian like Dr. B.C. Roy who has worked abundantly on Maratha rule in Orissa, has commented that the Maratha rule in Orissa was beneficial and peaceful. The Marathas could not be able to give a strong financial footing to Orissa because of the monopolistic economic policy and non-co-operation of the British as a neighbouring ruler.

Orissa during the Maratha rule was divided into two zones—Moghol Bandi consisting the territories lying between the river Suvarnarekha to Chilika and others were feudatory areas. Governors like Mirza Shale (1752-1759), Sheo Bhatt (1759-1764), Bhavani Pandit(1764-1768), Shambhuji Ganesh (1768-1770), Madhaji Hari (1773-1777), Raja Ram Pandit (1778-1793) and Sadasiv Rao (1793-1803) ruled Orissa from Cuttack as Headquarters.

In 1765, the East India Company got the Dewani of Bengal, Bihar and Orissa from the Mughol Emperor, Shah

Alam—but the British could not take over Orissa by force till 1803.

The Marathas used to collect the taxes from the Zamindars and people by coercion. There was no leniency in tax collection. They were also collecting taxes from the pilgrims who came to visit the Jagannath temple at Puri. They also collected exorbitant taxes on the exported salt to outside Orissa.

On the other hand the Marathas have rendered some beneficial works during their rule. In order to save the people from the recurrence of flood, they have built some strong embankments on the strategic places of rivers. They have advanced the taqabi loans to the needy farmers for cultivation and they have freed the people from collecting any loan and land tax who were severely affected by the flood or famine.

By nationality and instinct the Marathas were also Hindus. So they did not interfere in the administration of Jagannath temple. They paid utmost respect and devotion to the Hindu gods and goddesses and their temples.

The Marathas also did not allow the British to monopolise the salt trade in Orissa—as a result of which salt was available in plenty.

Thus we find a mixed feeling of good and bad of the Maratha administration in Orissa.

In October 1803, the British made a triangular attack upon the Maratha soldiers in Orissa. They overpowered the Maratha soldiers and occupied Barabati fort on 14th October 1803.

The British had set their foot in Orissa on 14th October in 1803 after a glorious victory against the Marathas in Barabati fort. They put an end to the Maratha rule of 52 years (1751-1803) in Orissa. The British did not rule Orissa according to the promulgated provisions of the Permanent Settlement of Lord Cornwallis nor did they look Orissa with leniency.

They could have united Ganjam, Koraput and agency areas with Mogholbandi and Sambalpur and would have ruled Orissa as a separate administrative unit or could have tagged entire Orissa (Ganjam, Koraput, Phulbani, Cuttack, Puri, Balasore and Sambalpur) with Bengal Presidency or Madras Presidency. But instead of doing neither, they vivisected Orissa into several fragmented territories and tagged separately with different Presidencies of Bengal, Central Provinces and Madras Presidencies. This administrative divisions had sub-divided the Oriya culture into several fragments.

After the occupation of Orissa in 1803, the British made Puri as their Head quarters. But as it was not equi-distance from all fragments, they shifted the capital from Puri to Cuttack in 1816 and ruled Orissa. Although Lord Wellesley directed the British military officers Lt. Col. Harcourt, Mr. Melville and Major Fletcher not to intervene in the affairs of Lord Jagannath and the Zamindars during the conquest of Orissa but they brought disaster upon the Zamindars, Paikas and the ryots after their occupation. They did not deal the problems of the Oriya people with sympathy or understanding, which ultimately flared into Paika Rebellion in 1817.

Paika Rebellion

The Paika Rebellion was an outstanding event in the early history of the British occupation of Orissa. We can term it as the First War of Indian Independence in a limited sense because many of the causes of the national movement are identical with causes of the Paik Rebellion of 1817. Orissa was the last territory in India which was subdued by force and Orissa was the first country to counteract the evil forces of injustice, exploitation, tyranny and oppression of the British Government. So the Paika Rebellion set an unparalleled example of the resistance movement to other suppressed Indians. Paika Rebellion was the pioneer movement in the entire annals of British Indian history—the forerunner of the Freedom movement in India.

Many factors had facilitated the Paika Rebellion in 1817.

The British officers did not introduce any provision of the Permanent Settlement of Lord Cornwallis who had fixed up the settlement at least for a period of 10 years. But they made temporary settlement every one-year or at best in two years. During this period from 1803 to 1817, the Government had done seven times the different settlements for which the Zamindars and the ryots faced a lot of difficulties. There was also an increase of land revenue due to temporary settlements. The assessment of land revenue was not done scientifically—rather the rate of tax was fixed at random by the Bengali Assessors. And whenever the Oriya Zamindars could not pay the revenue in Calcutta on prescribed day before the "sun set" the ownership of land is gone and the land of Orissa would be publicly auctioned in Calcutta and the big Bengali Zamindars of Calcutta would take the bid by paying the minimum to the Government. Thus many Oriya Zamindars were impoverished by the "sun set laws", and "absentee land lordism." They lost all their land the Zamindars of Bengal became the lords of Orissa land.

The British officers showed unusual sympathy to the Bengalis and hated the Oriyas. In 1817, the Commissioner of Orissa commented "The Oriyas were stupid and are inferior in knowledge to their Bengali counterparts". As the educated Bengalis helped and guided the British in their administration, the British officers reposed utmost faith and confidence in them.

The British officers enhanced exorbitantly the price of salt. The people of Orissa got the difficulty in getting it in spite of the increased price. They hijacked the price of salt from 25 paisa per 1 mound to Rs. 3.25 paisa. They made the monopoly of salt trade in Orissa.

Major Fletcher revived the land assessment in 1805 in accordance to which he deprived the Paikas of the rent-free hereditary revenue which they had been enjoying it as the soldiers much before. But the British government made the Paikas "beggars". They lost their jobs and their rent-free land was confiscated by the government for which they were reduced to the position of wage-earners having no stock of land or anything of their property. The peasants too were subjected to uncouth oppression at the hands of the corrupt tax collectors and police.

The general economic condition of the Paikas and Peasants of Khurda in 1817 was one of "extreme desperate wretchedness". They were obliged to live on herbs and water. Out of frustration, nearly 5000 to 6000 ryots have left Khurda for some other areas.

Mr. Trower, the Collector of Cuttack stated, "A system of extreme tyranny, violence and oppression has existed which has proved ruinous to the once flourishing Country".

The inhuman execution of Jai Rajguru in the grove of Medinipur in Bengal in 1804 also added fuel to the fire.

Buxi Jagabandhu Bidyadhar Mahapatro Bhramarabar Roy or the Buxi of the Raja of Khurda was also deprived of his. legitimate ownership of land of Rahang, Lembai, Sarai, Chabikud and Radhanga. Buxi had paid the land revenue and obtained the money receipts from the Tahasil office of Khurda—but the corrupt and dishonest Bengali Amalas have not deposited the amount in treasury. The main conspirator behind this was a Bengali—Sri Krishna Chandra Singh. When Buxi complained—it was found that the entire amount paid by Buxi was misappropriated in 1807-1808. Buxi was denied of his right on land because he has not paid the land revenue. Instead of punishing the corrupt Amalas, Buxi was punished. He became a pauper. He did not like to file a case against the government rather decided to raise a mammoth revolt against the injustice and exploitation of the British government. Thus the Paika Rebellion was launched on 1st April 1817 and Buxi

Jagabandhu became the undisputed leader.

The rebels tried to overthrow the British establishment from Khurda and then they were to go to Puri. So they invaded the Police station, treasury, Government buildings and attacked upon the British officers of Khurda.

The spirit of the Rebellion was further intensified when 400 Kandha Chauras of Ghumusar arrived Khurda. They pulled down many Government buildings, burnt them in Khurda and Puri- looted the treasuries. The rebels killed Sarbarakar Charan Patnaik—the traitor who hatched conspiracy against Buxi.

The Rebellion spread to Kunjanga, Pattamundai, Asureswar, Tiran, Rupsa, Astaranga, Banakud, Hariharpur, Gop, Pipli, Nimapada and Talapada.

The top leaders of the Paika Rebellion were Buxi Jagabandhu, Bamadev Pattajoshi, Narayan Paramguru, Pitabash Mangaraj, Madhusudan Sendha, Padmanav Chhotroy, Pinaki Bahubalendra, Birendra Patnaik, Loka Paika, Nath Pradhan and Madhu Bisoyi. Almost 268 persons were imprisoned.

Mr. Le Fevre, Major Hamilton, Captain Willington and Captain Kennel suppressed the rebellion by iron hand.

When the attempt to further continue the rebellion was foiled, the rebels gradually surrendered to the British except Buxi Jagabandhu. He hid himself and moved from pillar to the post in disguise. The British government declared a general amensty to Buxi if he would surrender. He ultimately surrendered to the British on 27th May 1825 and was kept under house arrest at Cuttack (the name of the place was known as Buxi Bazar). He was given a pension of Rs. 1200/- per year. Four years after his painful stay, he died on 24th January 1829.

Gopal Chhotrai, Vishnu Paikroy, Rama Singh, Nath Pradhan, Sachidananda Patnaik and Raghuram Nayak were sentenced to be hanged.

Thus one of the great movements against the British colonialism in India was subsided. But it opened the eyes of the freedom-loving people of India who gathered inspiration from this event to launch the subsequent movements against the British.

SEPOY MUTINY

After a long period of their colonial rule in India, the British Government faced another revolt in 1857 which is termed as the " Sepoy Mutiny of 1857". Though the mutiny flickered in a section of the Indian Sepoy in the barrack of Calcutta, it spread like a wildfire to other parts of India because many other causes like the Doctrine of lapse and the economic exploitation of the East India Company were involved in it. Two eminent heroes of Orissa—Surendra Sai and Chakhi Khuntia figured more prominently in the 1857 revolt against the British. Dora Bishoyi and Chakra Bishoyi of Bhanjanagar (Russell Konda) also rebelled against the British for social and economic justice.

The Sepoy Mutiny of 1857 was a turning point in the history of administration in India. The Mutiny was put down by an iron hand of the British Government. All the veteran leaders like Rani Lakshmi Bai of Jhansi, Tantia Tope, Nana Sahib, Kuanar Singh Chandan Hajuri, Surendra Sai were either killed or died. Several rebel leaders were imprisoned. The mutiny was a disastrous failure. But it opened the eyes of the British to the outstanding problems—the Indians were facing everyday in their life.

The mutiny put an end to the ignominious rule of the East India Company and inaugurated a new era of imperial rule of the Queen Victoria. The powers were transferred from East India Company to the British Queen and the Parliament. The designation of Governor General since 1772 was discontinued and Viceroys were appointed in their place. Lord Canning became the first Viceroy of India in 1857. The viceroys who ruled India from 1857 to 1947 were of different temperament and of different nature. They devised and applied their policies keeping in view of the prevailing circumstances of India and its people. Lord Ripon, under his Viceroyalty from 1880 to 1884 rendered immense services to the people in different fields of Local Self Govt.—law and justice, journalism and census of Indian population. He elevated the position of the Indians in all respects for which he was criticized and recalled to England.

But in general the British established a purely colonial administration in India and squeezed fabulous wealth from India. The history of British rule in India is the story of the uncouth economic exploitation of the Indians. On the issue of the continuous drain of fabulous wealth of India to England Mr. Montgomery Martin said in 1838, "That for half a century we have gone on draining from two or three and sometimes four million pound sterling a year from India, which has been remitted to Great Britain to meet the deficiencies of commercial speculation, to pay the interest of debts, support the home establishment and to invest on England's soil the accumulated wealth of those whose lives have been spent in Hindustan. I do not think it possible for human ingenuity to avert entirely the evil effects of a continued drain of three or four million pounds a year from a distant country like India and which is never returned to it in any shape.

Keeping aside the general administrative setbacks, the British Govt. had rendered colossal loss and inconvenience to the people of Orissa. For their administrative suitability, they vivisected Orissa into several territorial fragments and tagged them with different cultural units—Cuttack, Puri and Balasore were tied with the Bengal presidency. The district of Sambalpur was kept under the Central Provinces Administration, Ganjam, Phulbani and Koraput were placed under the control of the Madras Presidency. The 26 feudatory states were ruled by their respective kings and a British Political Agent supervised their nature of administration. The Oriya language was butchered by the British Govt. because the Persian language and the Bengali, Hindi, Telugu and Tamil languages were prevalent in all the fragmented Orissa territories. Not only the official transaction were made in Bengali, English, Hindi, Telugu and Tamil, but these languages were forceably imposed upon the Oriyas. There was a deliberate attempt to obliterate the Oriya language and culture in Orissa by the non-Oriya bureaucrats and the English. There was a naked invasion upon the Oriya language by an unworthy Bengali Teacher, Kanti Chandra Bhattacharya in 1878 of Balasore Zilla School, who commented that Oriya is not an independent separate language but it is a dialect of Bengali language. " This statement strained the Oriya-Bengali relations, idiot Bengali teacher was ignorant of development of Oriya literature through centuries. The Panchasakha of 15th century A.D, the writings of Dhananjay Bhanja, Upendra Bhanja, Kabisurya Baladev Rath, Fakir Mohan Senapati, Krishna Singh have already enriched the Oriya literature. Devoid of any knowledge about Oriya literature, this statement was unsound and was the sign of deliberate mischief of Kanti Chandra.

THE ORIYA MOVEMENT

The suffering of the Oriyas in different Presidencies was limitless and unbearable. So an organized attempt was made by some educated Oriyas—like Madhusudan Das, Brajasundar Das, Fakir Mohan Senapati, Madhusudan Rao, Nilamani Vidyaratna to safeguard the Oriya language. So the process of Orissa unification was first rooted in the language agitation in 1882 by Utkal Sabha. Petitions, applications and memorandums were profusely written to the Lt. Governors of Bengal, Madras and C.P. presidencies to pay proper position to Oriya language. Fakir Mohan Senapati, Madhusudan Rao and Radhanath Roy devoted their pens to the writing of countless Oriya Textbooks, Poems, Stories, Maths, Grammars and flooded the Oriya markets. The activities for the Orissa unification were hightened by an organized Utkal Union Conference of 1903. Unless the Oriyas of all fragmented territories of different Presidencies were solemnly united, there would be no hope for Orissa unification. So awareness of Oriya unity was created by organizing the annual meetings of the Utkal Union Conference at Berhampur, Paralakhemundi, Cuttack, Puri, Sambalpur.

The idea of Orissa unification was first rooted in the mind Sri Harihar Mardaraj—the king of Khallikote Estate. So he invited all the Oriya elites to the Rambha palace for a get-together to discuss informally the outstanding problems—the Oriyas were facing in different territorial fragments on 9th January 1902. The invitees who participated in the meeting were Madhusudan Das, Radhanath Roy, Fakir Mohan Senapati, Parasuram Patra, Gadadhar Bidyabhusan, Sadasiva Bidyaratna, Balaram Maharana and Maharaja Sri Ramachandra Bhanj of Mayurbhanj. All the members discussed the problems of Orissa—the education, Oriya language and administration. All the members also unanimously accepted the proposal for a next meeting to be held at Berhampur.

On 11th and 12th April 1903, the meeting was held at Berhampur — Shyam Sundar Rajguru of Paralekhemundi and the first Oriya Graduate of Ganjam district presided over the meeting. The important participants were—Madhusudan Das, Biswanath Kar, Nanda Kishore Bal, Fakir Mohan Senapati, Gopal chandra Praharaj, William Mohanty, Daniel Mohanty, A.P. Patro and Sribastsa Panda. This meeting was named as the "Ganjam National Conference" and later on in October 1903, it was changed into Utkal Union Conference.

The Inaugural function of the Conference was celebrated at Cuttack on 30th December 1903—Maharaja Sri Rama Chandra Bhanj of Mayurbhanj presided over the meeting and Madhusudan Das was the Secretary. This meeting was unique in the sense that the Ruling Chiefs of 30 feudatory and small principalities of Orissa have participated—the eminent Govt. officers and Commissioner of Orissa Division, Mr. K.G. Gupta. Delegates from all districts of Midnapur, Central Provinces, Andhra and Madras have participated. The delegates wore a special headgear of maroon colour on the head.

It is a long way for the Utkal Union Conference to travel since that day to 1920 when Gopabandhu Das on 31st December 1920 merged the Conference with the Indian National Congress. But the protagonists of the left out Conference continued to strive for the unification of Orissa. Madhusudan Das and Sri Krishna Chandra Gajapati single handedly pioneered the movement. They presented the memorandum and expressed the opinion of the Orissa people to Phillip-Duff Committee in 1924 and to the Simon Commission in 1928. The process of the movement for Orissa unification was on unabatedly.

The Phillip-Duff Committee after seeking the consensus of the people of Ganjam, Koraput and Phulbani submitted their report in favour of the annexation of Ganjam, Koraput and Phulbani with Orissa but the British Govt. turned down the report.

In 1931 January, Maharaja of Paralakhemundi went to London with the Raja of Khallikote, Rama Chandra Mardaraj, Lingaraj Panigrahy, Bhubanananda Das and Shyam Sundar Gantayat to participate in the 2nd Round Table Conference held during 1931. There he convincingly argued the case of Orissa unification in his brilliant speech. They met Sir Samuel Hoare—the Secretary of State for India.

It was the most successful participation of the Maharaja. The British Govt. there after appointed the O' Donnel Committee in 1931 with the other two members— H.M. Mehta of Maharashtra and T. Phokan of Assam to fix up the boundary of Orissa Province. Mr. O'Donnell was very much against the annexation of Ganjam and Koraput with the Orissa but the other two members favoured the annexation. The then Collector of Ganjam — Dixon in 1931 and Mr. Yeats— Census Superintendent of Madras were also opposed to this proposal. The report which was submitted ultimately to the British Govt. was twisted by O'Donnel. He recommended the annexation of all the territories of South Orissa except the two estates of Jeypore and Paralakhemundi. Again it was a travesty of truth. The man who has been fighting for unification since 1914 was excluded. But the Maharaja was not disappointed. He could understand the diplomacy of the British Officers. Once again he rushed to meet the in-charge Viceroy of Bengal. He explained all the details of his efforts in Orissa and England for unification. He left no stone unturned. Again he went to London to meet the Officers of the British Government and the M.Ps.

After his return he heard that a selection committee has been appointed by the British Govt. and Mr. Linlithgow was the Chairman. Mr. Linlithgow ultimately submitted the final report favouring the annexation of Jeypore and Paralakhemundi with Orissa.

The Indian National Congress did not manifest the minimum concern or interest for the Orissa unification. After the merger of Utkal Union Conference with Indian National Congress, Gopabandhu Das also did not take any concrete steps for unification. He died on 17th June 1928.

Under Sir John Austin Hubback—a committee was formed with other members. They were Madhusudan Das, Laxmidhar Mohanty, BNC Dhira Navendra, N.R Naidu, W.O. Newsam,

Nilamani Senapati, Loknath Misra and Gaur Chandra Dev, V. Ramaswamy was the Secretary of this committee.

This committee examined different feasibilities of the boundaries of the districts, their head quarters, the State Capital, High Çourt and University and finally submitted their recommendations on 20th December 1933. Cuttack as the Provincial Head quarters and for a High Court but no University. It was an irony that no member of the Administrative Committee urgently felt the necessity of a University in Orissa for higher education. Instead of November 27 1943 Orissa could have got the University at least 7 years before. Due to poverty, many Oriya students could not pursue their higher studies in Patna, Calcutta or Madras.

However, after a long period of strenuous struggle for 54 years (1882-1936), Orissa became a separate state on 1st April 1936. A draft order for creating Orissa as a separate Province was passed in the British Parliament on 21st January, 1936. The King Edward VIII, ultimately issued an order on 3rd March, 1936 to this effect. A new Province of Orissa was created on 1st April 1936 and the Home Department appointed Sir John Austin Hubback as the first Governor of new Orissa. Mr. Hubback took oath in presence of Sir Courtney Terrel—the Chief Justice of Bihar and Orissa High Court at the colourful inaugural function, which was held in the Ravenshaw College Hall at Cuttack.

On this occasion, the message sent by the King of England—Edward VIII was read out.

"The long cherished and natural desire of the Oriya people to be united after centuries of dependence upon other administration is thus fulfilled. It is my hope and expectation that the new Province will draw inspiration from the past and will prove worthy of the historic tradition of the land of Orissa".

But Madhu Babu passed away on 4-2-1934. He could not see his cherished dream of Orissa as a separate Province. Orissa became a separate administrative unit from Bihar (1912-1936) after 24 years with an area of 32693 sq. miles and a population of 8043681. It enjoyed some amount of autonomy and the right to elect their representatives according to the provisions of the Government of India Act of 1935.

2

Freedom Movement in Orissa

The Oriyas never seriously thought of Indian independence till 1920. They fought seriously for the unification of Orissa and safeguarded the Oriya language. So the history of the activities of Indian National Congress in Orissa from 1885 to 1920 was simply blank. Madhubabu, Gourishankar Roy, Hari Ballav Ghose, Janakinath Bose of Cuttack and Baikunth Nath Dey of Balasore and many other delegates attended the different annual sessions of the Indian National Congress every year. In 1894, Padmanavo Narayan Deva of Paralakhemundi along with B. Rajguru and Dewan Sadasiva Misra attended the Madras session of Indian National Congress. Shyam Sundar Rajguru, Dwipayan Roy and Gangadhar Khadanga attended the Pune and Calcutta sessions of Indian National Congress. Many delegates and visitors of Orissa attended the different sessions of Indian National Congress only to acquaint themselves with the proceedings and programmes of the Indian National Congress.

The Oriya delegates had no identity in Congress and they attended it only as the passive spectators.

In Dec. 29-30, 1920, Gandhiji made the Resolutions in the Annual Session of Indian National Congress at Nagpur, to launch the Non-Cooperation Movement against the British in India. A host of Oriya delegates attended this session such as Gopabandhu Das, H.K. Mahatab, Niranjan Patnaik. After their return, Gopabandhu Das merged the Utkal Union

Conference with the Indian National Congress at the Chakradharpur session of Utkal Union Conference of 1921. He constituted the Utkal Pradesh Congress Committee and the District Congress Committee to organise the Congress activities in Orissa. He enrolled 39,000 members and collected Rs. 21,000 by the end of June 30th, 1921 for the Congress party in Orissa. Thus Gopabandhu Das was the pioneer and the front leader of the Congress activities in Orissa. Niranjan Patnaik of Aska was the Secretary of the Utkal Pradesh Congress Committee.

Since the Non-Cooperation Movement of January 1921, the people of Orissa have most enthusiastically participated in the freedom movement of India till the last day of Indian Independence. In response to the clarion call of Gandhiji, the students of Orissa abjured the schools and colleges. The advocates did not attend the law-courts and many Govt. employees like Gopabandhu Choudhury, Pandit Nilakantha Das, Lingaraj Mishra, Surendra Nath Das, Md. Hanif gave up the services and mixed themselves with the mainstream of Non-Cooperation Movement in 1921. British goods were publicly burnt in crowded places to attract the people.

The two incidents galvanised the spirit of intense nationalism among the Oriyas in Orissa. The formation of the Utkal Pradesh Congress Committee by Pandit Gopabandhu Das in 1921 and the august visit of Gandhiji to Orissa on 21st March of 1921 inspired the people of Orissa to devote themselves to the freedom movement of India. Due to the active participation of the Orissa people the Non-Cooperation movement in Orissa became a tremendous success.

The second episode of the Gandhian era of the freedom movement in India was the Civil Disobedience Movement in 1930 Gandhiji made a historic journey as the pilgrim to the Dandi destination from Sabaramati Ashram on 12th March 1930. He walked all along the way of 240 miles accompanied by thousands of supporters and followers and reached Dandi on 6th April 1930. The he defied the salt laws by boiling the sea-water and obtained the salt. Sea and salt are the gifts of the nature to mankind. The British Govt. have got no right to put monopolistic restrictions on salt trade. This incident encouraged the satyagrahis all over India.

In Orissa too, the top leaders like Niranjan Patnaik, Rama Devi, Radhakrishna Biswasroy, A. Lakhmi Bai, Balaram Panda, Jagannath Misra, Sriharsa Misra, Dibakar Patnaik, Sashibhusan Rath, Banamali Moharana, Biswanath Das, Sarala Devi, Uma Charan Patnaik , H.K Mahatab, Surendra Nath Dwibedi, Bharat Behera, Raj Krishna Bose, Rabi Narayan Das, Mukunda Prasad Das and many others looted the salt godowns at Ganjam, Humma, Paradip, Chandipur, Dhamara, Inchudi and created insuramountable difficulties for the British to deal with. Many were arrested, beaten or sent to Chingelpet, Hazaribag and Madras Jails. They were later on released according to the terms of the Gandhi-Irwin Pact which was signed on 5th March 1931. The Civil Disobedience Movement was also crowned with a spectacular success in Orissa and it largely contributed to strengthen the stand of the freedom fighters of India.

The last phase of the Freedom Movement of India was the Quit India Movement of 1942. It marked the culminating point of the aggressive Indian nationalism when Gandhiji failed to achieve any significant results in two of the previous Movements of Non-Cooperation and Civil Disobedience. He gave the Slogan to "Do or Die" signified the bloodshed of the martyrs. When the deep and black clouds of Second World War were looming large in the Indian sky—the spirit of the Struggle Movement was volatile. So Gandhiji seized the opportunity and in order to surcharge the militancy, he launched the Quit India Movement. The All India Congress Working Committee decided in Bombay on 8th August 1942 to launch the most disastrous and final movement against the British colonialism in India. Gandhiji and other members declared that the British should withdraw all their powers and should quit India as early as possible.

Without a gap of preparations it was effective forthwith the next day on 9th August 1942. Having been defeated and frustrated by the Japanese naval forces in the Pacific Ocean, Indonesia, Burmese battle zones, the British Govt. took drastic measures to put down the August Revolution in India. Instantly on 9 August 1942, Gandhiji, Nehru, Azad, Sardar Patel and other top leaders of the Congress were put behind the prison bars. It was the vain hope of the Congress leaders that Mr. Linlithgow, the viceroy of India would invite Gandhiji for a dialogue or interview but he did not do it. Rather he took stern steps to suppress the movement by iron hand.

The message of the Quit India Movement spread like wildfire to the nook and corner of the Indian Sub-Continent. Every nationalist of India was inspired and blindly jumped into the horrors of the historic movement.

The freedom fighters in Orissa manifested their utmost sense of nationalism and supreme sacrifice of lives in their different activities of atrocities and destruction of public properties. They set fire different Govt. buildings, Police stations, Bungalows, Post offices, Railway Stations and pulled down the telephone wires, created barriers on the roads, looted the public offices and treasuries- attacked upon the police officers. They picketted before wine shops, ordinary grocery and cloth shops not to purchase any British goods. They disuaded the customers from purchasing the foreign goods. They burnt the foreign goods publicly. No Govt. employees attended their offices.

The first rank leaders who piloted the August Campaign in Orissa were many but the public participation in the movement was immense and spontaneous. Dr. H.K. Mahtab, Jagannath Das, Raj Krishna Bose, Biswanath Das, Rama Devi,

Sarala Devi, Malati Chowdhury, Biju Patnaik, Nabakrishna Chowdhury, Gopabandhu Chowdhury, Surendra Nath Dwivedi, Bibhudendu Misra, Niranjan Patnaik, Balaram Mohanty, Dibakar Patnaik, Harihar Das, Sriharsa Misra, Jugol Kishore Panigrahy, Maguni Das, Jagannath Misra, Radhakrishna Biswasroy, Lakhman Nayak, Muralidhar Panda, Lakshmi Narayan Mishra, Fakir Behera, Balaram Panda, Uma Charan Patnaik, Annapurna Maharana, Nanda Kishore Das, Rabi Narayan Das, Mukunda Prasad Das and innumerable others.

Terrible disturbances occurred in Eram Katasahi, Basudevpur, Bhandari Pokhari in Balasore district, Cuttack, Jajpur and Kendrapara in Cuttack district, Mathili, Pappadahandi in Koraput district. Besides, there were disturbances in almost all the districts of Orissa—but not violent as it occurred in Eram and Mathili. People resorted to violence and the police resorted to firing.

In the district of Cuttack the August Revolution first started at Ravenshaw College, some students on 14th August, 1942 launched a strike and set fire to the room of college office. The fire damaged many important official records and furniture. The students were arrested and were sent to jail.

Violent incident occurred at Kaipada—a village adjacent to Bari. The mob set fire the Post office and burnt it down. The police arrested some of the agitators. Thousands of people gathered immediately to demand for the release of the arrested persons. The police did not heed to their demands and in apprehension of further violence they fired at the crowd and killed five persons and many persons were injured.

At Ersama, Kendrapara, Tirtol, Balikuda and Jagatsinghpur, the agitators set fire the Dak-bungalows, Post offices, barracks etc.

But the August Revolution of 1942 took a violent turn at

Mathili in Koraput district and at Eram of Balasore district, Mathili and Eram would remain as the indelible memory for the supreme sacrifice of the martyrs for all times to come. Lakhman Nayak—an uneducated man of an obscure village of Borriguma was catapulted his image as the immortal martyr for his Mother land—India. His attempt to hoist the tricolour national flag on the top of the Mathili Police station on 21.8.1942 was foiled by a police inspector, Jogga Naikulu Dora, in charge of the Mathili Police station. Mr. Naikulu Dora fired at a short range and killed 12 associates of Lakhman Nayak on the spot. A weekly market was held on that day at Mathili. Lakhman Nayak was seriously injured by the bullets. The police mercilessly set fire the moustache of Lakhman and hit him by the baynots of the guns. Lakhman Nayak was senseless. Police thought him to be dead and left him in a gutter. But in the darkness of the night, he regained his consciousness and secretly fled away.

Next days, the police hunted the nearest villages and detected Lakhman. He was brought to the Berhampur jail. He was tried by an Indian Judge, V. Ramanathan, as a faithful dog of the British Govt. and sentenced him to be hanged. On 29th March 1943, Lakhman Nayak was hanged till death in the Berhampur jail before the sun-rise.

On 24th August 1942, thousands of tribal people assembled at Pappadahandi to protest against the police firing at Mathili and arrest of Lakhman Nayak. Without any warning for dispersal, the police fired at the crowd and killed several persons on the spot. Three persons later on died in the hospital.

Likewise, the police fired at the crowd of hundreds of villagers at Eram in the South Balasore district on 28 September, 1942. The people have gathered there to listen to their leaders for future course of action of the Revolution, but the police was determined to punish them because the people had snatched away some postal bags from the peon. The police fired at the thick crowd of the place and killed 29 persons on the spot and hundreds of people were injured.

Bhandari Pakhori was also burst into an open violence on 17th August 1942. The mob surrounded the local police station and beat one of the constables and the rest fled away. The people not only burnt the police station but destroyed a wooden bridge nearby which prevented the police and people from outside.

These were the most violent tragic incidents in Orissa which took away many precious lives.

In totality in the entire India by the end of 1943, 91836 persons were arrested.. 1060 persons were killed by police firing at different places. More than 2000 were seriously injured. The mob destroyed 208 police stations, 322 Railway stations and 945 Post offices.

The Quit India Movement exhibited the unusual strength and unity of the Indian people. The British Govt. did not yield to the demands of the Indian leaders but whiled away the issues till the end of the Second World War in August, 1945. The British Govt. won the glorious victory against Axis Powers. Mussoline was killed. Adolf Hitler committed suicide in his bunker on 30th April 1945. America dropped inhumanely bombs on Hirosima on 6.8.1945 and on Nagasaki on 9.8.1945 and killed instantly lakhs of Japanese.

After the World War, elections took place in England. Fortunately Winston Churchill was set aside. The people voted for the Labour Party to form Ministry. Clement Attlee became the Prime Minster of England who was sympathetic to India. Mr. Wavell was recalled and Attlee deputed Lord Mountbatten as the last Viceroy of India in March, 1947 with a special instruction that he should grant independence to India by June 1948.

After his new assignment, Lord Mountbatten observed that the situations in India were extremely inflammable and antagonistic due to the violent communal riots in August, 1946 in Noakhali, Calcutta and other parts of India which ravaged the lives of millions. So Mountbatten explored the possibility that in a shortest period of time, he should grant Independence to India instead of June 1948. He convened a meeting of the top leaders of all political parties in India at New Delhi. Mr. J. L. Nehru, Sardar Ballabhbhai Patel, Acharya Kripalani, Md. Ali Jinah, Baldev Singh and Liaqat Ali Khan attended the meeting and accepted the terms and conditions of the Mountbatten Plan. Then Mountbatten flew to England and laid before the Parliament on 5th July, 1947, a Bill—Indian Independence Act of 1947 providing for the establishment of the two Dominions of India and Pakistan. The Indian Independence Act ultimately came into force from the mid-night of the 14th August, 1947. Mr. Jawaharlal Nehru was sworn in as the first Prime Minister of Independent India on the mid-night of 14th August 1947. Next day on 15th August, 1947 the Nation celebrated the Independence Day. Mr. Mountbatten became the first Governor General of Independent India.

3

Integration of Princely States

It is difficult to decipher the definite dates of the origin of the Feudatory states of Orissa. Because no royal dynasty came to be established in a particular contemporary period. Besides, the genesis of the royal dynasty is associated with the legends and myths than any reality. As for instance, the King of Mayur Bhanj is born out of the peacock-egg and was brought up by Basista Saint. Likewise many such obscure stories are connected with the royal dynasties of all the feudatory states of Orissa. Mostly it has been referred that they were the descendents of the Rajputs.

But most of the feudatory states were founded during the 9th and 10th century A.D. Gradually, they remained as the subordinate kings under the Imperial Gangas and the Gajapati Kings of Kapilendra Dev, Purusottam Dev and Prataprudra Dev. The Mughol Emperors, the Marathas and the British ultimately collected heavy tributes from them. During the regime of the British Govt., all the ruling chiefs of the feudatory states fell victim to the ruthless economic exploitation and their sufferings were limitless. Those feudatory states which were ruled indirectly by the British Govt. through their Political Agents were 26 in number and they were:

(1) Athagarh (2) Athamalik (3) Bamanda (4) Badamba (5) Boud (6) Bonai (7) Dasapalla (8) Dhenkanal (9) Gangapur (10) Hindol (11) Kalahandi

(12) Keonjhar (13) Khandapada (14) Mayurbhanj (15) Narasinghpur (16) Nayagarh (17) Nilagiri (18) Palalahada (19) Patna (20) Rairokhol (21) Ranapur (22) Sonepur (23) Talcher (24) Tigria (25) Sareikala (26) Kharasuan.

The feudatory states were also known as the Tributary Mahals. They lie between 22° 34' and 19° 2' N and 82° 32' and 87° 11' E and have a population of 3173395 and covered an area of 28125 square miles in 1901.

The fate of the feudatory states was altered in 1803 when the British took possession of Orissa by conquest from the Marathas. The British vivisected the entire Orissa in to four parts—the districts of Cuttack, Puri and Balasore were tagged with the Bengal Presidency. Ganjam, Koraput and Phulbani were placed under the Madras Presidency; Sambalpur was also tied with C.P administration. And the feudatory states were ruled by their respective the Political Agents of the British Government supervised rulers and their administration. The Feudatory Chiefs danced with the sweet tunes of the British Government. The British Government regulated all their powers.

Sareikala and Kharsuan—two other Oriya dominated feudatory states were treated as the Ping-Pong balls in the court of Bihar and Orissa. And ultimately because of the inefficient leadership of the Oriya leaders, Sareikala and Kharswan were tagged with the Bihar state.

The British after their conquest of Orissa in 1803 changed the pattern of the general administrative system of Cuttack, Puri, Balasore, Sambalpur because they were previously ruled by the Marathas. But the British did not interfere in the matters of administration in the feudatory states of Orissa. The British were convinced that there was definitely a separate administrative code for every individual feudatory state. And it was not urgent to abruptly change their pattern of

HERE IS A STATEMENT OF THE HEADQUARTERS, POPULATION AND SQUARE MILES OF THE FEUDATORY STATES OF ORISSA IN 1901

	Name of the States	*Capital*	*Population in 1901*	*Square miles in Area*	*Emblem*
1.	ATHAGARH	ATHAGARH	43784	168	RADHA KRISHNA
2.	ATHAMALIK	KAINTIRAGARH	40753	730	KADAMBA FLOWER
3.	BAMANDA	DEOGARH	123378	1988	SHANKHA (Conch-shell)
4.	BADAMBA	BADAMBA	38260	134	
5.	BOUD	BOUDAGARH	88250	1264	PEACOCK
6.	BONAI	BONAI	38277	1296	PEACOCK
7.	DASAPALLA	KUNJABAN	51987	568	PEACOCK
8.	DHENKANAL	DHENKANAL	273662	1463	FISH
9.	GANGAPUR	SUNDARGARH	238896	2492	DIETY JAGDAL
10.	HINDOL	HINDOL	47180	312	DEGGA
11.	KALAHANDI	BHAWANIPATNA	350529	3745	COBRA
12.	KEONJHAR	KEONJHARGARH	285758	3096	PEA-FOWL
13.	KHANDAPADA	KHANDAPADA	69450	244	TIGER'S HEAD
14.	MAYURBHANJ	BARIPADA	610383	4243	PEACOCK
15.	NARASINGHPUR	NARASINGHPUR	39613	199	SCORPION
16.	NAYAGARH	NAYAGARH	140779	588	TIGER'S HEAD
17.	NILAGIRI	NILAGIRI	66460	278	FLOWER KORRALA
18.	PALALAHADA	PALALAHADA	22351	452	COBRA
19.	PATNA	PATNA	277748	2399	CHAKRA (QUOIT)
20.	RAIROKHOL	RAMPUR	26888	833	SHANKA-PADMA
21.	RANAPUR	RANAPUR	46075	203	SWORD
22.	SONEPUR	SONEPUR	169877	906	CHAKRA (DISCUS)
23.	TALCHER	TALCHER	60432	399	TIGER
24.	TIGIRIA	TIGIRIA	22625	46	FIVE WEAPONS

administration. So the British Govt. adopted a clever policy of conciliation and leniency. They tried to put them in the good humour to rule upon the subjects. And whenever the expediency arose, the British Govt. intervened in the feudatory administration and put pressure upon the Kings to solve the problems. The British left all the administrative, executive and judicial powers to the Kings and Zamindars of the Garjatas and collected annual tributes from them.

On 5th February 1814 a new office of the Superintendent of Tributary Mahals was created to exercise control over the powers of the Kings and Zamindars of Orissa. The British Govt. dealt cleverly the multifarious problems of the regicide and murder of any leader by the Kings, popular uprising of the people due to economic exploitation of the Kings etc.

PRAJA MANDAL MOVEMENT (1938)

Only a handful of Kings or Maharajas of feudatory states were compassionate and considerate to the subjects. The Maharaja of Mayur Bhanj, the King of Bamanda were sensitive and sympathetic to the public. Apart from a few almost all the Kings and Zamindars tortured the people by bethi unpaid labour presents, economic exploitation, excessive land revenue and Rasad. The subjects had no rights to protest. No freedom was accorded to the subjects to move to the court of law. All were ruthlessly suppressed. The Kings of Dhenkanal, Nilagiri, Ranapur and Talcher were very selfish and tortured the subjects maximum.

In protest of the ruthless administration of the Kings, the first meeting of the people of the Garjata was held in 1913 at Cuttack. Radhanath Rath, Madhusudan Patnaik and Balukeswar Acharya took the initiative, but nothing could be achieved.

Sporadic movements started in Dhenkanal in 1922 under the leadership of Maheswar Subahu Singh and Purnachandra

Mahapatra in Nilagiri in 1928, Boudh in 1930 and at Talcher in 1932. But they achieved nothing.

The Second Praja Mandal Conference was held on 23/24 June 1937 at Cuttack under the Presidentship of the Congress leader—Pattavi Sitaramayya. Several resolutions were adopted but the behaviours of the Kings remained unchanged.

In the same year in 1937, the Princely states were categorized according to their territorial jurisdiction and status in to "A", "B" and "C".

In the Group A, the following states were placed—Dhenkanal, Keonjhar, Mayur Bhanj, Bamanda, Boudh, Gangapur, Patna, Kalahandi, Sonepur, Sareikala and Nayagarh.

Group B consisted of Athagarh, Badamba, Narasinghpur, Athamalik, Hindol, Dasapalla, Khandapada, Kharsuan, Redhakhol, Talcher, Bolangir and Nilagiri.

In the group C, Palalahada, Ranapur and Tigiria were placed.

To relieve the burden of the heavy taxation bethi, beggary, Rasad and social exploitation of the people, an Enquiry Committee was formed at Cuttack under the headship of Hare Krishna Mahatab. Lal Mohan Patnaik and Balawanta Rai Mehta were the members. Mr. Saranga Dhar Das became the Secretary. This committee approved the public demands as true. The subjects expressed their opinion and reaction without any fear. But the Kings did not change their ruthless policy.

Ultimately the people became revolting and formed "Praja Mandal" to protest against the unjust administration of the Kings. This Praja Mandal Movement shook the foundation of the royal dynasty of Dhenkanal, Talcher, Nilgiri and Ranapur. The movement spread like the wildfire.

Nilagiri of Balasore—under the dynamic leadership of Kailash Mohanty and Banamali Das of Nilagiri revolted against the King on July 11, 1938. The subjects denied paying land revenue. The King arrested the rebels and penalised with fines. Mr. H.K Mahatab, Political Agent Bazellegate and D.M of Balasore mediated the issue and the King accepted some public demands.

Dhekanal

Thousands of people started a movement against the misrule of the King of Dhenkanal. H.K. Mahatab, Nabakrishna Choudhary, Sarangadhar Das, Brajakishore Dhal and Malati Choudhury delivered speeches in the gathering.

But in spite of that the sepoys of King and British police started the lathi charge and beat the people on 13th September 1938.

Here itself, the rebel boy Baji Rout of only 12 years old refused the British constables to cross the river by a boat. Having been irritated by the adamant behaviour, the police ultimately shot Baji Rout dead on 11th October 1938. Baji Rout became immortal as Martyr in the annals of Orissa History.

The British Govt. took away the powers from the King and Bethi was abolished. The land revenue was reduced from 4 annas to 1 anna only.

Talcher

Under the leadership of Mr. Pabitra Mohan Pradhan, the Praja Mandal Movement was started at Talcher in 1938 November. The rebels demanded the abolition of bethi, "Magana" presents and rasad. H.K. Mahatab requested the King and the King agreed to accept some demands. Krutibash Rath and Maguni Pradhan helped the rebel subjects in procession and slogans.

Ranapur: January 5th-1939

But the Praja Mandal Movement took a violent turn at Ranapur. The people were intensely aggressive and inflammable. The sense of protest was profound. Thousands of people in a procession reached the palace and rented the air by loud slogans to abolish the unjust taxation, beggary, bethi and Rasad. The King was terribly afraid to see the rebellious subjects. And he immediately called for the Political Agent—Mr. R.L. Bazellegate who was staying with his wife in circuit Bunglow of Nayagarh. He had recently come from Sambalpur to study the situations of Praja Mandal Movement at Ranapur. Mr. Bazellegate moved with a military van towards Ranapur via Ludhadua village. He was obstructed on the way by the rebel subjects by a barricade of trunks of the big trees. But he removed them and reached the palace. He saw Dibakar Parida and Raghunath Mohanty delivering speeches to the gatherings.

The British constables dispersed the people by the lathis and baynots of the guns. Many people were also wounded. It was rumoured that some persons were killed. Mr. Bazallegate wanted to know actually how many persons were killed by his constables. So he proceeded towards the bullock cart where the wounded persons were seated. Meanwhile the frenzied mob started a skirmish-push and pull started. Mr. Bazellegate out of fear fired one bullet—As ill luck it was the bullet of his pistol hit a man, Arjun Rout who died on the spot. This crime led the people to commit violence and they chased after Bazellegate. Bazellegate tried to hid himself behind the wheel of a bullock cart. But the mob ceaselessly beat him to death at 5 P.M on 5th January 1939. This unfortunate death of Mr. Bazellegate moved the British Govt. and puzzled the entire administration.

H.K. Mahatab who reached the spot immediately asked all the villagers of Ranapur and the adjacent villages to evacuate otherwise the results would be disastrous. Within a moment, all the villagers ran away helter and skelter leaving the entire areas desolate. Thereafter, Mr. Buden came with hundreds of Sepoys with loaded guns to Ranapur—but found none.

Mr. Dibakar Parida and Raghunath Mohanty were tried by a special Magistrate Mr. B. Sivaraman at Ranapur Tahasil office. 27 persons were convicted for life imprisonment and Mr. Dibakar Parida and Raghunath Mohanty were sentenced to capital punishment. They were taken to the Bhagalpur Jail in Bihar. On 4th April 1941, at 4 A.M, they were hanged to death. Even the dead bodies were not handed over to their parents. Mr. Dibakar Parida and Raghunath Mohanty remained as the unforgettable characters in the struggle for justice and truth.

This movement also spread to Mayur Bhanj (1940), Bolangir, Sonepur, Bamanda, Redhakhol and Gangapur.

After this tragic incident of Mr. Bazellgate's death, the movement was subsided. And on 9th August 1942, the Quit India Movement engulfed the entire India. The Second World War also left the trails of tragedy of death and destruction in the world.

In the mid-night of 14th August 1947, India achieved independence from British. But the problems and hazards of the post-independence era devastated the entire nation of India. India was vivisected into two territorial fragments—India and Pakistan. The rivers of blood flooded the entire Indo-Pak border.

The process of integration of the Rajas and Maharajas was started by the then Home minister of India—Sardar Ballav Bhai Patel. Harekrishna Mahatab who was the Prime Minister of Orissa also appealed to the entire feudatory Chiefs of Orissa to merge themselves with Orissa or India.

There were altogether 565 great Kingdoms in India. And

Orissa had 26 feudatory states. Sardar Patel did not only officially send letters but he himself went to all the Rajas and Maharajas of India to persuade them to merge with the Indian Union.

Sardar Patel came to Cuttack on 13th December 1947 with V.P. Menon. On 14th December 1947, at 10'O clock, Patel met the "B" class Rajas of Athagarh, Baramba, Dasapalla, Hindol, Khandapada, Kharsuan, Narasinghpur, Nilagiri, Palalahada, Rairokhol, Ranapur and Talcher in the presence of H.K Mahatab, V.P Menon and the Chief Secretary of Orissa in a Conference. There Sardar Patel and Menon appealed to them in a most persuasive arguments. He also assured to protect the privileges of the Rajas and Zamindars. Which they were enjoying since time immemorial.

V.P. Menon extended the hope of Privy Purse to the Rajas for their maintenance in future.

Both of them also made the Rajas fearful of the rising Praja Mandal Movement in the state, which would ultimately lead them to pauperism.

In the afternoon session, they met the "A" class Rajas and Maharajas of Bamanda, Boudh, Dhenkanal, Gangapur, Kalahandi, Keonjhar, Mayur Bhanj, Nayagarh, Patna, Sareikala and Sonepur. Patel and Menon explained to them about their future predicaments in the equal terms they had convinced the "B" class Rajas at 10 A.M. Sardar Patel explained:

> "The Orissa states were like ulcers on the body of the province and that they must either be cured or eliminated. If they listened to his advice, they could be cured otherwise they might find themselves uprooted by the people."

The Kings asked for sufficient time to think over it—but nothing could be done on 14-12-1947 till the mid night.

Next day on 15-12-1947, the King of Dhenkanal decided to merge with the Indian Union. Gradually all the Rajas of Feudatory States expressed their willingness for merger. On 23rd December 1947 in exercise of the powers conferred by the Extra-Provincial Jurisdiction Act of 1947, the Govt. of India delegated all the powers to the Govt. of Orissa to implement the instrument of Merger. All the Rajas put their signatures on the instrument of Merger and it became effective from 1st January 1948. But the Maharaja, Pratap Chandra Bhanj of Mayur Bhanj did not sign. He pleaded that the state powers have already been transferred to a popularly elected body and the state council is already formed to make laws for Mayur Bhanj. Sardar Patel did not listen to his arguments and turned down his representation. Ultimately the Maharaja signed the instrument of Merger on 17th October 1948. The Govt. of India took over the Mayur Bhanj state on 9th November 1948. Mayur Bhanj merged with India on 1st January 1949. One year after the merger of other Orissan kings.

Regarding the fate of Sareikala and Kharsuan, these two feudatory states were handed over to Bihar on 18th May 1948. Since that day, till to day there is a rift between Orissa and Bihar and it will continue to be in future.

With the merger of Mayur Bhanj state, the process of integration of Princely states was completed. Out of this merger, 13 districts were created in Orissa. H.K Mahatab was the Prime Minister of Orissa when India got independence on 15th August 1947. All the Rajas and Maharajas were paid privy purses by the Govt. of India as promised during the accession. The amount of privy purses was fixed in accordance with the annual income of the Rajas from their estates. All the Kings and Maharajas all over India enjoyed this Privy Purse uninterruptedly from the day of their merger to 1971. This amount was not sufficient to their maintenance—but still then they used to receive the payment thinking that India now is a democratic state. But all on a sudden in 1971 a sword hanged over their heads. Mrs. Indira Gandhi—the then Prime Minister of India, 1971 abolished the Privy Purse by an Ordinance. Sri V. V Giri was the President of Indian Republic who was voted to the position in July 1969 by the support of Mrs. Indira Gandhi. V.V Giri later on gave his consent to the Act on 28-12-1971.

The Rajas and Maharajas of different Estates ran to Delhi and launched "Dharana" in front of the Parliament—but Indira Gandhi did not yield to their demands. Ultimately the payment of Privy Purse to the Rajas was discontinued.

4

Political History of Orissa (1936-2000)

Orissa assumed a separate constitutional status on 1st April 1936. The long cherished desire of the Oriya people was fulfilled. The area of the new province of Orissa was confined to 32,695 square miles.

From the 1st April 1936 to 31st March 1937, there was no Govt. in Orissa. So it was ruled by the Governor with an Advisory Council. The Governor was Sir John Austin Hubback and the Advisory Council consisted of B.B. Gopinath Bisoyi, Mandhata Gorachand Patnaik, Maharaja Krishna Chandra Gajapati of Parlakhemundi, Harihar Das, Godavarish Mishra, AT Panthulu, Brajananda Das, Birabara Narayan Dev Narendra, S A Jalil, Nikunja Kishore Das, Radharanjan Das, Braja Mohan Panda, Jagannath Das, Lokanath Mishra, B. Das, P.T. Mansfield-Finance Secretary, Lakhmidhar Mohanti.

The general election in Orissa was held in January 1937. The arrival of Pandit Jawaharlal Nehru on 10th November, 1936 boosted the election campaign of the Congress party. He addressed a number of political meetings at Salepur, Kendrapara, Jagatsinghpur, Cuttack, Puri and Berhampur.

Besides, the Indian National Congress, the United Party and the Orissa Nationalist Party contested in the first election. The election started from 18th January 1937 and continued up to 23rd January 1937. Out of 60 seats, Congress Party won

36 seats and the 24 seats were distributed among the Nationalist Party of Raja of Parlakhemundi, the United Party by Shailendra Narayan Bhanjadeo of Kanika and the Independents led by the Raja of Khallikote—Rama Chandra Mardaraj.

As a rule, the Congress Party was to form the Ministry but as there was a faction between H.K. Mahtab and Nilakantha Das, the Congress did not do so. Nilakantha Das was eliminated. And the Congress Party elected Biswanath Das as a leader of the Party. Mr. Austin Hubback invited Mr. Das to form the Cabinet but Biswanath Das asked for an assurance from the Governor that he should not interfere in the affairs of state administration and the popular Govt. The Governor turned down the request of Mr. Das, so Biswanath Das did not form the Ministry.

Interim Ministry of MKCG of Parlakhemundi 1-4-1937

The Governor therefore invited Maharaja Krishna Chandra Gajapati Deo, the leader of the United Party to form the Govt. The Raja took oath as the first Prime Minister of Orissa knowing fully well that his Govt. has got no majority in the house. He had got two other ministers—Mandhata Gorachand Patnaik and Moulavi Latifur Rehman. This Govt. cannot prove his majority in the Assembly floor. So the Raja tendered his resignation on 19th July 1937. The Govt. did nothing except whiled away the period of four months.

Ministry of Biswanath Das Congress Party — July 1937 to 1939

Mr. Biswanath Das took oath as the Second Prime Minister of Orissa on 19th July 1937. Two other ministers—Nityanand Kanungo as the Minister of Revenue and Bodharam Dubey as the Minister of Education sworn in simultaneously. This Govt. lasted up to 4th November, 1939. During this short period, the Govt. passed a number of Bills in the legislature notable of them were the Orissa Money Lenders Act, Orissa Cooperative Land Mortgage Bank Act, Hindu Religious

Endowment Act and the Orissa Prevention of Adulteration and Control of Sale of Food Act. Biswanath Das also provided adequate relief to the peasants of Orissa. During the thick of the Second World War, Mr. Das resigned on 4-11-1939 from the Ministry because the Indian Congress Party decided not to co-operate the British Govt. in the war efforts in any way. The Governor took over the administration and imposed his rule in Orissa.

During this period the Praja Mandal Movement was also launched against the injustice and exploitation of the Rajas of different feudatory states. The British Govt. decided to extend all possible help to the Rajas to put down the movement.

Meanwhile Dibakar Patnaik of Ganjam also formed a Provincial Unit of the Forward Bloc in Orissa in March 1940 as a part of Subash Bose and himself became the Secretary.

In October, 1940 Pandit Godavarish Mishra formed an Association as Orissa Congress Swaraj Dal and himself became the President. Nilakantha Das has dissociated himself from the Congress Party in November 1940. Both the leaders tried their most to form a Coalition Govt. in Orissa but they were not successful.

The Governor took charge of the administration of Orissa from 4-11-1939 to 23-11-1941.

Coalition Ministry (24-11-1941)

Ultimately Maharaja Krishna Chandra Gajapati formed the Coalition with the help of the Nationalist Party, Muslim League United Party, Independents and the dissidents of the Congress Party on 24th November 1941. Godavarish Mishra and Abdus Sevan Khan became the Minister of Education and Law respectively. The Governor of Orissa, Sir Hawthorne Lewis who joined on 1st April, 1941 after Sir John Austin Hubback administered the oath of confidence on them. This

Coalition Govt. lasted from 24th November 1941 to 19th June 1944. The Maharaja submitted his resignation on 20th June 1944 and it was accepted on 29th June, 1944.

The important landmark of the regime of Maharaja during his short span of tenure was the adoption of the Utkal University Bill. Pandit Godavarish Mishra as the Education Minister prepared the bill in consultation with Dr. Shyama Chandra Tripathy—the principal of Ravenshaw College and the DPI of Bihar and Orissa State and the Utkal University Bill was unanimously accepted by the legislature on 23rd June 1943. Accordingly the new Utkal University and the only University in Orissa was established on 27th November 1943. It was the crowning achievement of the Coalition Govt. of Maharaja Krishna Chandra Gajapati. It not only opened a new vista for higher education but saved the promising youngmen and girls of Orissa from a great economic burden.

Although the Coalition Govt. took another measure to establish the High Court in Orissa, the British Govt. did not take any prompt decision in this regard. The Coalition Govt. resigned on 20th June, 1944. The proposal was dropped.

The SCB Medical College at Cuttack was given a definite shape and recognition by the Govt. of Maharaja and it was established in 1944.

An attempt to form another ministry by Congress was made futile. The Governor imposed his rule in Orissa from 29-6-1944 to 22-4-1946.

In 1946 April elections were held under limited franchise. The Congress Party won 47 seats and Harekrishna Mahtab was selected as the leader of the Party. Biswanath Das was debarred from contesting in the election because he spent more than the sanctioned amount of rupees in Baliguda Constituency as a Poll Agent of the Congress Party.

H.K. Mahtab

The new Ministry under Mahtab took oath on 23rd April, 1946 with Nabakrishna Chowdhury, Nityanand Kanungo, Lingaraj Mishra and Radha Krishna Biswasroy.

Many new faces like Sadasib Tripathy, Biju Patnaik, Nilamoni Routroy, Dinabandhu Sahu and Biren Mitra appeared in the political scenario of Orissa during this period.

Lal Mohan Patnaik and A. Lakhmi Bai were elected uncontested as the Speaker and Deputy Speaker of the Orissa Assembly respectively.

H K Mahtab was the Prime Minister of Orissa on 15th August, 1947 when India achieved her Independence.

Mahtab continued to rule Orissa from 23rd April 1946 to 12th May 1950. And he left Orissa for Delhi to accept the portfolio in the Central Cabinet.

The period of H K Mahtab in Orissa as the Prime Minister was conspicuous because his Govt. rendered valuable services to the people of Orissa. He tackled the inflammable situations in Orissa between the Hindus and Muslims on the issue of the Partition of India on 15th August 1947.

This Govt. undertook a number of projects in Orissa and ultimately completed them. The first and foremost of all the projects was the construction of the Hirakud Dam on Mahanadi near Sambalpur town. The foundation work of the Dam was already laid by the Governor, Sir Howthorne Lewis in 1945. Some of the Congress Leaders of Sambalpur like Bodhiram Dubey, Laxmi Narayan Mishra and Shankar Prasad Misra launched an anti-Hirakud Dam agitation with the people of Sambalpur district. Even Rajendra Narayan Singhdeo—the Maharaja of Bolangir Patna also supported the agitation and demanded a separate state for the Western Orissa people. But this agitation did not last longer. It gradually fade away.

The Govt. of Orissa entered into an agreement with the Central Govt. for financial help in November 1947. The Hirakud Dam ultimately became a reality. Along with it, we got abundant facilities of hydro-electricity power and irrigation to some thousand hectors of land. Besides, this dam saved the people from the disaster of flood.

In view of the necessity of the huge amount of cement for the construction of the Hirakud Dam, the Orissa Govt. simultaneously established a Cement factory at Rajgangpur.

The Hirakund Dam after completion of construction was inaugurated by the then Prime Minister, Jawaharlal Nehru on 13th January 1957.

Another notable achievement of Sri Harekrishna Mahtab was the selection of the State Capital-Bhubaneswar. Different places like Rangeilunda (Ganjam) Choudwar and Mancheswar were proposed to be the State Capital at different periods by different personalities but Mahtab discarded all the proposals and selected Bhubaneswar—the historic and Temple city as the State Capital. On 30th September 1946, the State Legislature passed a resolution whole-heartedly in this respect. On 10th October 1949, the Capital was shifted from Cuttack to Bhubaneswar. The French Architect who had already designed the Chandigarh Secretariat was also engaged in designing the Secretariat at Bhubaneswar. His name was Mr. Le Corbusier. All the Govt. offices including the Legislature started functioning in the temporary rented houses. During the Second Five Year Plan (1957-1962) the construction works of Secretariate, Legislative building, Raj Bhavan and the Orissa Museum were geared up. Along with them, works of the Zoological garden at Nandan Kanan, Rabindra Mandap and Kalamandap were also started. A huge number of Departments such as Orissa Sahitya Academy, Sangeeta Natak Academy and Lalit Kala Academy of Orissa Govt. were established. The Utkal University which was functioning at Ravenshaw

College Cuttack since 1943 was shifted to Bhubaneswar during the academic session of 1962-63.

Now Bhubaneswar is the most flourishing city in Orissa. Innumerable flats, Govt. and private buildings and industries have dotted the city. But it has left the most devastative effect upon the ancient temples of Bhubaneswar. The influx of the countless people and pilgrims from different parts of Orissa and India, the overcrowd of the local inhabitants, the floating population, the employees of the Orissa Govt. innumerable Govt. and private buildings, flats, industries, International Airport at Bhubaneswar, frequent travel of bus services, trucks, tourist cars, private cars, two wheelers, scooters, three wheelers, locomotive engines, trains, the smoke of different industries, the stone-crushing machines adjacent to Bhubaneswar city have destroyed the temples of Bhubaneswar. The drugs, opium, brown sugar, wine, Ganja are profusely used by the reckless educated youths. Unsocial and anti-social activities, rape, theft, robbery goondaism, are the usual features of the Bhubaneswar city. It became a den of the anti-social people. The hypocrites live in the spiritual citadel of Bhubaneswar.

Mahtab rendered immense services to Orissa for setting up of different industries and multi-purpose projects. This Govt. sponsored to implement the Machhakunda Duduma Project in Koraput district. There was also an anti-Machhakunda Dam agitation in 1946. But the Govt. insisted to have it and on 12 September 1946, Mahtab passed a resolution in Orissa Assembly to work out the Machhakunda Project.

The Congress Govt. under Mahtab drew the attention of the Central Govt. to finance some large-scale industries in Orissa in 1946. The most important industries were—Textile Mill and Kalinga Tubes at (Choudwar), Sugar Mill, Iron and Steel works, Jute Mills, Pottery works, Paper Mills, Cement Factory, Orissa Mining Corporation, Refractories at Jharusuguda and Belpahar, Ferro Manganese Plant at Rayagada

& Joda, Kalinga Iron Works at Barbil, Aluminium Plants at Hirakud. Due to these factories, Orissa a got impetus for improvement of industries and economic condition.

Mahtab set up the Orissa High Court at Cuttack on 26.7.1948 with the approval of the Central Govt.—the All India Radio Station at Cuttack on 28 January 1948. And Mahtab himself inaugurated the AIR. Those who have pursued the matter for the establishment of AIR were Kabichandra Kalicharan Patnaik, Dr. Artaballav Mohanty, Lakhmi Narayan Sahu & Bhubananda Das. Mahtab also set the work in motion for Barabati Stadium. Bhairab Chandra Mohanty was the main instrumental for pioneering the works of Barabati Stadium.

As it was the most tense situation in India after the Quit India Movement and Second World War, the British Govt. was sandwiched by different adverse and opposite forces in the world. The elections in England after the Second World War set Winston Churchil aside from the corridor of powers. The Labour Party under the stewardship of Clement Attlee came to power. There was a green signal already given for granting Independence to India. So the preparation for drafting a new Constitution for India was started from November 1946. Eminent personalities from all parts of India were selected to constitute the Constituent Assembly to draft the Indian constitution. There were as many as 957 persons were nominated as the members of the Constituent Assembly. The members of Orissa who were selected to the Constituent Assembly were—Biswanath Das, Hare Krishna Mahtab, Bodhram Dubey, Bhubanananda Das, Malati Choudhury, Maharaja Krishan Chandra Gajapati, Lakhmi Narayan Sahu, Raj Kishore Bose, Shantanu Kumar Das and many more. Dr. Rajendra Prasad was the Chairman of the Constituent Assembly. Dr. B. R. Ambedkar mainly drafted the Constitution.

On the 15th August 1947, Independence dawned upon India. On occasion of Independence, the Orissa State

Legislature met jubilantly on 27th August, 1947 morning. Dr. Kailash Nath Katju, the Governor of Orissa was the first Constitutional Governor after Independence who addressed the members of the Assembly floor in Cuttack. The members passed a resolution of joy and happiness and paid homage to the martyrs of the National Movement who have laid down their precious lives for their motherland.

The first Cabinet was formed in India after Independence under the Prime Ministership of Jawaharlal Nehru. (Governor-General-Lord Mountbatten from midnight of 14.8.1947 to 17 June 1048 and C. Rajgopalchari 17 June 1948 to 25th January 1952-Governor-General).

1. Pandit Jawaharlal Nehru—Prime Minister, External Affairs—Commonwealth Relations Scientific Research.
2. Sardar Ballabh Bhai Patel—Home-Information and Broadcasting
3. Dr. Rajendra Prasad—Food and Agriculture
4. Maulana Abul Kalam Azad—Education
5. Sardar Baldev Singh—Defence
6. Jagjiban Ram—Labour
7. Dr. C.H. Bhaba—Commerce
8. Rafi Ahmed Kidwai—Communications
9. Raj Kumari Amrit Kaur—Health
10. Dr. B.R. Ambedkar—Law
11. Shanmukham Chetty—Finance
12. Shyama Prasad Mukharjee—Industries and Supplies
13. N.V. Gadgil—Works, and Powers.

Amalgamation of Princely States with Orissa

After Independence on 15th August 1947, the amalgamation of the Princely States with Indian Union all over India paused the greatest problem to Sardar Ballabh

Bhai Patel who assumed the portfolio of the Home Dept. Due to his strenuous efforts and the unflinching cooperation of the Congress leaders of different states, the process of amalgamation of the Princely States was completed. Basically in Orissa, there were 26 feudatory states and they were categorised as "A" "B" "C" in late 1937. The category of "A" comes the following feudatory states—Mayur Bhanj, Bamanda, Dhenkanal, Patna Boudh, Gangpur, Patna, Kalahandi, Sonepur, Sareikala & Nayagarh.

And the category "B" states were—Athagarh, Badamba, Narasinghpur, Athamalik, Undol, Dasapalla, Khandapara Kharswan, Redhakhol, Talcher, Balangir and Nilagiri.

The category of "C" are Palalahada, Ranapur and Tigiria.

On 14th December 1947, Sardar Ballabh Bhai Patel met the Rulers of the Feudatory states of Orissa at Raj Bhawan, Cuttack-with H K. Mahtab-the Chief Minister of Orissa. In the morning session of his conversation Patel discussed the accession of the feudatory states of 'A' 'B' classes with India and in the afternoon session, he met the other rulers. All the 23 Feudatory Chiefs agreed to sign the Instrument of accession with the Indian Union except the Maharaja of Mayur Bhanja, Sri Pratap Chandra Bhanja. He pleaded that he has already established a representative and responsible Govt. for the people of Mayur Bhanj state and there was also a Prime Minister and a popular Assembly in Baripada which looked after the administration. But Sardar Patel set aside the claim of Pratap Chandra Bhanj. Maharaja still did not agree to sign the agreement.

The merger of 23 feudatory states of Orissa with Indian Union was made effective from the 1st January 1948.

Sardar Patel very ardently warned the Rulers of the feudatory state because the Praja Mandal Movement against the Ruling Chiefs of States in Pre-Independence period was the manifestation of the people's anger and dissatisfaction. The people were also gradually aware of their rights and the exploitation of the kings. These were the words of Sardar Patel :-

> "The Orissa States were like the ulcers on the body of the Prince that they must either be cured or eliminated. If they listen to his advice, they could be cured otherwise they might find themselves uprooted by the people".

Then Sardar Patel left Cuttack for Raipur. Gradually, all the kings of the feudatory states signed the documents of merger.

Meanwhile the economic and political conditions of Mayur Bhanj became miserable. The hastily constituted responsible Govt. of Bhanj did not function well. Sarat Das was the Prime Minister of Mayur Bhanj. The so-called selfish officers of Pratap Chandra Bhanj squandered the exchequer of the state and led to utmost bankruptcy. The selfishness of the officers, the lack of abundant experience to run the responsible Govt. were the causes of the downfall of the Govt. Due to such hostile circumstances, Pratap Chandra Bhanja decided to put his signature on the merger agreement and went to Delhi. There he signed the agreement on 17 October 1948 and handed over the administration of state to the Central Govt. Mr. D.V. Rege I.C.S. was appointed as the Chief Commissioner of Mayur Bhanj on 9.11.1948 who stayed at Baripada. Ultimately the merger of Mayur Bhanj with India became effective from 1.1.1949. Thus the long process of amalgamation of feudatory states of Orissa with India was completed.

The Mahtab Ministry has also passed two important Bills in Orissa legislature-(1) Orissa Opium-smoking Bill on 31 March 1947 and (2) Bihar and Orissa Excise (Orissa

Amendment Bill) on 2nd June 1947 to check the unbridled use of opium and intoxicants.

The days of Mr. Mahtab as the Prime Minister (Chief Minister) of Orissa did not last longer, Surendra Nath Dwivedi Nabakrisha Choudhury, Gopabandhu Chowdhury, Nityananda Kanungo launched a movement to oust Mahtab from power. Radhakrishna Biswasroy—the PWD Minister resigned on the issue of the corruption charges in July 1948. Mahtab took Lala Ranjit Singh Bariha, Raj Krishna Bose and Sadasiv Tripathy into Ministry. But the political situation of Orissa was extremely volatile. Other charges against Mahtab on the issue of the destiny of Sareikala and Kharsuan of not amalgamating with Orissa were levelled against him which undermined his prestige. Meanwhile the High Command of Congress Party decided to insert Mahtab in the Nehru Cabinet. So Mahtab resigned as the Prime Minister (CM) on 12th May 1950 and left for Delhi. Nabakrishna Choudhury was chosen as the Chief Minister to succeed Mahtab on the recommendation and beseechful requests of Mr. Bijayananda Patnaik and Biren Mitra.

Nabakrishna Choudhury

Nabakrishna Choudhury remained in the office as the Chief Minister of Orissa from 12 May 1950 to 18th October 1956. Nabakrishna Choudhury was good as a man but ineffective as the administrator. Under the new constitution of India, the Central Govt. had conducted its first general election from 20th December 1951 to 15 January 1952. The elections for Lok Sabha and Orissa State Assembly were simultaneously held. There were 20 MPs for Lok Sabha and 140 MLA for the state Assembly. Although Congress Party did not win the overwhelming majority but managed to get the support from six independent MLAs and formed the Congress Ministry of 74 MLAs. Nabakrishna Choudhury took oath as the Chief Minister on 20 February 1952.

The Ganatantra Parishad led by R N Singhdeo got the second largest seats, Many said that the Ganatantra Parishad is a political party of the Kings and the Aristocrats. So it commanded respect in Gadjat areas where as the Congress bagged maximum seats in the Coastal districts of Orissa.

Biju Patnaik sincerely wanted to enter into the Orissa Cabinet under N.K Choudhury, but Mr. Choudhury prevented the entry of Biju Patnaik for which Biju Babu was dissatisfied. And ultimately Biju Babu, Biren Mitra, Nilamani Routroy left Nabakrishna Choudhury and joined hands with Mr. Mahtab. Mahtab was elected as the MP to Lok Sabha. Mr. Mahtab had joined as the Minister of Industry and Supply in the Nehru Cabinet from 1950 to 1952. Mahtab was asked to leave it for which he was greatly disappointed: Nehru advised Mahtab to devote time in the organisational aspect of the Congress Party and appointed him as the Secretary of the Congress Parliamentary Party in which post he continued (1952-1955) until he was appointed as the Governor of Maharashtra.

The times of Nabakrishna Choudhury as the Chief Minister of Orissa from 18th February 1952 to 18th October 1956 was a period of political turmoil, intrigues and conspiracy. Nabakrishna Choudhury was basically a man of simplicity, a character of peaceful disposition who hated the nasty politics. Besides the Bhoodan Movement of Vinoba Bhave and the participation of Nababābu's wife, Malati Choudhry in the Bhoodan Movement diverted the attention of Nabakrishna Choudhury.

The unexpected artificial and natural events like the "Nepalibaba" of Ranthalei village near Anugul, the Naga Sadhu-police conflict at Puri town (1955) and the Daleighai Flood (1955) shook the administration of Nabakrishna Chowdhury.

The great setbacks Nabakrishna Choudhury faced were the failure of the fixation of Orissa boundary with Sareikala and Kharsuan before the Central Boundary Commission appointed by the Central Govt. in November 1953. Secondly he could not utilise the allotted money for the developmental works in Orissa within a stipulated period of time for which the money was refunded. Besides Naba Babu was mostly dissatisfied with the unbecoming conduct of his Associates and the party.

In view of these adverse circumstances, Nabakrishna Choudhury resigned from the post of Chief Minister on 18th October 1956 Dr. H.K. Mahtab relinquished the post as the Governor of Maharashtra and accepted the post as the Chief Minister of Orissa on the very same day, Nabakrishna Choudhury gave up politics for ever and spent the rest of his life at "Malati Ashram" in Anugul (Dhenkanal). He died on.

On the other hand, Mahtab was hoodwinked by the Congress Party who was not taken into Nehru Cabinet. Out of disappointment, Mahtab once again wanted to come back to Orissa politics. So Mahtab since 1952 to 1956, through his daily news paper, "Prajatantra", began to vehemently criticise Nabakrishna Choudhury and his views on different problems of Orissa. Many other supporters of Mahtab also made Mr. Choudhury the target of their scathing criticism. In politics, nobody is a friend and nobody is an enemy but the self-interest of the person reigns supreme in life.

Nabakrishna Choudhury could not rebuff the united attack of Mahtab and his supporters. The Congress High Command—UN Dhebar replaced Choudhury.

Soon after Mahtab became the Chief Minister of Orissa, the second general elections in India were held from 24th February 1957 to 14th March 1957. The Congress Party under the leadership of Mahtab got only 56 seats out of 140 in

Orissa Assembly. It gave a great setback to the Congress leaders in India, but Mahtab in order to give an impression to the Central leaders, tried to form a Coalition Govt. with the PSP (11 seats) and CPI (9 seats). The Coalition Govt. was formed with Mahtab as the Chief Minister. But this period was the darkest period in the history of Orissa—"a period that witnessed intense politicking furious horse-trading and rampant corruption." Mahtab out of greed of the political power did everything which he would not have done.

A scandal against Mahtab rented the entire air of Orissa Politics that Mahtab has illegally granted mining lease to M/s Serajuddin as the Mining owner in Orissa. This scandal gradually gathered intense momentum in Orissa. The MLAs were traded as horse in the market places—always there was a defection in Assembly. The MLAs exchanged blows and used the most unparliamentary words—Physical assault torn the Punjabi and shirts of MLAs one another. Under such a hectic political scene in Orissa, Mahtab resigned in May 1958. Singdeo claimed the support of the majority of MLAs and wanted to be the Chief Minister of Orissa but the Governor Mr. Y.N. Sukhtankar (1957-1962) did not accept the resignation of Mahtab nor did he invite R N Singhdeo to form any Ministry.

After a few days, another political device was explored. Mr. Biju Patnaik persuaded R N Singhdeo to form a Coalition Govt. R.N. Singhdeo who was anxiously waiting for an opportunity to come himself and the Ganatantra Parishad to the notice of the Orissa public readily agreed. Mahtab once again became the Chief Minister and R.N. Singhdeo became the Finance Minister. The new Coalition Govt. came into existence on 22 May 1959.

Biju Patnaik who was the architect of the Coalition Govt. wanted to be taken into the Cabinet of Orissa, but Mahtab stabbed Biju Patnaik from rear and whiled away the process of inserting Biju into his cabinet Biju Patnaik out of disgust turned hostile to Mahtab and vomited poison against Mahtab and illustrated his anti-Mahtab activities.

Fortunately, Biju Patnaik holds position of the President of the Utkal Pradesh Congress Committee. He now projected the images of modern agriculture. Science and technology and a better industrialization in Orissa. By this, Biju Patnaik created a public opinion in Orissa and motivated the people in favour of his dynamic leadership. When the political situation in Orissa was turned to his favour, he formed a sub-committee in September 1960 consisting of Banamali Patnaik, Biswanath Das and Biren Mitra to study the works of the coalition Govt. and prepare a report. This committee submitted an adverse report against the Coalition Govt. and suggested to dissolve the ministry and imposition of President's rule. No budget was presented in the Assembly Ultimately the Coalition Govt. was dissolved on 24-February-1961. And the President's rule was imposed.

The Governor A N Khosla invited R N Singhdeo to from a Ministery—but he expressed his inability. The President's rule was imposed till 23 June 1961.

The mid-term election was held in Orissa in 1961 in the month of June Biju Patnaik invigorated the hopes and aspirations of the people of Orissa by his spectacular promises. He invited the top Congress leaders from centre for political propaganda in the meetings of different constituencies.. This charismatic personality created a hallow in the mind of the voters of Orissa. In the mid term elections, the Congress party emerged with the overwhelming majority of 82 seats out of 140, Ganatantra Parishad 37 and P.S.P. 10 seats only. Biju Patnaik became the natural choice of the legislative party and took oath as the Chief Minister of Orissa on June 23 1961.

Biju Patnaik materialized more Projects and Plans what he promised during the electioneering. It can be said that the period of Biju Patnaik is a landmark in the history of Orissa. He tenaciously worked and created a legacy of his life work.

Biju Patnaik as the Chief Minister of Orissa rendered commendable services to the people of Orissa during his regime (June 1961 to October 1963). The most important of them was the setting up of the Paradip Port, Thermal Power Plant in Talcher, the MIG Factory at Sunabeda and Balimela Project. He established several mills—the factories and Paper Mills. Two technical schools at Aska and Chouduar were established. Another memorable institution he set up was the Regional Engineering College at Rourkela. Students from all over India came to study in this institution Sainika School at Bhubaneswar is Biju Patnaik's creation. Scholarships to the students of Engineering, Medical and Art and Architecture, and Education were awarded. So he has created innumerable Doctors, Engineers, Lecturers, painters and has given appointments to countless youths at Kalinga Textile & Kalinga Tubes at Chouduar, Biju Patnaik unhesitatingly extended financial help to the school students to purchase Text Books, Bicycles, and to the Patients for their treatment. So Biju Patnaik would be remembered by all due to his magnanimous character and philanthropic inclination.

Biju Patnaik established State Planning Board of Orissa to undertake different development works. Biju Babu did not encourage "Red-tapism" and "bureaucratic procrastination" which clogged the progress. "What is good to the People and to State" must be done forthwith. And so he has done it. But that Biju Patnaik due to his old age and corrupt administrative machinery could do absolutely nothing during his second tenure of Chief Ministership of Orissa from 5th March 1990 to March 1995. Red-tapism and bureaucratic procrastination which were discarded by Biju Patnaik in 1961-1963 now clogged the wheel of progress in Orissa in 1990-1995. The octopus of corruption clamped the employees, bureaucrats and political leaders of Orissa.

In October, 1963, the ghost of Kamraj Plan necessitated Biju Babu to step down from the corridor of powers. Under the Kamraj Plan some top leaders of Congress Party all over India were pulled down to devote their time, skill and energies to strengthen the Congress Party. With the stepping down of Biju Babu from Chief Ministership, the downfall of the Congress Govt. began in Orissa. It also put an end to the glorious period of Orissa. It led me to think that Kamraj Plan is the most ruinous and dubious. Due to the departure of Biju Patnaik, no other developmental works in Orissa could be done. So Kamraj Plan rendered a great loss to Orissa. Biren Mitra is not Biju Patnaik nor is he a proper substitute. The techniques of works and the scientific outlook of Biju Patnaik could not be inherited by Biren Mitra. Biren Mitra could succeed the chair of Patnaik and nothing else.

Biren Mitra

After a brilliant period of Biju Patnaik, Biren Mitra started a darker phase of Orissa administration. He began to do all works in the "durbar style" of traditional Kings of feudatory states. Many of his colleagues and enemies began to criticize him for the alleged crime of the involvement of his wife in the business deal with M/S Serajuddin, the mine-owner taking a sum of Rs. 16 lakhs of rupees as bribe. All the leaders like Mahtab, R N Singhdeo, Pabitra Mohan Pradhan criticized this deal and suggested to probe this corruption by CBI. In November, 1964, the CBI submitted the reports implicating Biren Mitra's involvement in corruption and misuse of powers.

In September, 1964, the Govt. of Biren Mitra could not tackle the students strike. From a very trivial cause, it flared into a strike of great magnitude. A student of Engineering school, Cuttack gave an transistor to a mechanic for repair in the Station Bazar near M.S. Law College. The customer did not pay the requisite amount for the repair to the mechanic. So the mechanic one day caught the customer in a saloon where the customer was being shaved by a barber and demanded the money. Then they went to the shop of mechanic where there was a hot exchange of words between them. The shop-keeper assaulted the student. This incident ultimately brought the students of Law College, Ravenshaw College to the spot. The students burnt and looted the different cloth shops, stalls.. Police began lathi charge—entered into the Law Hostel and Ravenshaw College. The students threw stones at the police. Then entire College square of Ravenshaw College was turned into a battle field. The student strike spread like a wildfire throughout Orissa. The students got into the Assembly Halls and created nuisance by destroying the furniture and files etc. All colleges were closed down sine die. In a firing at Cuttack some persons were seriously wounded and some were killed. The students mob set fire the house of Satyapriya Mohanty—the then Education Minister and attacked the houses of Biren Mitra and Biju Patnaik. There was a tremendous uproar and student indiscipline in entire Orissa.

In the long run, the Govt. of Orissa agreed for a judicial enquiry under S. Burman, Justice of Orissa High Court and compensation to the affected students. All the students who were arrested during the strike were released. But the Govt. became unpopular. It could not function as before, Biren Mitra finally resigned as Chief Minister on 1.2.1963.

The resignation of Biren Mitra puzzled the political situation of Orissa. All the top leaders of Orissa were experimented and found guilty of their misuse of political powers and position. A case against H K Mahtab on Kendu leaf was launched from 1958 and that case was dismissed in 1981 for want of sufficient documents and death of many witness. A case against any political leader in Indian democratic setup is a gimmick.

Sadasiv Tripathy

Ultimately an honest and gentleman of the tribal district

of Koraput was chosen as the Chief Minister of Orissa from the Congress Legislative Party—Mr. Sadasiva Tripathy who took oath on 19th February, 1965.

Having been frustrated Mr. Pabitra Mohan Pradhan and H.K. Mahtab left the Congress and formed a new Political Party as "Jana Congress" on 3th May 1966. Pabitra Mohan was nominated as the President and a few MLAs and MPs were the numbers. Mahtab tried to align himself and Party with Ganatantra Parishad to fight against the Congress.

Mr. Sadasiva Tripathy as the Chief Minister of Orissa found himself in the series of adversities. Biju Patnaik operated the adverse force by his remote control.

The dissident Congress leaders Swatantra Party (earlier Ganatantra Parishad) and the Jana Congress jointly brought innumerable charges of corruption against the Ministers of Sadasiva Tripathy, Biju Patnaik also created problems for Tripathy by writing letters to the Congress High Command—Kamraj Nadar. Sadasiva Tripathy took it as the most insulting issue and asked the Ministers to resign. Many Ministers resigned.

Under such hectic and adverse political situations, elections for the Orissa Assembly were held on 21th February 1967. For electioneering propaganda, Mrs. India Gandhi as the Prime Minster of India paid a visit to Orissa. On 8th February, 1967 in a mammoth gathering of thousands of spectators at Bhubaneswar Indira Gandhi addressed but during her speech some indisciplined youths created chaos and threw stones at Indira Gandhi. The stone hit the nose of Mrs. Indira Gandhi and there was bloodshed. The entire audience was stunned to see it. I was also one of the spectators in that meeting standing far away from the pavilion. The police arrested some youngmen. This incident took place at the large field in front of the Secretariate—now Indira Park. The opposition parties, Swatantra Jana Congress and PSP took the utmost advantage of this troubled waters. The results of the elections exposed the disastrous defeat of the Congress Party. The pre-election manifesto of the Swatantra and Jana Congress caught the imagination of the voters and both the parties were voted to power with Swatantra—49 and Jana Congress—26 seats in the Assembly of 140 seats.

R.N. Singh Deo

According to the pre-election agreement, Mr. Rajendra Narayan Singhdeo of Swatantra Party was elected as the Chief Minister of Orissa. And this Coalition Ministery formed with other top leaders of both the parties. Mr. Pabitra Mohan Pradhan became the Deputy Chief Minister. It was for the first time that the post of Deputy Chief Minister was created in Orissa politics. This Coalition Ministry took charge of the Orissa administration on 8th March 1967 with 19 Ministers. In a Coalition Ministry, there were frequent conflicts and dissatisfaction on the issue of the distribution of portfolio positions and Govt. policies. In spite of this, this Govt. lasted for a period of 3 years and 10 months.

During the period of the Coalition Govt. corruption as the national Institution could not be abolished rather it was deep rooted. The Govt. faced the Teachers strike (College) and a great student strike. Mr. Banamali Patnaik was the Minister of Education who ruthlessly put down the strike of the College Teachers—the police beat the teachers and the tents where they launched Dharana before the Minister's bunglow were uprooted. Not even a single demand of the College teachers was fulfilled.

Likewise the students strike was also suppressed by an iron hand of Rajendra Narayan Singhdeo. During the period of wanton strike, somebody was killed in the SCB Medical College, Cuttack. On this issue, the Chief Minister threatened the student leaders for general arrest. Later on the strike was called off.

This Coalition Govt. of Rajendra Narayan Singhdeo brought the age of superannuation of the Govt. employees from 58 years to 55 as a result of which many Govt. servants were retired. This Govt. also abolished the land-revenue of the people.

The year 1969 saw the tumultous events in national history of India. The Indian Congress was bifurcated into Congress(R) and Congress (O)—on the issue of the Presidential election in July 1969 of Varah Giri Venkat Giri. It was a triangular fight among V.V. Giri, Sanjiva Reddy and C.D. Deshmukh. Mrs. Indira Gandhi did not support Sanjiva Reddy rather encouraged the acting President V.V. Giri to contest in the Presidential election. V.V. Giri was the acting President in the event of the death of Dr. Zakir Hussain. Mr. Nijalingappa—the President of Indian National Congress—backed the candidature of Sanjiva Reddy. Ultimately in the Presidential election, V.V. Giri won the victory. The Congress (O) Party consisted of Moraraji Desai, Kamraj Nadar, Nijalingappa, Atulya Ghose, S.K. Patil, Congress (R) Party consisted of Indira Gandhi, Jagajivan Ram, Y.V. Chavan, C Subramaniam, Nandini Satapathy. This division of Congress Party left the tremendous impact upon the functioning of the Govts. of other provinces. Many leaders were in a tupsy-turvy to which Party they would lean.

Mrs. Indira Gandhi also got the ordinance signed by V.V. Giri for the abolition of the Privy Purses of the Rajas and Maharajas of India. The Privy Purse, which was being given to the Kings of India since 1947 was discontinued in 1971. The Rajas and Maharajas staged a "dharana" in front of the Parliament in support of the Privy Purse but Indira Gandhi turned a deaf ear to this.

Indira Gandhi also nationalised 14 Private Banks in India by an ordinance.

This Coalition Govt. worked with understanding till

January 1971. Rajendra Narayan Singhdeo abolished land revenue and guaranteed absolute freedom to the bureaucrats to deal with the financial problems. This Ministry did not pick up any Industrial Projects and did not revive the old and sickly industry. R.N Singhdeo closed down the Panchayat industries which negated the economic standard of the rural people.

Taking the political vendetta, R.N. Singhdeo directed to set up "Enquiry Commission" under H.R. Khanna against the charges of corruptions and irregularities committed by the Ministers of 1961-67. This committee submitted its report on 15th January 1969.

The Second Enquiry Committee under J R Mudholkor, a retired judge of the Supreme Court was also set up to probe into the charges of Sadasiv Tripathy H.K Mahtab, N K Choudhury, R N Singhdeo and Shantanu Kumar Das. This Committee submitted its report to the Chief Minister but the Chief Minister did not publish it.

Another Enquiry Committee under Sarjoo Prasad was also established to particularly find out the corruptions against H K Mahtab on the eve of 1971 elections.

All the findings of the Enquiry Commissions are though found to be true but no minister has ever been punished in Orissa or in India. R N Singhdeo wasted a huge amount of public money and valuable time in digging out the corruption charges. He could not devote his mind, energy and public money for the development of the health, education, energy, roads and many other subjects.

In Orissa, the Congress Party was also divided into two fractions. Sadasiv Tripathy retired from State Politics permanently on the ground of ill health. He died on 10.9.1980.

Biju Patnaik was also very critical about the activities of

Mrs. Indira Gandhi and leaned more towards Morarji Desai. The only Congress leader who sided with Mrs. Indira Gandhi was Binayak Acharya of Berhampur. Indira Gandhi also showed unequivocal support and help to Mrs. Nandini Satapathy who was also a Deputy Minister of Information and Broadcasting in the Central Cabinet.

The resignation of Biju Patnaik from Congress Party was inevitable when the Congress High Command turned down his claim for Rajya Sabha seat in March 1970. Biju Patnaik took this issue as a great humiliation and resigned from the Congress. Thereafter he formed a new Political Party as "Utkal Congress" according to the decision of the meeting, which was held on 16 May 1970. The Congress Party was divided into two in Assembly. The Utkal Congress had 22 members and was recognised as the Opposition Party of the Assembly.

H.K. Mahtab was not fully satisfied with the functioning of the Coalition Govt. because R N Singhdeo as the Chief Minister did not listen to the advice and suggestions of Mahtab nor Mahtab was induced into the Cabinet. Besides Pabitra Mohan Pradhan was also hankering after powers in the Cabinet. So Mahtab wanted to withdraw from the Coalition Govt. so he made preparations and requested Nandini Satapathy to take Mahtab and his followers. Nandini Satapathy discussed with Indira Gandhi about this proposal. Indira Gandhi accepted it. Mahtab as a political opportunist immediately resigned from the Jana Congress. He and some of his followers were admitted into Congress on 22-January-1971. After it, Mahtab demanded to have the Assembly with Parliamentary elections in March 1971. The followers of Mahtab were Banamali Patnaik, Man Mohan Tudu, Surendra Nath Patnaik. All the Jana Congress Ministers resigned from the Coalition Cabinet of R N Singhdeo on 5th January 1971. R.N. Singhdeo as the Chief Minister also resigned on 9th January 1971.

Orissa was then put under the President's Rule from 12.1.1971 to 2.4.1971. The Governor of Orissa was Dr. Shoukatulla Shah Ansari who was a Dentist by Profession.

Biswanath Das

The Indian Parliament was dissolved on 27th December 1970. V.V. Giri thereafter issued notifications for a fresh election and simultaneously the Orissa Assembly election was to be held. The elections were held on February 1971. The "Garibi Hatao" slogan of Mrs. Indira Gandhi left a deep impact upon the voters. But Congress or any other party did not get overwhelming majority to form ministry single-handed. So once again the attempt to form the Coalition Govt. was started. Biju Patnaik of Utkal Congress, R N Singhdeo of Swatantra and Siddhilal Murmu of Jharkhand discussed together about the possibility of a united party to form the Ministry. Ultimately they forged to form the Ministry. But Biju Patnaik and R.N. Singhdeo did not like to be the Chief Minister of Orissa. So they searched for an agreeable candidate and discovered Biswanath Das—who was by that time retired as the Góvernor of Uttar Pradesh and living a lonely life in Cuttack. On April 3rd 1971 at 9 P M Biswanath Das took oath as the Chief Minister of Orissa along with 14 other ministers.

According to the Constitutional provisions a candidate has to be elected to the Assembly within a period of six months. Ultimately Mr. Das was elected to the Assembly from the Rourkela constituency. The rival candidate of Mr. Das was Binayak Acharya in Rourkela who was then the leader of the Opposition Party in Orissa Assembly.

Biju Patnaik was miserably and desparately defeated by his rivals in four constituencies of Bhanjanagar, Bhubaneswar, Khurda and Chouduar for Orissa Assembly and one Lok Sabha seat of Aska Constituency. It was the greatest mortal blow to Biju Patnaik in his entire political career.

Biswanath Das could not swim safely in the troubled waters of Orissa politics. Dr. Mahtab, his followers and the Congress leaders like Binayak Acharya, Braja Mohan Mohanty, Banamali Patnaik, CPI leaders, and PSP leaders tried to pull him down from the powers. So in a most organized conspiracy of vandalism, they misbehaved Biswanath Das in the Assembly premises. Meanwhile the two prominent PSP leaders—Prasanna Kumar Das and Banka Behari Das left the PSP Party of India and joined hand with Congress. They began the naked "horse-trading" and gained over two ministers of United Govt. Mr. Gangadhar Pradhan, Fisheries & Animal Husbandary and Dambarudhar Majhi, PWD and Transport along with other six MLAs as a result of which the majority of MLAs reduced to minimum. Besides, Biswanath Das was an old man of 82 years old who did not like to shoulder the burden of the Govt. So after a hectic period of 14 months, he resigned from the Chief Minister on 13.6.1972.

Virtually, after the resignation of Biswanath Das, Binayak Acharya was to be the Chief Minister of Orissa. The next probable candidate was Nilamani Routroy who joined the Congress later on. But both the prospective candidates were eclipsed. The Governor, Joginder Singh was the henchman of Indira Gandhi. Indira Gandhi instructed the Governor Singh to keep Mr. Acharya and Mr. Routroy aside and paved the way for Mrs. Nandini Satapathy to be the Chief Minister of Orissa. Accordingly, Joginder Singh acted.

Nandini Satapathy

Nandini Satapathy who by that time was the member of the Rajya Sabha and holds the post of the Minister of State in the Indira Gandhi Cabinet. Although Nandini Satapathy was previously a branded Communist in Orissa. Indira Gandhi out of political necessity reposed confidence in the Communist leaders in Delhi politics and provided them ample privileges and opportunities. Nandini Satapathy therefore pushed herself into the corridors of powers and was nominated as the Chief Minister of Orissa. She took oath on June 14th 1972 and a host of other Ministers was induced. Later on Nandini Satapathy was elected from Cuttack Constituency.

Nandini Satapathy wanted to rule Orissa arbitrarily and without other's cooperation except the Communist Party. So she did not accept the proposal of Biju Patnaik to include some members of Utkal Congress. The Communist members supported her.

The Nandini Govt. could not achieve any respect and cooperation from the people of Orissa because she could not render any beneficial services to the public. She was thoroughly indulged in hooliganism, corruption, conspiracy, dishonesty, goondaism and malafied activities. Due to her pressure only, H K Mahtab was suspended from the Congress Party.

Once again the Trio—Mahtab, Biju Patnaik and R N Singhdeo hatched a conspiracy to topple down the Nandini Govt. Nilamani Routroy who was a member of the Nandini Council of Ministers became a trump card to be played for the downfall of the Nandini Govt. along with other 21 MLAs. All the 22 MLAs withdrew their support from Nandini Govt. and joined hands with Utkal Congress. Nandini Satapathy lost the majority in the Legislature and ultimately she resigned as the Chief Minister on 2.3.1973. The Governor of Orissa was Basappa Danappa Jatti (as B D Jatti).

Biju Patnaik anxiously met the Governor at his Raj Bhavan to form the Ministry with 71 MLAs-but B D Jatti did not comply with his request. He implored the kindness of the President V.V. Giri who imposed President's Rule in Orissa on March 3rd 1973.

Mid-term elections were held in Orissa on 22-24 of February 1974. The total member of Assembly seats was increased from 140 to 147 after reallocation of voters in different Constituencies.

The elections resulted in no Political Party secured majority. The Congress Party owned 69 seats only and Nandini Satapathy was once again selected to head the Ministry with the support from the Communist Party. The Prominent Communist Legislators of Assembly who extended unequivocal support to Nandini Satapathy were Sri Lokanath Choudhury (Erasama), Sadananda Mohanty (Kabisuryanagar) and Harihar Das (Aska). In lieu of their support Nandini Satapathy showered on them the unlimited privileges and comforts. They were supplied with Fiat Cars for their personal use and she paid huge amount of money. Nandini took oath for the second time as the Chief Minister on 25.2.1974 and continued to be in power till 16.12.1976.

Nandini Satapathy

Just as a replica of Indira Gandhi, Nandini Satapathy also started an era of ignominious rule in Orissa in the line of thoughts and actions of Indira Gandhi. And it was during her regime that V.S. Mathews (the Chief Secretary of Orissa) and Dr. Sri Rama Chandra Dash (Professor of Political Science-Utkal University) were given compulsory retirement. She ruthlessly put down her opponents and critics and utilized the office, power and pressure to further her interests, her relatives and Indira Gandhi.

The dramatic emergence of Jaya Prakash Narayan in Indian politics was a terror to the position and powers of Indira Gandhi. Though the movement of Jaya Prakash was first aimed at the injustice, irregularity, corruption and conspiracy of the Gaffur Govt. in Bihar, but the movement spread all over India as the wildfire. The fiery speeches of Jayaprakash and the techniques of organising innumerable meetings all over Indian peninsula caught the imagination of the people. Lakhs of people were attracted to his magnetic personality. It became a "Revolution of JP in Indian politics. The Indian people were mesmerized by his revolutionary and inflammable speeches. And this JP Movement shook the edifice of the throne of power of Indira Gandhi. And she gradually observed as the Prime Minister that almost all the public-spirited people were inclined to Jaya Prakash Narayan. The entire political atmosphere of India was surcharged with a deep sense of righteousness and alertness of the people. Indira Gandhi was extremely frightened.

Jaya Prakash Narayan visited Orissa and addressed the mammoth meetings at Jharusuguda, Sambalpur on 30 March 1975. All the dissident members of Congress Party and new members of Swatantra, Utkal Congress gathered round Jaya Prakash Narayan. He also attended the meetings at Dhenkanal and Baliyatra field of Cuttack Town. The Nandini Govt. did not allow the organizers of JP meeting in front of the Secretariate. JP addressed a meeting at the school area of unit No. 1 in Bhubaneswar. JP was welcomed as the Messiah to the suffering mankind.

Banka Behari Das and Braja Mohan Mohanty were ousted from the circle of powers of Nandini Satapathy who ultimately formed an alliance with Janaki Ballav Patnaik and Trilochan Kanungo to topple the Nandini Ministry.

Meanwhile the judgement of the Hon'ble justice Jag Mohan Lal Sinha of Allahabad High Court was propounced where he implied Indira Gandhi to be guilty for utilising the Uttar Pradesh Govt. officials and machinery for her electioneering at Rae Bareilly MP Constituency and won the victory. Her rival Contestant, Mr. Raj Narayan filed a case against Indira Gandhi for her alleged role in Election. Mr. Sinha found Indira Gandhi to be guilty from witness and official documents and punished that Indira Gandhi could not contest in any election as a candidate for at least a period of six years. This judgement was just like a bolt from the blue. Many members of the cotterie of Indira Gandhi suggested to appeal to the Supreme Court. Indira Gandhi personally wanted to obey the judgement of the Judge and to keep herself aloof from the politics. But her son, Sanjay Gandhi decided to take the case to the Supreme Court. In the Supreme Court, the judges were reshuffled. Mr. A.N. Roy who was the Junior Judge in the Supreme Court superceded three Senior judges and posted as the Chief Justice of the Supreme Court. A.N. Roy paid back to Indira Gandhi the honour, the promotion she has bestowed upon him. A.N. Roy negatived the judgement of Mr. Sinha and made Indira Gandhi innocent and free from the allegations Raj Narayan lavelled against her.

All the days do not smoothly go with happiness. The dark clouds have gathered round the head of Nandini Satapathy. Attempts were made to topple her Cabinet by Janaki Ballav Pattnaik and Banamali Pattnaik. They convinced Sanjay Gandhi who was there the most undisputed man in India. He could make and unmake things in India.

Indira Gandhi whenever keenly observed that the people of India were gradually inclining to Jaya Prakash Narayan and the situation was intensely inflammable. She declared "National Emergency" in India on 15th June 1975.

The period of Emergency covered almost two years from 15th June 1975 to 22.3. 1977. It was the darkest period in the political history of India. All the top leaders of India J.P., H.K. Mahtab, Morarji Desai, Nabakrishna Choudhury were imprisoned in different jails. Some leaders were tortured in jails. Indira Gandhi throatled the press. No press was allowed to publish any independent news. The press brought one type of news from the "News Bank" founded by Indira Gandhi. The police took over the administration of India and in some cases the police also killed some persons due to their excessive torture. The entire India became a burning cauldron. The emergency terrified all the people of India and the people wanted a relief from this dragon of Emergency.

Mrs. Nandini Satapathy posed herself as the most powerful lady in Orissa and gave an impression to the people of Orissa that she was more powerful than Indira Gandhi. As Indira

Gandhi was termed as "Indira is India" by the then Congress President Mr. Hemakanta Barua, Nandini Satapathy herself was also regarded as the "rising sun of Asia". Nandini could not be Indira. Sanjay Gandhi did not tolerate this caption of Nandini and obtained the permission from his mother. Nandini Satapathy was mercilessly sacked on 16.12.1976.

Binayak Acharya

And there was a vacuum of power in Orissa for 13 days. The President Fakruddin Ali Ahmed imposed President Rule in Orissa. And during this period the Congress Party searched for a leader to head the Ministry in Orissa. Ultimately the choice fell upon Sri Binayak Acharya—who had entered into politics after the teachership of the Municipal High School at Berhampur. Binayak Acharya took oath as the Chief Minister of Orissa on 29.12.1976.

The times of Binayak Acharya from 29.12.1976 to 25 June 1977 were eventless. The spirit of emergency of Indira Gandhi began to fade away. The people of India were restless and hopeless. Some of the closest Congress leaders without feeling the pulse of the Indian people advised Indira Gandhi to put an end to the Emergency and declare for general Parliament elections which were overdue to be held in March 1976. Indira Gandhi advised the President Fakruddin Ali Ahmed to dissolve the Indian Parliament on 18 January 1977.

Elections were held in India from 16.3.1977 to 20.3.1977. Out of 542 seats the Janata Party secured 271 seats. Raj Narayan in the Rae Bareilly Lok Sabha Constituency defeated Indira Gandhi herself. The Emergency was lifted from 21 March 1977 and a new Central Cabinet was formed on 24 March 1977 under the stewardship of Mr. Morarji Desai—an old and veteran Congress leader during the Nehru Regime.

Nilamani Routroy

Mid term Elections were also held in Orissa on 10th June

1977 for 147 seats. In this elections, the voters of Orissa rejected the Congress Party for its Emergency and voted the Janata Party to power. After a long period of discussions, Nilamani Routroy was selected as the leader of the Party who ultimately took oath as the Chief Minister of Orissa in the post-emergency period on 26 June 1977 with 9 Cabinet Ministers and 6 Rastra Ministers. The Governor of Orissa in those days was Hara Charan Singh Brar.

Due to the division and subdivision in the four party Coalitions Govt. in Centre, Mr. Morarji Desai was upset. Choudhury Charan Singh and Raj Narain withdrew their support from the Desai Govt. which ultimately led to the collapse of the Govt. Mr. Morarji Desai tendered his resignation on 27th July 1979.

Mr. Charan Singh appealed to the President Mr. Sanjiv Reddy to form the Govt. Surprisingly Mrs. Indira Gandhi who was by that time confined in Tihar Jail for her alleged involvement in Maruti Car Company sent congratulatory message with the support to Charan Singh Govt. Therefore, Charan Singh took oath as the Prime Minister of India on 28th July , 1979 Mr. Biju patnaik was the Cabinet Minister with the steel portfolio. Mrs. Indira Gandhi was the political wizard and played the game to pull down the Charan Singh Govt. She withdrew her support and Charan Singh Govt. was collapsed like house of cards on 20 August 1979 just twenty two days after the formation of his Govt. A Prime Minister of 22 days only was also worshipped in India by the bogus politicians and public.

The immediate and successive collapse of the two Central Govt. in Delhi left a deep impact upon the Orissa politics. The ideological difference between Biju Patnaik and Biswabhusan Harichandan as a RSS member grew wider. Nilamani Routroy having been obliged by the circumstances dropped Mr. Hari Chandan and Prahallad Mallick from his Cabinet.

Nandini Satapathy who was once upon the undisputed and unequivocal during the emergency was now arrested on the alleged collection of huge amount of money from the Govt. treasury and private parties. Two years after her trial, she was ultimately released on 4 Dec. 1980 by the order of Prime Minister, Indira Gandhi.

The Indian politics was always paradoxical. So Orissa. All the leaders pull others by their selfish interests. In the general elections of India in January 1980 Mrs. Indira Gandhi and her Congress (I) was once again voted to power. In India there was and is always a negative voting by the people. Because no Political Govts. function to the satisfaction of the people. They are so blindly involved in their party scrabbling and interests, that they forget the voters or work adversely against the interests of the people for which the Govt. in power is doomed to downfall.

As Mrs. Indira Gandhi won the victory in 1980 general elections, she decided to topple the Orissa Ministry of Nilamani Routroy. The Nilamani Govt. was dismissed on 17th February 1980. The President imposed his rule on Orissa upto 9th June 1980. Elections in Orissa were held on 31st May, 1980 for 147 seats in the Assembly.

In the elections, almost all the Non-Congress Political Parties were wiped out. The Congress won an overwhelming majority of 117 seats—a record in the entire political history of Orissa. Janaki Ballav Patnaik by that time who was nominated as the PCC President and enjoyed the rank of Cabinet Minister in the Indira Cabinet, was sent to Orissa to head the Ministry as the Chief Minister. Later on he was elected as a MLA from the Athagarh Constituency on 23 November 1980.

J. B. Patnaik

Sri Janaki Ballav Patnaik no doubt was crowned as the Chief Minister of Orissa for a full term of five years from

1980 to March 9, 1985. During this period Janaki Govt. did not work to the satisfaction of the people of Orissa. The superfast Nilachala Express from Bhubaneswar to New Delhi or the Bhubaneswar-New Delhi direct plane fight had nothing to do with the common people of Orissa. They wanted bread or rice, peace, discipline and justice, employment, moderate market price, etc. but the Govt. was involved in suppressing the press and building the Castle at Rameswaram regardless of any law, reaction of the people, or shame. One of Janaki's Minister—Mr. Basant Biswal overpowered the Chief Minister and did whatever he liked to do. Janaki Ballav Patnaik kept mum and dumb. Basant Biswal committed all financial irregularities in the Govt.

One of the memorable events of Janaki's regime was the cold-blooded murder and rape of Chhabirani Mohapatra in the river-bed of Biluakhai in the district of Cuttack. She was the wife of a Correspondent—Mr. Naba Kumar Mohapatro of "Pragatibadi" newspaper. Janaki Ballav Patnaik played a foul game in politics.

He was also a perfect liar. To hoodwink the people of Orissa, Janaki Ballav Patnaik gave a loud slogan that he would establish one thousand industries in one thousand days with one thousand crore of rupees. It was the greatest political hypocricy the people of Orissa have not yet forgotten. He did absolutely nothing in the field of Industry in Orissa. Anyhow, he completed 5 years as the Chief Minister because all the leaders of other Political Parties were defunct and inactive in Orissa.

The brutal assassination of Mrs. Indira Gandhi on 31st October, 1984 was the greatest blow to Congress. The Indian people forgot the atrocity and exploitations of Mrs. Indira Gandhi during the darkest chapter of national emergency in 1975 to 1977. The followers shed tears at her inhuman death.

Immediately after death fresh elections were held in India.

Mr. Rajiv Gandhi got sympathy votes from the people and formed the Ministry at the Centre and himself became the Prime Minister.

In Orissa too, in the 1985 elections in March, the Congress Party was once again voted to power and Mr. Janaki Ballav Patnaik took oath as the Chief Minister of Orissa successively in two terms on 10 March 1985. The period of the Janaki Govt. from 1985 to February 1990 was also useless. During the Second term as the Chief Minister, Janaki Babu did nothing for the welfare of the people. It was the golden period for Janaki Babu who successively became twice the Chief Minister-but intimately he cheated the voters of Orissa. He built his own nest firmly by satisfying the top Congress leaders in Delhi. He also thought that after the death of Mrs. Gandhi, there was no such powerful Congress leader who could dismiss him as the Chief Minister of Orissa. So he indulged himself in all types of nefarious illegal and erratic activities in Bhubaneswar. He patronized corruption in administration and politics. He favoured the worthless and useless goondas to further his political interests. He suppressed the persons who criticized his Govt. and activities. It was reported that Mr. Janaki Ballav Patnaik was involved in the suicide case of Miss Rani Mallik who wanted to be an air-hostess and surrendered herself to Janaki. She having been frustrated committed suicide.

Janaki Babu was also criticized for his having illicit relations with a lady of Bhubaneswar—Sebarani Das who was kept in the OSEB Guest House at Sahid Nagar, near Vani Vihar Square, BBSR.

The leading English weekly of India "The Illustrated Weekly" published these two sex scandals of Janaki Babu and his Govt. and supporters tried to block the circulation of the Weekly in Orissa market and burnt many Illustrated Weekly copies in cuttack and Bhubaneswar. Ultimately the Editor of the Illustrated Weekly begged excuse and Janaki

Babu withdrew the case, which he had filed immediately after the release of the Weekly in the markets.

The period of 10 years (1980-1990) was enough for Mr. Janaki Ballav Patnaik to achieve miracles in enterprises and achievements for the good of the people. Unnecessarily, the Ministers and MLAs were fed by the public money. It was a period of misdirected energy and useless expenditure for the MLAs. Whereas Janaki Babu repeatedly refers that he has given the stable Govt. Political stability of Govt. did not mean the economic welfare of the people. It was the dullest period in the political history of Orissa.

The people expected many things but got nothing. Janaki Babu was asked to resign by Rajiv Gandhi, the Congress High Command and accordingly he vacated the office and Mr. Hemananda Biswal entered into the office of Chief Minister on 7th December 1989. Mr. Biswal became a stop-gap arrangement—a Stephene prior to the Assembly elections which were held on 28 February 1990—a Chief Minister of 82 days only.

By a negative voting, Janaki Babu, Hemananda and Congress Party were once again voted out of power on 28th February 1990 elections in Orissa. Biju Patnaik won a thunderous victory in this election. He got 123 seats in the elections out of 147. Biju Patnaik set an unparalleled record of his political victory in Orissa. After the longest period of 27 years, Biju Patnaik returned to Orissa politics as the Chief Minister. He took oath on 5th March 1990 which coincided his birthday.

Biju Patnaik

The tenure of Biju Patnaik from 5th March 1990 to February was also useless because his Govt. was fully unsuccessful to do anything good for the people. The people of Orissa were very much optimistic that Biju Patnaik would do unlimited welfare activities for the people. Because the people of 1962-

63 are still alive who have seen the miraculous works of Biju Patnaik as the Chief Minister, But Biju Patnaik at the age of 74, did not possess that juvenile spirit and zeal to work. Besides there was a sea change in the nature of the employees and the administration of the Orissa state. Corruption reigned supreme—every body was trying to build his selfishness. There was no sign of honesty, sincerity, obedience and dedication of the employees of the state. Biju Babu was already haggard and difficult to manage the welfare of the state with a wretched and rotten administration of the state. So he gave a slogan to the people to beat those officers who were not efficient in doing the public welfare. Some officers were also beaten in their Govt. offices and outside. It created an administrative problem and deadlock. The officers criticized the slogans of Biju Patnaik Through beating the officers, the people achieved nothing. It ended in smoke.

Biju Babu had got tremendous weakness for women for which many women cultivated relations with Biju Babu and squeezed fabulous profits and privileges. Kiran Bala Mangaraj was one of such women who became the Chairman of the Bhubaneswar Municipality by the grace and patronage of Biju Patnaik.

One of the notable works he has done for the Labour class people of Orissa was to fix up the rates of wages to be paid to the daily labourers. He fixed up the rate of Rs. 25/- for ordinary labourer, Rs. 30/ for half-skilled labourer, Rs. 35/- for skilled labourer and Rs. 40/- for super-skilled labourer. Somehow this rate of wages gave a relief to the labourers who were working under meagre-rates.

Though Biju Babu did not improve the economic condition of the people or the administrative efficiency of the employees of the state but he could divide the entire Orissa state and raised the number of districts from 13 to 30 districts. Some large districts like Cuttack, Balasore, Sambalpur, Koraput,

Puri were divided and new 17 districts were created. The division and subdivisions of the districts did not improve any caliber of the officers nor did it reduce the burden of the people but some new IAS, and IPS and OAS officers were appointed. Till-to-day the Govt. office of Collectors, IPS and OAS officers are still running in the rented houses. Because of the scarcity of funds, no quarters have yet been built.

During the regime of Biju Babu nearly 200 drunkards died of drinking poisoned-liquor in Cuttack town in May 1992.

With patience, Biju Babu spent 5 years in power without any visible achievements.

After the expiry of his term of 5 years—elections for Assembly were held in March 8th 1995. By a negative voting-Biju Babu and his Janata Party was rejected by the voters and brought the Congress Party again to power. The people were so disgusted with the works of the ruling Govt. and party during the tenure of 5 years that they voted once again the rejected leaders of the yester years. That is the trend of the voters and the political traditions of the state. But in neither way the voters are benefited. They are disappointed and would remain like this forever. No Govt. can do anything in the prevailing circumstances with the corrupt Ministers & employees of the state. The voters will always be the political victims of the corrupt and selfish Ministers.

J.B. Patnaik

In the 1995 election, P.V. Narasingh Rao was elected from Berhampur Lokasabha Constituency. He played a mischievous role in Orissa politics. The voters of Orissa and the dissatisfied Congress aspirants did not like Janaki Patnaik to contest in any election, P V Narasingh Rao accepted the complaints of the Congress men and set Janaki Babu aside. Janaki Babu did not contest. So all the top leaders aspiring for Chief Ministership and other Congress men tried their best to win in the elections-And ultimately Congress Party won 79 seats out of 147. Whenever the proposal for Chief Ministership arose-P. V Narasingh Rao as the Congress President pushed Janaki Ballav Patnaik and made him the Chief Minister of Orissa who took oath on 15th March 1995. The other legislators shouted against this hypocricy of Narasingh Rao & Janaki Babu. But elections were already over by now and they can not dissolve the Assembly. So reluctantly they accepted Janaki Babu. Later on Janaki Babu was elected to the Assembly from Begunia Constituency. Janaki Babu as an old shrewd and Veteran Congress leader led the Journey of politics upto January 1999. During his third phase of Chief Minister,, he entered into an agreement with TISCO to establish an Iron and Steel Plant near Gopalpur in the district of Ganjam,, but he was not successful because of the vehment opposition from the local people of Chamakhandi and several other villages of this area. The TISCO acquired a huge area of land for the Steel Plant. Now proposal is pending in the dustbin of time.

Janaki Babu made extensive tour to Israel, America, Korea, Thailand, Malayasia to import knowledge and techniques of irrigation and improved type of agriculture in Orissa. The official tour was successful and more colourful with the public money but no improvement in Orissa agriculture and irrigation was done for which many agricultural graduates are moving jobless in Orissa.

But good days are very transitory. In 1997 July 11, the Advocate General of Janaki Ballav Patnaik, Mr. Indrajit Roy was involved in the rape case of Smt. Anjana Misra, a divorcee of Mr. Subash Misra who was the Indian Forest Officer Many top IPS officers Surendra Nath Swain, Amiya Kumar Tripathy were summoned to investigate the case and furnish a report. Many women cells and the opposition leaders demanded the resignations of Indrajit Roy. Ultimately it became a serious political issue. The matter was referred to the Congress High Command-Sonia Gandhi who ultimately removed Mr. Janaki Ballav Patnaik and placed Sri Giridhar Gamango as the Chief Minister of Orissa in January 1999.

Indrajit Roy was sentenced 3-year rigorous rigorous imprisonment and a fine of Rs. 5000/- in February 2000 by a CBI Judge.

Another sex scandal which centered round the Janaki Govt. and himself, was the unexpected and mysterious death of Sri Jayadev Panda—a junior advocate of Indrajit Roy. It was alleged that Janaki Babu had illicit relations with the wife of Jayadev Panda, Mrs. Babita Panda in Bhubaneswar at Dharam Vihar. This was also a darker aspect of Janaki Ballav Patnaik's character.

On January 22, 2000, the Adivasis burnt Mr. Steins and his two sons to death at Manoharpur in Keonjhar district.

Likewise such unexpected events in Orissa defamed Janaki Babu and his Govt. and ultimately he was dropped. Sri Giridhar Gamango became his next successor who was nominated by Sonia Gandhi. Gomango took oath on 17.2.1999 at Raj Bhavan. Within six months after his assumption of the post of Chief Minister, Mr. Gomango was elected from the Laxmipur Constituency of Koraput district.

A "Changu Master" became the Chief Minister of Orissa.

The condition of Orissa Administration during the regime of Giridhar .Gomanga February 1999-2000-December was miserable. The top IAS officers,'OAS officers and all employees of the Secretariat did not respect the new Chief Minister. Mr. Gomango was mainly an M.P. in Delhi who did not know the fundamentals of administration and had a poor knowledge about the complicated affairs of Orissa. Administration became stand still. No file work was done in the Secretariat. The employees started making merry and dosed on the office tables.

Apart from the general apathy of the employees, in the State, the Super Cyclone on 16th October, 1999 in Ganjam and 29th October 1999 in the north and Coastal Orissa devastated the lives and conditions of people. Thousands of people were washed away by the waves of the Bay of Bengal. All the rivers were awfully flooded. Lakhs of birds, cows, oxen and buffaloes were killed. Houses were demolished. All the standing paddy plants and trees were uprooted. There was a tremendous hue and cry-slogans and demand for food, relief houses and water. Unexpected relief materials of rice, cloths, blankets, utensils, polythenes sheets, money from all over states of India and foreign countries are poured into Orissa. Because of the lack of administrative cooperation, propensity sincerity, honesty, many trucks loaded with relief materials returned. Many food materials were perished. Because the relief was not properly and adequately distributed. The Gomango Govt. could not tackle the post-cyclone situations in Orissa. There was utmost anarchy, indiscipline, non-cooperation, and negligence from the Govt. side. The NGOs rendered valuable services to the cyclone-affected people and areas by providing them cooked food, clothes, medical help, utensils etc. The Gomango Govt. was criticized and condemned by all sections of the people of Orissa. The MLAs and people condemned the inability of Giridhar Gomango. The top leaders of the Congress Party hatched a conspiracy against Mr. Gomango and Gomango was asked to resign. Mr. Hemananda Biswal, a man of western Orissa took oath as the Chief Minister of Orissa on 6th December 1999.

Meanwhile Biju Patnaik passed away on 7 April 1997 in the Escort Hospital of Delhi. His dead body was brought to Bhubaneswar and then he was burnt at Swargadwar, on the Puri sea-beach. Biju Babu did not like his two sons—Prem Patnaik and Naveen Patnaik and one daughter—Gita Patnaik to make them the politicians. Sri Prem Patnaik is a businessman. Naveen Patnaik a renowned author in English. And likewise Gita is also a prolific writer. But after the death of Biju Patnaik, the selfish Janata leaders dragged Biju Babu's son Naveen Patnaik to the nasty politics.

On 26 December 1999 the Janata Dal was divided into two political groups. Prasanna Acharya, Prasanna Patasani, Padmanav Behera and Arjun Sethi supported Naveen Babu. Ashok Das, P.C. Ghadei, Nalini Kanta Mohanty, Surendra Nayak, Narasingh Misra belonged to other group.

Naveen Patnaik contested in the Aska Loksabha Constituency, which was vacant due to the death of Biju Patnaik. Though Naveen was new to the politics, he was elected to Loksabha on two grounds. He is the son of Biju Babu and he got sympathy votes for the death of Biju Patnaik. He was twice elected to Lokasabha from Aska Constituency and became the Cabinet Minister of Steel in the Atal Behari Cabinet in New Delhi. But he did not do anything for Aska people nor his father.

The period of Hemananda Biswal as the Chief Minister lasted from 6th Dec. 1999 to March 4,2000, only for 3 months 18 days. This Govt. was just like a stepen Govt. which could do nothing in Orissa. The incalculable monetary relief which was poured into Orissa from the foreign Govts. and NGO were evaporated and plundered in Orissa.

On 20 February 2000 the Assembly elections were held in Orissa. The voters were displeased and dissatisfied with the functioning of the Congress Govt. and the care-taker Govt. of Gomanga and Hemananda. They voted the Congress leaders out of power and brought the BJD political parties to power.

Naveen Patnaik

As it was a Coalition Govt. in consultation with both the

members of the BJP and BJD, the Chief Minister would be elected. Ultimately it is decided to put the Crown of the Chief Minister on the head of Mr. Naveen Patnaik who was the Cabinet Minister of Atal Behari Govt. in Centre.

To pay respect to his father Biju Patnaik, Naveen Patnaik also took oath as C.M. on 5th March 2000, which was the birthday of Biju Patnaik. When the new Govt. of BJP-BJD came to power, they found the Govt. had got no economic balance-but drained away to the deficit of 14000 crores of rupees. In the name of Public Service to the cyclone affected people of Orissa, the Hemananda Govt. plundered all the public money and left the Govt. treasury simply bankrupt. Due to the Congress and BJP-BJD rivalry, the common people of Orissa are suffering from uncouth economic miseries. No developmental works under the BJP-BJD Govt. are being undertaken so far. The Naveen Govt. abruptly and inhumanly sealed the opportunity of any appointment of the educated youths of Orissa, but allowed the Govt. and non-Govt. Colleges, Institutes to produce thousands and thousands of students every year. If the Naveen Govt. would not appoint and fill up the vacancies of different posts under the Govt. of Orissa, what would be the future of the educated youths. It is a heinous crime of the Govt. of Orissa. In the name of economic bankruptcy, the Govt. of Orissa cannot avoid the employment and development in Orissa.

Naveen Patnaik divided Janata Party and created a separate Political Party. The new Party is named as the Biju Janta Dal or BJD. The strong Janata leader-Bijoy Mohapatra was expelled from the BJD.

Mr. Naveen Patnaik being the son of Biju Babu does not know Oriya—a tragedy to Oriya people. But the question arises-how long Naveen Babu would survive in the name of his father without feeding the Orissa people with food and employment?

5

People and Festivals of Orissa

Orissa is a state of mixed population of different castes, tribes and different religions. There is a great influx of Bengalis, Telugus, Tamils and Hindi-speaking people from different neighbouring provinces and from Rajasthan and Gujarat. This migration of different Non-Oriyas into Orissa was made possible uninterruptedly during the long rule of the British Govt. from 1803 to 1947 and the vivisection of Orissa into three major territorial fragments and tagged them with Bengal Presidency, Central Provinces and Madras Presidency. As Orissa was educationally back ward, many educated, semi-educated and illiterate people of the neighbouring states rushed in to officials. Orissa and manned the machinery of the Govt. with the British Many of the Bengalis, Telugus and Tamils owned vast landed properties in Orissa and established their supremacy and Zamindari. They asserted their influence and hegemony upon the illiterate Oriya people of Orissa. Very often they exploited the people of Orissa and built their fortune here. As the famous historian Rakhal Das Banerjee summarised:

> "In fact, Bengalis of a low type ruled Orissa for nearly half-a-century after the conquest. Having control of judicial and executive work, the Bengalis found Orissa an easy means to get rich quick. Hundreds of Orissa noblemen were ruined and their ancient heritage passed into the hands of the Bengali Zamindars."

Even after the separation of Orissa from Bihar on 1st April 1936, very few Non-Oriyas left Orissa for Bihar, M.P. Bengal, Andhra Pradesh and Madras. It is increasingly difficult for them to dispose their vast landed properties and palatial buildings in Orissa. The Bengalis have got their vast Zamindaris in Balasore, Jagatsinghpur, Jajpur, Cuttack, Kendrapara, and Mayur Bhanj. The Telugus and Tamils have occupied many fertile land and villages in Ganjam and Koraput. Due to the sunset laws, all the lands of the Oriya Zamindars were publicly auctioned in Calcutta for which the Oriya zamindars became paupers and the Bengalis became the Zamindars of the Orissa soil. Absentee landlordism developed in Orissa. Even Nobel laurate, Rabindra Nath Tagore had also Zamindari in Orissa. The Telugus and Tamils occupied vast lands in Ganjam and Koraput districts and became the Zamindars.

The famous historian Abul Fazal of Akabar's Court and later on Mr. Sterling (1822) who was the District Magistrate of Cuttack have given a very sordid account of the nature of the Oriya people.

> "Orissa as a nation are justly described by Abul Fazal to be very effeminate that is why they are extremely deficient in many spirit. The Oriya has long had an unenviable reputation as a weak, effeminate and stupid creature. That the industry and enterprise are as foreign to them as opium eating and noonday sleep to the English husbandmen. That there are few districts in India where the natives are so listless and idle as in this as long as the poorer classes have food enough to eat from the day-to day, they will not exert themselves to get more or make provision for an evil hour. Hence the misery, disease and starvation occasioned by dearth of grain. Generally speaking, the people are kindly and good humoured, easily controlled and remarkably law-abiding. Outside

> Orissa, they have a reputation for good work as domestic servants, peons, and coolies and their readiness to migrate and find employment as carpenters, panka-pullers and palanquin bearers and in other kinds of labour."

This statement I inserted in this book not to offend the Oriya race but to awaken them from the drudgery, stupidity and disunity to unity, industry and selflessness so that every Oriya at least thinks seriously about the prestige and prosperity of Orissa. Everybody and all historians have gone through the above statement, but nobody was aware to publish it.

Beside this, the Muslims and converted Christians also have got their homes and hearth in different towns and villages of Orissa. By force and persuasions many Oriya families became Muslims and Christians in the past. And at present Christian fathers still adopt their conversion policy in the remote areas of the Koraput and Phulbani, Mayur Bhanj, Keonjhar and Sundargarh and converted the Tribals into Christianity for which the criminal offences occur.

Marwaris as a business class migrated from Madhya Pradesh, Gujarat, Rajasthan and began to live at Rairangpur, Baripada, Sambalpur, Bolangir, Balasore, Puri, Cuttack, Ganjam and Koraput in Orissa. Their business flourished very luxuriantly and they have become multi-millionaire in Orissa.

Migration of population is mainly facilitated by three major causes (1) Marriage with a local lady (2) Trade and Business as the British have done in India (3) Service or Employment. These three obligations bind the migrated people with the land, customs and people of that locality by which they permanently settle there.

Orissa is rich in resources but the Oriyas are poor. There is an abundant deposit of Iron-ore, Bauxite, Gold, Diamond, Ferro-Chrome, forest products and extensive seacoast. But the Oriyas, due to their laziness, indifference and lack of driving ability do not harness the mines of iron-ore, gold, diamond and bauxite and left them to the Non-Oriya businessman. Even the Govt. of Orissa is so apathetic and useless, that no concrete steps have been taken to explore them. The Oriyas do not exploit the extensive seacoast of Bay of Bengal or Kalinga Sagar for profitable purposes. The vast deep forest of Similipal, Koraput and Phulbani are left useless. Unauthorised deforestation has left the areas desolate. Mr. Sterling the Collector of Cuttack described the Oriyas as the Bohemian race of England — the meaning of which is—the people of free and easy habits not industrious at all.

Orissa became a colony of the Non-Oriya businessmen. The Marwaris of Rajasthan and Gujarat and the Punjabis control the markets of Orissa in dealing in different essential commodities. Gradually, they too entered into the politics of the State and contested in the elections and became the Minister of Orissa.

The migration of the Bengali refugees into Orissa during the recent decades has also created insurmountable problems to the local people. Adivasis of Raighara in Koraput and in the coastal districts of Balasore, Cuttack and Puri. They gradually encroached the land of the Adivasi, Oriyas and Govt. land and began to permanently settle there. They inserted their names into the electoral rolls of the Govt. of Orissa a by manipulation and claimed all the rights as the bonafide citizens of that locality. And the Govt. of Orissa is so stupid and inactive that no serious steps have yet been taken to oust them from the land. It will tend to continuous struggle and armed conflicts between the local people of Koraput and Cuttack and the refugee-Bengalis.

The land of Orissa means where most of the Oriya live and Oriya is the spoken language of the people.

Among the population of Orissa, the Oriyas occupy the

POPULATION OF DISTRICTS IN 1991 CENSUS

Sl. No	*Name of the District*	*Total Population 1981*	*1991*	*Density per square km.*
1.	Angul	783734	961037	154
2.	Balasore	1357727	1696583	955
3.	Baragarh	1032354	1207172	979
4.	Bhadrak	895081	1105834	985
5.	Bolangir	1061727	1230938	987
6.	Boudh	268366	317622	981
7.	Cuttack	1649790	1972739	919
8.	Deogarh	197671	234238	84
9.	Dheṇkanal	797053	947870	206
10.	Gajapati	420402	454708	118
11.	Ganjam	2267407	2704056	311
1.2	Jagatsinghpur	861698	1014242	514
13.	Jajpur	1136093	1386177	480
14.	Jharsuguda	368251	446726	203
15.	Kalahandi	946573	1130903	135
16.	Kandhamal	448914	546281	71
17.	Kendrapara	981219	1149501	451
18.	Keonjhar	1114622	1337026	161
19.	Khurda	1134523	1502014	520
20.	Koraput	859133	1029986	130
21.	Malkhangiri	335169	421917	68
22.	Mayurbhanj	1581873	1884580	181
23.	Nabarangapur	680952	846659	160
24.	Nayagarh	683392	782647	184
25.	Nuapada	392619	469482	138
26.	Puri	1103130	1305365	428
27.	Rayagada	608751	713984	94
28.	Sambalpur	682700	809017	121
29.	Sonepur	397386	476815	203
30.	Sundargarh	1337871	1573617	162

Source: Statistical outline of Orissa-Govt. of Orissa 1999.

95% of the total population and the rest are the Muslims, Christians, Marwaris, Sikhs, Telugu, Tamils, Bengalis, Biharis, Chinese and other people of different Indian states. The different industrial bases of Rourkela Steel Plant, NALCO at Anugul and Damanjodi, Paradip Port, Golabandha, Choudwar and Chandipur Military and rocket complex are full of non-Oriya service men. Besides, Cuttack, Puri, Bhubaneswar, Berhampur, Baripada, Rairangpur, Sambalpur, Bolangir, Balasore, Bhawanipatna attracted many non-Oriya businessmen who have unexpectedly flourished in enterprises. Many Bengalis have built luxurious hotels on the sea- beach of Puri. Here is a table of the distribution of population of different religions and S.T. and S.C.

Population by Religion and Their Percentage to Total Population of Orissa

Sl. No	*Religion*	*1951*	*1961*	*1971*	*1981*	*1991*
1.	Hindu	14318411 (97.76)	17123194 (97.57)	21121056 (96.25)	25161725 (95.42)	29971257 (94.67)
2.	Muslims	176338 (1.20)	215319 (1.23)	326507 (1.49)	422266 (1.60)	577775 (1.83)
3.	Christians	141934 (0.97)	201017 (1.15)	378888 (1.73)	480426 (1.82)	666220 (2.10)
4.	Sikhs	4163 (0.03)	5030 (0.03)	10204 (0.04)	14270 (0.05)	17296 (0.05)
5.	Buddhists	969 (0.01)	454 (neg)	8462 (0.04)	8023 (0.03)	9153 (0.03)
6.	Jainas	1248 (0.01)	2295 (0.01)	6521 (0.03)	6642 (0.03)	6302 (0.02)
7.	Other religion and religion not stated	2883 (0.02)	1537 (0.01)	92977 (0.42)	276914 (1.05)	411733 (1.30)
						31659736

Population of Scheduled Caste and Scheduled Tribes in Orissa—(Districtwise) 1991 Census

Sl. No	Name of the District	S.C population (.000)	% of S.C to total population of of the dist	S.T. population (.000)	% of S.T. to total population of the district
1.	Anugul	161	18.82	112	11.68
2.	Balasore	315	18.57	179	10.57
3.	Baragarh	223	18.44	236	19.58
4.	Bhadrak	240	21.71	19	1.69
5.	Bolangir	189	18.39	271	22.06
6.	Boudh	62	19.64	41	12.92
7.	Cuttack	359	18.19	69	3.49
8.	Deogarh	34	14.60	78	33.31
9.	Dhankanal	152	16.06	120	12.68
10.	Gajapati	40	8.77	218	47.86
11.	Ganjam	484	17.91	79	2.93
12.	Jagatsinghpur	220	21.72	6	0.61
13.	Jajpur	317	22.87	103	7.40
14.	Jharusuguda	77	17.15	142	31.83
15.	Kalahandi	192	17.01	327	28.88
16.	Kandhamal	100	18.21	281	51.51
17.	Kendrapada	228	19.83	5	0.40
18.	Keonjhar	154	11.49	595	44.52
19.	Khurda	205	13.62	77	5.14
20.	Koraput	138	13.41	522	50.67
21.	Malkangiri	84	19.96	246	58.36
22.	Mayur Bhanj	132	6.99	1091	57.87
23.	Nabarangapur	128	15.09	468	55.27
24.	Nayagarh	108	13.78	47	5.96
25.	Nuapada	62	13.09	169	35.95
26.	Puri	242	18.56	4	0.27
27.	Rayagada	102	14.28	400	56.04
28.	Sambalpur	138	17.07	284	35.08
29.	Sonepur	105	22.11	45	9.50
30.	Sundargarh	138	8.78	798	50.74

Social Systems

Since the time immemorial, the caste system still prevails in Orissa. There are four major castes as Brahmin, Kshatriya, Vaisya, and Sudra. In the Brahmin caste also, there are several categories among them—(1) The Samanta Brahmin (2) Halua Brahmin (3) Bhadri Brahmin and (4) Sarua Brahmins. When the caste rigidity was strictly practised by them, the Samanta Brahmins did not dine with other Brahmins and did not establish matrimonial alliances. But with the progress of civilization and the necessity of the brides and grooms, all the barriers were let loose.

The Brahmins hold the key position in the society because they perform the Puja, Homa, other rites and rituals of marriage with austerity and observe celebacy in the etiquettes and in life. Gradually, the Brahmins entered into the vices of the age, they began to lose their morality, superiority in the society. The modern age and politics smashed the inequality between man and man, and the leaders promulgated the reservation policy, which made the higher castes of people beggars and paupers. Below the Brahmins, the Kshatriyas occupy the next rank in the society. They no longer fight as the Paikas against the enemies in traditional methods of warfare like swords, spears, shields, armours, on horseback. So naturally they came back to cultivation and service. The Kshatriyas and subsequently Khandayats have got different identity in different parts of Orissa and the surnames also vary from region to region.

The Karans as the writer class enjoy the superior position in the society. They hold the important position in the administration of the Orissa State as the I.A.S, O.A.S, I.P.S, Doctors, Engineers and Lecturers. The Karan caste is evolved later on.

Along with the people of these castes, there are some people of different sub-castes as—Badhei, Bania, Rangini,

Gouda, Gudia, Kachara (Bangles), Kansari, Kumbhar, Kamara, Mali, Teli, Sundhi, Roula (Pujari), Bhandari, Matibasa, Nolia, who live in all the districts of Orissa. The scheduled castes and people like Pana, Bauri, Chamar, Dandasi, Dewar, Dhoba, Dom, Hadi, Jaggati, Kandara, Keuta, Khadala, Patra tanti, Sauntia, Siyal (Toddy trappers) live almost in all districts. But the Santal, Bhumija, Kolo, Ho, Kandha, Paraja, Gadaba, Soara, Munda, Oraon, Koya, Ladha, Mankidi, Mirdhas, Pentia, Kharia, Gond, Dharua, Bhuyan, Binjhal and Mahali live in the districts of Mayur Bhanj, Keonjhar, Sundargarh, Dhenkanal, Sambalpur, Phulbani and Koraput

It is estimated that ninety-three types of scheduled caste people are there in the Orissa state and 62 different scheduled tribes. Their social behaviour is not uniform.

In addition to this, the Christians, Muslims, Sikhs, Telugus, Tamils, Gujarati, Bengali, Bihari, also live together in Orissa. According to the census of 1991, the ratio of the different religions is like this—Muslims -1.83 (population-577775), Christians-2.10 (population-666220), Sikhs-0.05 (population-17296), Buddhists-0.03 (population-9153). As West Bengal and Andhra Pradesh are situated as the neighbouring states, most of the influxes into Orissa are the Bengalis and Andhrites.

Marriages

Marriages are solemnized in accordance with the Vedic principles among the own castes in the Hindu society by a Brahmin. Monogamy is the prevailing pattern of the marriage. Polygamy is also practised, but in a very secret manner. Although the Dowry Prohibition Act is enforced in Orissa, most of the brides are willfully murdered either by strangulation of throat, terrible beating, immolation by the in-law members, uncouth torture for which the bride commits suicide.

Polygamy is adopted in the Muslim family and among the Tribal people.

Child marriage, widow remarriage, divorce-marriage, intercaste marriages are not encouraged in higher castes. The Orissan society accepts it with much reluctance. But due to mutual love of woman and man, such marriages are being prevalent.

Divorce cases are now more frequent and member of such cases is rapidly increasing. Marriage at present is not a sacred bond but a commercial alliance. Where there is more dowry, there is the ready acceptance of the bride by the groom and his parents.

Registration marriages are also being held among the grown-up boys and girls in the marriage offices of all the district headquarters.

Inter-regions and inter-cultural marriages like the Oriya-Telugu, Oriya-Tamil, Oriya-Sikh, Oriya-Bengali are also performed. Ordinarily the brides of higher castes prefer the high salaried grooms or serving in foreign countries etc.

The Muslims perform their marriages between cross cousins or between parallel cousins.

Christian marriages are solemnised in different churches according to the Christian principles of marriages.

The marriages, birth ceremony, thread-ceremony, name-giving ceremony and the funeral rites of the higher castes are indispensably performed by the Brahmins. No such functions are observed without enchanting the Vedic hymns by the Brahmins. On the other hand, such equivalent functions of the lower castes or the scheduled castes and scheduled tribes are performed by their headman or by low cast Brahmins.

Languages

All the states of India are reorganized on the linguistic basis on 1956 and find a place in the schedule VIII of Indian Constitution. The regional spoken languages are as Bengali in West Bengal, Telugu in Andhra Pradesh, Tamil in Tamilnadu. Likewise the Oriya is the dominant spoken language of Orissa. 90% of the total population of Orissa speaks Oriya—an Indo-Aryan language of India.

As the states of West Bengal and Andhra Pradesh flank Orissa state on the northern and southern sides, more Bengali and Telugu people rush into Orissa for service, business or labour. 2.28 per cent of Telugu and 1.51 per cent of Bengali population live in Orissa of its total population-Hindi (1.10 per cent), Urdu (1.31 per cent), Punjabi (0.08 per cent), Malayalam -(0.05 per cent), Tamil -(0.04 per cent) and Gujarati (0.06 per cent) only.

Among the Tribal people, the Kondha speak Kui in Phulbani, Khand (0.89 percent). There are also Koya language, Bhumija, Bonda Paraja, Godaba, Juanga, Kharia, Kol and Munda.

In Mayur Bhanj district, late Mr. Raghunath Murmu of the village Dandbash P.O. Tamal Bandh P.S. Rairangpur has invented a new script called "OL Chiki" sometimes in 1940 for the Santals. In 1960's and 1970's some books on drama (Bidu Chandan). Myths and alphabates were published and they were widely circulated among the Santals of Bihar, West Bengal M.P. and Orissa. Pandit Raghunath Murmu was regarded as the "Guru Gomke". Except this OL Chiki of the Santals, no other tribals have got their own scripts. The languages of these tribes exist in the position of the spoken language only.

The spoken languages in Orissa also vary from region to region and persons to persons. The people of Mayur Bhanj and north Balasore districts are mostly influenced by the Bengali language and Hindi. The people of coastal districts of southern Balasore, Cuttack, Puri and Ganjam speak Oriya in a polished manner, which is different from the tone and pronunciation of the people of Western Orissa and Koraput.

The people of Ganjam are also influenced by the Telugu language. Besides this, the Bengalis, Marwaris, Punjabis, Telugus, Tamils, Hindi, Muslims, speak in both the languages of Oriya and their mother languages. In order to attract the customers, the Traders and Businessmen speak in the mother tongues of the customers, so the businessmen are versatile in different languages.

FESTIVALS OF ORISSA

No festival in Orissa is uniformly and strictly celebrated in all the districts by its people. And no festival is celebrated on the fixed date of the English calendar. The dates are fixed according to the Hindu astronomical calculations of day, time, planet, "Graha" and traditions of Hindustan. The variation of festival is mainly because of the difference of temperament of the people, the disintegration of the joint family, the highly educated modern brides and the awfull involvement of modern men in different commercial enterprises.

Not that the modern men have got no money to celebrate the festivals, but they lack the interests of doing it. Most of the Oriya festivals are associated with the rural life of the people. Orissa is a land of villages, but now the rural life is completely shattered. All the educated and semi-educated couple run with their families to the nearest towns and cities leaving the old haggard parents in the villages. Relating to the agriculture and cultivation, the people of the villages used to celebrate the Akshaya Trutiya, Raja festival, Manabasa(Lakhmipuja), Bandana where the peasants and their families worship the cows, bulls and oxen and feed them cakes.

If we categorize the different festivals in monthwise, there are more than 60 festivals in Orissa connected with the different Gods and Goddesses. Rakhi Purnima and Durga Puja festivals are not indigenous in Orissa. Rakhi Purnima has been imported from the Northern India whereas the Durga Puja is brought from the West Bengal. Orissa is no doubt a cradle of the Shakti cult. The mother Goddess is worshipped everywhere in Orissa in different names. These Goddesses are not universal but local. So the local people worship them for good health, good fortune and longer life. Due to widespread and speedy bus and train routes, the people begin to worship the distant gods and goddesses. Lakhs of coconuts are daily sent to the Ghata Tarini of Ghata Gan of Keonjhar district from different places of Orissa.

The different Shakti Pithas in Orissa are-Mangala of Kakatpur (Puri), Charchika of Banki (Cuttack), Sharala of, Krijanga Bimala of Puri, Chandi of Cuttack, Biraja of Jajpur, Bhattarika of Badamba, Bhadrakali of Bhadrak, Samaleswari of Sambalpur. Kichakeswari of Khiching, Narayani, Khambeswari, of Ganjam and Tarini of Taratarini Ghatagan (Keonjhar) are famous in Orissa. There are ten-handed, eight-handed Devi statues in Orissa who are worshipped throughout the year with bananas, coconuts, vermillion, ghee and flowers.

As we find twelve months in the Christian calendar from January to December there are also twelve Oriya months in Orissa. In each month the Oriyas celebrate two and three festivals. Of course, the people of different states observe different festivals. In Orissa too, some festivals are very much localized. The Sital Sasthi or the marriage of Siva and Parvati is celebrated in Sambalpur district with much pomp and grandeur; whereas the people of other districts do not. The Dhanuyatra is also observed in Bargarh and Sambalpur gorgeously where Sri Krishna killed Kansa. Dance programmes, the presentation of modern songs, Dalkhai dance, explosion of crackers, illumination of buildings, different stalls of handicrafts are the main attractions of the Dhanuyatra. Thousands of people throng round the festival.

The Thakurani Pooja of Berhampur lasts more than fifteen days. The entire Berhampur Town is bustled in to ecstasy

The parents make up their children in different mythological characters of Rama, Sita, Krishna, Hanuman. The Tiger dance is the most popular and difficult to enact.

The following are the festivals connected with each month of the Oriya race and the Christian calendar.

1.	Baisakha April and May)	:	Pana Sankranti, (Bisub Sankranti) Akshaya Trutiya, Chandan Yatra, Chaitra Parba
2.	Jyestho May and June)	:	Jhamu Yatra, Raja Festival, Sital Sasthi, Snana Yatra
3.	Ashadha (June and July)	:	Rathayatra, Bahuda Yatra, Chitalagi Amabasya
4.	Shrabana (July and August)	:	Jhulan Yatra, Rakhi Purnima
5.	Bhadrab (Aug. and Sep.)	:	Ganesh Puja, Janmastami, Ananta Brata, Somnath Brata, Sunia, Radhastami
6.	Aswina (Sept. Oct.)	:	Biswakarma Puja, Dussera festival, Kumar Purnima, Gajalaxmi Puja.
7.	Kartika (Oct. and Nov.)	:	Deepavali, Onla Navami, Raso Purnima
8.	Margasira (Nov. and Dec.)	:	Prathamastami, Manabasa, Lakhmi Puja, Baliyatra
9.	Pousa (Dec. and Jan.)	:	Dhanu Jatra, Shambo dasami, Makar festival, (Mayur Bhanj, Keonjhar and Balasore)
10.	Magha (Jan. and Feb.)	:	Magha Saptami, Saraswati Puja.
11.	Phalguna (Feb. and March)	:	Sivaratri, Dol Purnima
12.	Chaitra (March and April)	:	Rama Navami, Sivaratri, Dandayatra (Ganjam)

In the past, it was a source of immense pleasure to celebrate the festivals at home sitting together all the members of the joint family by blowing the conch-shells and "Hula huli" by women. Then we used to eat the consecrated food or the "Prasad." But gone are the days of the joint family of the village. Now all the modern families are disintegrated and scattered from one another. Self-interest widens the difference between the sons and fathers and among the different brothers, which has shattered the unity of the family. It is an irony that a high salaried son celebrates his birthday in the town with his wife, children and invites friends leaving his old and haggard parents in the village. The so-called son owes his origin and birth to them who are neglected in the village.

Most of the functions are associated with the mythological characters and sequences. As there were no Cinema Halls, Radio and other modern entertainments in the past the people were celebrating these festivals every month with dances and dramas. They prepare different cakes, khiri and wear new clothes. These festivals were the principal sources of entertainments and happiness. The modern sources of entertainments are of different kinds—TV, Tape Recorders, VCP, Computers, brake dances, extensive use of wines, clubs, the organized festivals, outing to different places, brothel houses and Valentine days.

The modernization and urbanization have deprived the urban people from celebrating the rural festivals. As for instance, the celebration of Lakhmi Puja on last Thursday of Margasira is the most serene occasion for the Oriya families in the villages. Lakhmi- the goddess of wealth and prosperity is being worshipped by the head of the women of the family. Lakhmi Purana of Balaram Das is read. Different types of cakes are prepared. The women clean the home premises with the cowdung water and then the premises are ornamented by different "Jhuti" as flowers, the feet of the Lakhmi, conch-shell and different designs of "Murujas" which enhances the beauty of the front door, varandha, corridor and premises. But in a multi-storeyed apartment of the flat in the towns or cities, such decoration is a remote possibility. So the modern men have given up the celebrations of all the village festivals and celebrate the birth-festivals, marriage anniversary, Xmas festival, New Year's Day, cocktail party and valentine day with bafe.

The old traditions and taboos of society were shattered. And the life is now modernized and westernized. Man is bound to live in isolation and alienation and enjoys life in optimum and ecstasy but this material happiness will not last longer.

6

Administrative Structure in Orissa

Orissa though fragmented was ruled by the British for 144 year (1803-1947). They conquered Orissa from the Marathas on 14th October, 1803 and ruled in different capacity up to the mid-night of 14th August, 1947. They selected Puri as the capital in 1803 but they found it difficult to rule Balasore from such a long distance. So they shifted to Cuttack in 1816. Since then Cuttack had been the nerve center of all the activities of Orissa till 1949. On 10th October 1949, the capital of Orissa was shifted from Cuttack to Bhubaneswar. The legislature and all functions of the Govt. of Orissa was carried on temporary basis in the rented buildings at Bhubaneswar, and the secretariat building and the legislature are built in the model of the Chandigarh Secretariat of Punjab state. The designer of the Orissa Secretariat was a French Architect Mr. Le Corbusier.

On 1st April 1936, the districts of Cuttack, Puri, Balasore, Ganjam, Koraput and Sambalpur were amalgamated. Sambalpur was brought from the Central Provinces on 19th July 1905. Cuttack, Puri and Balasore, which were a part of Bihar since 1912, April 1st were separated from Bihar and Ganjam, Koraput and phulbani were brought from the Madras presidency. Thus formed a new Orissa state with 6 districts of Cuttack, Puri, Balasore, Sambalpur, Ganjam and Koraput. Cuttack was the Capital . Later on other 7 districts were created.

The Govt. under several Prime Ministers functioned in Orissa from 1936 to 1947 amidst mutual adversities and bickering among Maharaja Krishna Chandra Gajapati, Biswanath Das, Nabakrishna Choudhury and Harekrishna Mahatab etc. No Govt. during this period lasted the full term of 5 years. As many as 5 ministries functioned during 11 years. The British Govt. also did not encourage the local Govt. to do any developmental works because of their involvement in the Second World War (1939-1945).

After the Independence of India the Orissa Govt. devoted times and energy to persuade the feudatory Chiefs to merge themselves with India. And this process was completed on 1st January 1949.

The new Indian Constitution was promulgated on 26th, January 1950. And the first general elections for Lok Sabha were held in January 1952. But the functional politics and the mutual rivalry among the Congress leaders in Orissa did not end. The rivalry became rampant.

Nature of Administration

Although we were independent on 15th Aug. 1947, our process of thoughts, education and administration were so deeply moulded by the British systems that every British element is ingrained in the Indian soil. So it is rightly said that the administration in India is British in origin and taste.

We have changed certain names of the bureaucrats in our vernacular language, but the spirit and pattern of the British administration is still in vogue in India. The only difference is that before 1947 almost all the high ranked officers of the British Govt. were the Europeans, the English only. The administration was strictly controlled by the British local Govt. but after Independence all the posts from top to bottom are filled by the Indians.

After the introduction of the competitive Exams of I.A.S.,

I.P.S., O.A.S., O.F.S., and O.P.S. in Orissa and India, a new set of bureaucrats was appointed to run the administration of the Central and local administration. The examinations are conducted by the Orissa Public Commission and Union Public Service Commission annually to select the qualified and meritorious candidates for the State Administration. ICS is replaced by IAS Exams. These IAS Officers are appointed as the District Magistrates of 13 districts and head the different Departments of the Orissa Govt.—the Finance, Education, Health, Agriculture, Irrigation, Roads and Buildings, Animal and Husbandry, Revenue, Tourism, and as many Departments as Govt. desire to open. They play the key role in the State Administration during the early post-Independence decades. But with the passage of time, when the Politics reigned supreme in determining every policy of the Govt. the IAS Officers have became simply "yes men" of the corrupt politicians and Ministers. In the present administrative setup, the IAS Officers simply maintain their position and prestige vainly, submitting themselves to the wishes of the Ministers. In a welfare state the Ministers, MLA's and the bureaucrats must look to the benefits of the people by whom they are voted to powers, but nothing good is done for the people. And the people are left to the vagaries of their fortunes. They live in harassment, exploitation and oppression.

The spirit of the British style, vanity of the officers and red tapism still continue. The more our independence is growing older, the greater is the degree of corruption, insincerity, dishonesty, hypocrisy and irresponsibility of the Indian people, leaders and officers. In all offices, corruption is deep-rooted and nationalized in India. Every irregular work is being done in the office with the knowledge of the Govt. for this only the entire administrative machinery is wretched and rotten in India. Corruption has retarded the wheel of progress.

The Chief Minister, his Council of Ministers, the top

bureaucrats, the clerks and the peons run the administration of the entire Province. In the different Assembly Sessions of Orissa, several Bills are passed by majority of votes of the legislators and after receiving the consent and signature of the Governor, the Bills are turned in to Acts and later on they are enforced from a particular date. As the Executive officers, the top bureaucrats of different Department execute the work in the districts. Therefore there are different offices of different Departments in the Secretariat at Bhubaneswar. These Departments send the proposal for developmental works to the District Magistrates of the districts.

District Administration

There were 13 districts in Orissa up to 1990 since the Independence. But after the Assembly elections in February 1990, Janata Party under Biju Patnaik came to power. The people of different districts demanded the divisions of the larger districts. Keeping in view the public demand, Biju Babu as the Chief Minister of Orissa divided the 13 districts in to 30 districts. Some big districts like Balasore, Cuttack, Puri, Ganjam, Koraput, Kalahandi, Sambalpur, Sundargarh and Dhenkanal were split into separate small territorial fragments and increased the number of 13 districts to 30 districts.

The entire Orissa State is divided into three Administrative Units and is placed under the control of the Revenue Divisional Commissioner. The old districts of Mayur Bhanj, Keonjhar, Balasore, Cuttack, Puri are placed under the supervision of the Revenue Divisional Commissioner. The Head quarter is at Cuttack. The districts of Ganjam, Koraput and Phulbani are under the control of the RDC — the official Head Quarter is at Berhampur and the RDC of Sambalpur exercises powers in the districts of Sambalpur, Sunargarh, Dhenkanal, bolangir and Kalahandi.

In every district, an IAS officer is appointed as the District

MAP OF ORISSA - 2002

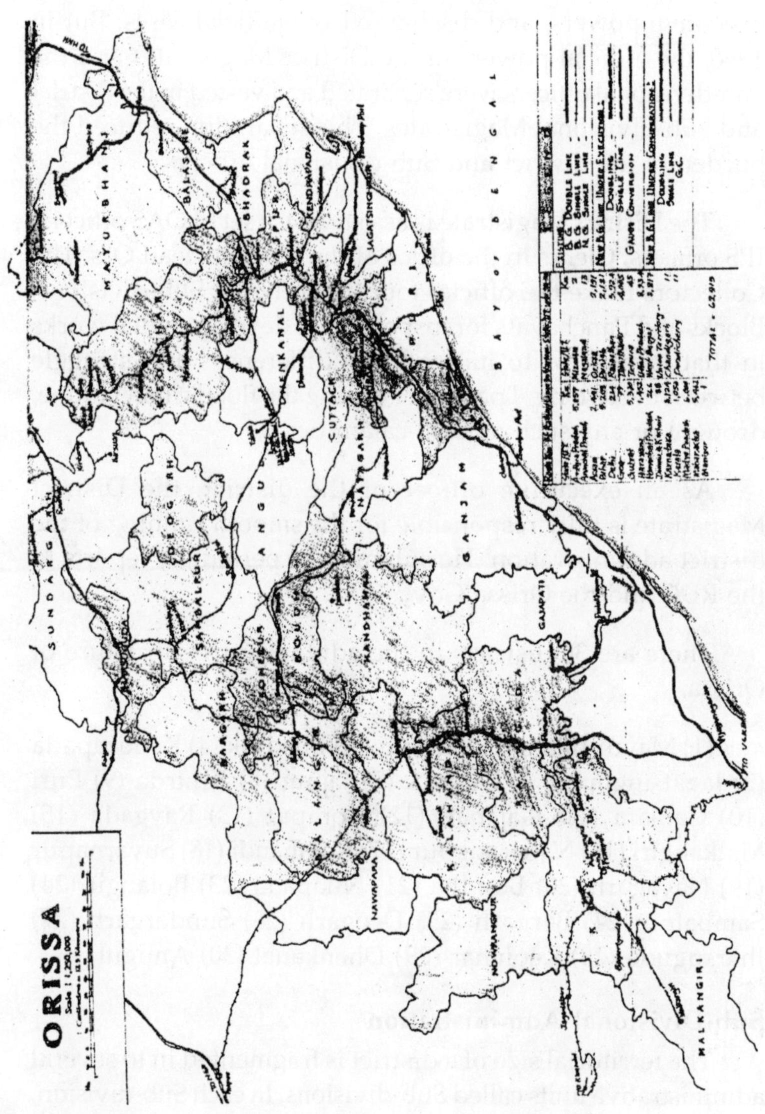

Magistrate with the overall responsibilities to run the district administration at the district Head quarters. Till 1959-1960, the District Magistrates were exercising the judicial and the executive powers, and discharged the judicial cases. But in 1960, the judicial powers of the District Magistrates and the Sub-divisional officers were separated and vested in the district and Sub-divisional Magistrates. This separation reduced the burden of the district and Sub-divisional officers.

The District Magistrate is assisted by a set of OAS officers, IPS officers, Clerks in the office of the District Head Qrs. The Collectors make the official tours to different Sub-divisions, Blocks and Panchayats for inspection of developmental works in that locality or to mitigate the differences and struggle between the two rival parties or during the floods, fire, famine, drought or any such natural calamities.

As an executive officer of the district, the District Magistrate is fully responsible for the smooth running of the district administration. He submits the periodical reports to the RDC and the Orissa Govt.

There are 30 districts in the administrative structure of Orissa.

(1) Mayur Bhanj (2) Balasore (3) Bhadrak (4) Kendrapada (3) Jagatsinghpur (6) Cuttack (7) Jajpur (8) Khurda (9) Puri (10) Ganjam (11) Gajapati (12) Koraput (13) Raygada (15) Malkangiri (16) Nabarangpur (17) Kalahandi (18) Suvarnapur (19) Nayagarh (20) Boudha (21) Nuapada (23) Bolangir (24) Sambalpur 24) Bargarh (25) Deogarh (26) Sundargarh (27) Jharsuguda (28) Keonjhar (29) Dhenkanal (30) Anugul.

Sub-Divisional Administration

The territorial size of a district is fragmented in to several administrative units called Sub-divisions. In each Sub-division, a Sub-divisional Officer either IAS or OAS is posted as the Executive officer. He runs the administration from the office

DISTRICTS OF ORISSA-1994

Sl. No.	*Name of the Districts*	*H.Qrs*	*Square . Kms*	*Population*
1.	Mayurbhanj	Baripada	10,410	1871796
2.	Balasore	Balasore	3076	1692439
3.	Bhadrak	Bhadrak	2788	1103882
4.	Kendrapara	Kendrapara	2546	1146470
5.	Jagatsinghpur	Jagatsinghpur	1759	933296
6.	Cuttack	Cuttack	3915	2043338
7.	Khurda	Khurda	2818	1497846
8.	Puri	Puri	3055	1925562
9.	Nayagarh	Nayagarh	3954	776786
10.	Ganjam	Chatrapur	8033	2684379
11.	Gajapati	Parlakhemundi	3056	458741
12.	Koraput	Koraput	8534	1055842
13.	Rayagada	Rayagada	7585	714599
14.	Nabarangpur	Nabarangpur	5135	808215
15.	Malkangiri	Malkangiri	6115	420950
16.	Nuapada	Nuapada	3408	463325
17.	Sonepur	Sonepur	2284	476410
18.	Bolangir	Bolangir	6552	12227345
19.	Boudh	Boudh	3444	31663
20.	Phulbani	Phulbani	8510	858553
21.	Sambalpur	Sambalpur	11689	1484765
22.	Baragarh	Baragarh	5832	1203630
23.	Deogarh	Deogarh	2781	2930273
24.	Kalahandi	Bhawanipatna	3197	1128659
25.	Sundargarh	Sundargarh	9942	1568442
26.	Jharsuguda	Jharsuguda	2203	444744
27.	Jajpur	Panikoili	2885	1380203
28.	Keonjhar	Keonjhar	8336	1315626
29.	Dhenkanal	Dhenkanal	4597	942672
30.	Anugul	Anugul	6346	958003

ADMINISTRATIVE SETUP OF ORISSA—1999

Number of Sub-divisions, Tahasils, CD Block, Towns, Police Station, Gram Panchayats and Villages in Different Districts of Orissa

Sl. No.	*Name of District*	*No. of Subdivision*	*Gram Panchayats*	*No. of Tahasils*	*No. of CD Blocks*	*No. of Urban local bodies*	*No. of Police Stations.*
1.	Anugul	4	180	5	8	3	20
2.	Balasore	2	257	7	12	4	19
3.	Bargarh	2	196	8	12	3	14
4.	Bhadrak	1	166	6	7	2	12
5.	Bolangir	3	241	6	14	4	13
6.	Boudh	1	58	2	3	1	6
7.	Cuttack	3	278	11	14	4	34
8.	Deograh	1	53	1	3	1	4
9.	Dhenkanal	3	172	6	8	3	11
10.	Gajapati	1	106	3	7	2	9
11.	Ganjam	3	444	14	22	18	25
12.	Jagatsinghpur	1	165	4	8	2	7
13.	Jajpur	1	242	6	10	2	11
14.	Jharusuguda	1	60	2	5	3	9
15.	Kalahandi	2	195	7	13	3	12
16.	Kandhamal	2	144	4	12	2	15
17.	Kendrapara	1	205	7	9	2	7
18.	Keonjhar	3	244	8	13	4	20
19.	Khurda	2	153	7	10	5	22
20.	Koraput	2	196	7	14	4	20
21.	Malkangiri	1	77	3	7	2	8
22.	Mayur Bhanj	4	316	9	26	4	28
23.	Nabarangpur	1	148	4	10	2	10
24.	Nayagarh	1	143	4	8	2	9
25.	Nuapada	1	93	2	5	2	6
26.	Puri	1	204	7	11	4	16
27.	Rayagada	2	140	4	11	3	12
28.	Sambalpur	3	133	4	9	4	19
29.	Sone Pur	2	80	4	6	3	7
30.	Sundargarh	3	170	8	17	4	11

of the Sub-divisional Head Qrs. with a group of different Officers like B.D.O, Engineer, Tahasildar, the clerks and peons.

He combines both the powers as a Revenue officer and Executive officer.

He arranges official tours to different Tahasil offices of the semi-urban areas to inspect the revenue collections and the other developmental works of the Tahasil areas. He directly works under the instructions of the District Magistrate. The S.D.O. furnishes the periodical reports about the development and failure of the different Govt. Projects and works. The S.D.O. also reports to the D.M. about any unusual incidents, lawlessness or any natural calamities.

He maintains law and discipline in the Sub-division. To assist him there are other Govt. officers like Divisional Superintendent of Police, BDO's, Engineers, Land settlement officers etc.

Tahsildar

The Tahasildar of a particular Tahasil area looks into the collections of the land revenue through Revenue Inspectors and settle the land-disputes, demarcates the Govt. land or grazing land. His office issues the permanent "Patta" to the original owner of the land or plots after the verification of sale-deeds and purchase documents.

On the other hand, the Block Development officer of his area is the only executive officer who looks into the development works of roads, education, agriculture, and other developments in the rural areas.

According to the recommendations of the Balbant Roy Mehta Committee, the old District Boards, local Boards were dissolved. And in its place, three tier system of local self. Govt. was established—in the district level—the Zilla Parishad, in the Sub-divisional level- the Panchayat Samiti and in the Village level- the Gram Panchayats.

The Panchayat Samities and Gram Panchayats look to the grass works of the village about the Primary education, the rural roads, clubs, rural libraries etc.

The members of the Panchayat Boards and Panchayat Samities are elected by the people on the adult suffrage basis. Mr. Biju Patnaik during the tenure of his Chief Ministership made the 1/3rd representation of women candidates in all the local bodies of Zilla Parishad, Panchayat Samities and Village Panchayats. But there are hardly any woman to discharge all the official duties successfully as the office bearers. On her behalf either her husband or any other relative is functioning ultimately leads to the conflicts among the members of the Samities. In some cases, the women office bearers are being man-handled and misbehaved in the offices, which leads to the criminal offences.

For all the rural developmental works, whatever money is allotted, a sizable amount of grant is being swallowed by producing false vouchers without any work being done.

State Police System

There was no such remarkable Police Dept. in Orissa during the British rule from 1936 to 1947. The British Govt. maintained the law and order situations in the ordinary or extraordinary circumstances in Orissa. The Praja Mandal Movement which was started in 1938 was put down by the British soldiers in collaboration with the feudatory Chiefs. The British Govt. was the protector of the vested interests of Chiefs of the Gadjats. Baji Rout of Dhenkanal was shot dead on 11th Oct. 1938. On the charges of the murder of Mr. Bazellgate at Ranapur, Dibakar Parida and Raghunath Mohanty were hanged to death in Bhagalpur Jail-Bihar. During the Quit India Movement, hundreds of freedom fighters were imprisoned and hundreds of Satyagrahis were killed indiscriminately.

But after the Independence and after the merger of the States with Orissa, the Police Dept. was entirely reorganised and redesigned.

In the entire state of Orissa, one Police officer namely the "Inspector General of Police" is appointed as the Chief in the hierarchical Police ranks and positions. The I.G. inspected the entire Police administration in this state. To help him, several (D.I.G.) are appointed in different Police circles of Berhampur, Cuttack and Jharsuguda. Several districts are tagged with the office of the D.I.G.

Apart from the state level police officers, a Senior Police Officer as Superintendent of Police is appointed in every district of Orissa, who looks after the general Police administration of a particular district. Below him the positions of Assistant Superintendents of Police, Deputy Superintendent of Police, Inspectors, Sub-Inspectors, Assistant Sub-inspectors, Havildars and Constables are subsequently created. The works and duties are accordingly distributed and the area of police zone for their functional operations.

Due to the overpopulation and the growth of the rate of crimes in the Orissa state, a separate Intelligence Dept. is created to investigate the cases. In order to send the secret and confidential messages to the distant districts, a wireless unit is also established in every district and Sub-divisional head quarters. A pigeon service is introduced at Rairangpur in the district of Mayur Bhanj. The trained Pigeons carry the messages in paper -tied in then-legs and fly to the destinations.

The Police officers are not adequate in proportion to the growth of crimes of modern times. The Police Dept is not properly supplied with the deadly A.K. Rifles or other guns and scientific materials to combat and suppress the armed revolts or agitations. The criminals own the most deadly weapons of Pistols, hand-grenadges, AK-47 Rifles, Rifles, guns, bombs, and they overpower the Police officers during raids or violence. The criminals safely escape without being caught by the police. Of course, the police ultimately arrest the criminals through the detectives or acquiring knowledge from the circumstantial evidences.

The cases of murder, rape, sex scandals, burning the newly abduction, brides due to dowry, theft, robbery, loot, demands for ransom, rampant corruption are the burning issues to the Police Dept. of Orissa.

Besides this, the violent activities of the terrorists and the Naxalites are the challenges to the Police Dept.

Apart from the inferior quality of defensive and offensive weapons of the Police Dept, the objectionable interference of the corrupted and wretched Ministers and the so-called legislators help to increase the crimes in the state. Having been obliged by the Ministers, the Police officers set free the criminals. The criminals take shelter under the umbrella of the Politicians. The Politicians utilize the services of the branded goondas, criminals and unsocial workers during the elections. They threaten the voters and the candidates to win in the elections by criminal voting and rigging.

In a democracy, corruption cannot in any means be uprooted because democracy always tends towards corruption. So Democracy and corruption are inseparable—both are complementary to each other. By loud slogans of the Ministers, corruption can never be uprooted.

ORISSA ASSEMBLY SEATS AND MEMBERS OF PARLIAMENT

Sl. No.	*Name of the districts*	*Name of Constituency*	
1.	Mayur Bhanj	(1)	Karanjia
		(2)	Joshipur
		(3)	Bahalda
		(4)	Rairangpur
		(5)	Bangriposi

Sl. No.	*Name of the districts*	*Name of Constituency*	
		(6)	Kuliana
		(7)	Baripada
		(8)	Baisinga
		(9)	Khunta
		(10)	Udala
2.	Balasore	(1)	Bhogarai
		(2)	Jaleswar
		(3)	Basta
		(4)	Baleswar
		(5)	Soro
		(6)	Simulia
		(7)	Nilagiri
3.	Bhadrak	(1)	Bhadrak
		(2)	Dhamanagar
		(3)	Bhandaripokhari
		(4)	Chandabali
		(5)	Basudevpur
4.	Kendarapara	(1)	Ali
		(2)	Pattamumdai
		(3)	Rajnagar
		(4)	Kendrapara
5.	Jagatsinghpur	(1)	Tirtol
		(2)	Erasama
		(3)	Balikuda
		(4)	Jagatsinghpur
6.	Jajpur	(1)	Sukinda
		(2)	Korai
		(3)	Dharmasala
		(4)	Bari Derabisi
		(5)	Binjharpur
		(6)	Badachana
		(7)	Jajpur

contd...

Sl. No.	Name of the districts	Name of Constituency	
7.	Cuttack	(1)	Kishore Nagar
		(2)	Mahanga
		(3)	Salepur
		(4)	Govindapur
		(5)	Cuttack Sadar
		(6)	Cuttack Town
		(7)	Choudwar
		(8)	Banki
		(9)	Athagarh
		(10)	Badamba
8.	Khurda	(1)	Balipatna
		(2)	Bhubaneswar
		(3)	Jatni
		(4)	Chilika
		(5)	Khurda
		(6)	Begunia
9.	Puri	(1)	Pipili
		(2)	Nimapara
		(3)	Kakatpur
		(4)	Satyabadi
		(5)	Puri
		(6)	Bramhagiri
10.	Nayagarh	(1)	Ranapur
		(2)	Nayagarh
		(3)	Khandapada
		(4)	Dasapalla
11.	Ganjam	(1)	Khallikote
		(2)	Chatrapur
		(3)	Aska
		(4)	Bhanjanagar
		(5)	Hinjilicut
		(6)	Jagannath Prasad
		(7)	Kabisuryanagar
		(8)	Berhampur

Sl. No.	*Name of the districts*		*Name of Constituency*
		(9)	Gopalpur
		(10)	Soroda
		(11)	Kodala
		(12)	Chikiti
12.	Gajapati	(1)	Mohana
		(2)	Ramagiri
		(3)	Parlakhemundi
13.	Koraput	(1)	Koraput
		(2)	Pattangi
		(3)	Kotpad
		(4)	Jeypur
14.	Rayagada	(1)	Rayagada
		(2)	Bisamkatak
		(3)	Gunupur
		(4)	Laxmipur
15.	Nabarangapur	(1)	Kodinga
		(2)	Nabarangapur
		(3)	Dabugaon
		(4)	Umarkote
16.	Malkangiri	(1)	Malkangiri
		(2)	Chitrakonda
17.	Nuapada	(1)	Nuapada
		(2)	Khariar
18.	Suvarnapur or Sonepur	(1)	Sonepur
		(2)	Binika
		(3)	Bira Maharajpur
19.	Bolangir	(1)	Titalagarh
		(2)	Kantabanjhi
		(3)	Patnagarh
		(4)	Saintola
		(5)	Loisinga
		(6)	Bolangiri

contd...

Sl. No.	*Name of the districts*	*Name of Constituency*	
20.	Boudh	(1)	Boudh
21.	Kandhamala	(1)	Baliguda
		(2)	G. Udayagiri
		(3)	Phulbani
22.	Sambalpur	(1)	Sambalpur
		(2)	Kuchinda
		(3)	Redhakhol
23.	Sundargarh	(1)	Sundargarh
		(2)	Rajgangapur
		(3)	Biramitrapur
		(4)	Rourkela
		(5)	Bonai
		(6)	Raghunath Palli
		(7)	Talasara
24.	Kalahandi	(1)	Dharamgarh
		(2)	Kokasara
		(3)	Junagarh
		(4)	Bhawanipatna
		(5)	Kesinga
		(6)	Narla
25.	Bargarh	(1)	Padmapur
		(2)	Melechhamunda
		(3)	Bejipur
		(4)	Bhatali
		(5)	Bargarh
26.	Deogarh	(1)	Deogarh
27.	Jharsuguda	(1)	Brajaraj Nagar
		(2)	Laikera
		(3)	Jharusuguda
28.	Keonjhar	(1)	Champua
		(2)	Patna
		(3)	Kendujhar
		(4)	Telkoi

Sl. No.	*Name of the districts*	*Name of Constituency*	
		(5)	Anandapur
		(6)	Ramchandrapur
29.	Dhenkanal	(1)	Dhenkanal
		(2)	Hindol
		(3)	Gondia
		(4)	Kamakhyanagar
30.	Anugul	(1)	Anugul
		(2)	Palalahara
		(3)	Athamalika
		(4)	Talcher

There were 60 seats for Orissa Assembly in 1936 and after the formation of Orissa state on 1st January 1949 and introduction of the first general election in India in February 1952, the number of seats was increased to 140 and the members elected to the Lok Sabha were 20 and Rajya Sabha was 10.

Whenever the member of seats to Orissa Assembly was increased from 140 to 147 in 1971, the number of MP seats was also increased from 20 to 21 that is one member to the Lok Sabha will be elected from a Parliamentary Constituency comprising of 7 Assembly Constituencies.

The seats of Orissa Assembly are distributed among the 13 districts as follows:

Name of the district	*Total no. of seats*	*SC*	*ST*	*(General)*
Cuttack	26	5	*	21
Puri	16	2	*	14
Balasore	12	2	—	10
Sambalpur	12	2	2	8
Ganjam	15	2	1	12

contd...

Name of the district	*Total no. of seats*	*SC*	*ST*	*(General)*
Koraput	14	1	10	03
Phulbani	4	1	2	01
Mayur Bhanj	10	*	9	01
Keonjhar	6	1	4	01
Dhenkanal	8	2	0	06
Bolangir	9	2	*	07
Kalahandi	8	2	01	05
Sundargarh	7	*	5	02
Total	147	22	34	91

After the first general election of India in February 1952, the following was the composition of the Orissa Assembly.

Congress	—	68
Ganatantra Parishad	—	31
Socialist Party	—	10
Communist Party	—	1
Forward Bloc	—	1
Independents	—	23
		140

Second General Elections

			Mid-term elections, 1961
Congress	36	—	82
Ganatantra Parishad	51	—	36
Communist Party	09	—	04
PSP	11	—	10
Independents	13	—	08
	140	—	140

Fourth General Elections Feb. 1967

Congress	—	31
Swatantra	—	49
Jana Congress	—	26
PSP	—	21
CPI	—	7
CPI (M)	—	1
SSP	—	2
Independents	—	3
		140

Fifth General Election: March 1971

Congress	—	51
Swatantra	—	36
Utkal Congress	—	32
PSP	—	4
Communist(I)	—	4
Jharkhanda	—	4
CPI(M)	—	1
Jana Congress	—	1
Congress (N)	—	1
Independents	—	6
		140

Sixth General Election: March 1974

Congress (R)	—	70
Pragati Dal	—	33
Swatantra	—	21
SSP	—	2

SPI	—	2
CPI	—	7
CPI(M)	—	3
Jana Congress	—	1
Independents	—	8
		147

After emergency in 1977, the elections were held in Orissa. Orissa Assembly consisted of

Janata Dal	—	117
Congress	—	22
CPI	—	2
CPI (M)	—	2
Independents	—	4
		147

The Nilamani Routroy Ministry was dissolved and the elections were held in February 1980. The Orissa Assembly: -

Congress (1)	—	118
Congress (U)	—	2
Janata	—	13
CPI	—	4
Janata (JP)	—	3
Independents	—	7
		147

J.B. Patnaik—Chief Minister

Ninth General Elections—after murder of Mrs. Indira Gandhi: March 1985

Congress	—	118
Janata	—	19
BJP	—	1
CPI	—	1
Independents	—	6
		147

J.B. Patnaik—Chief Minister

Elections in two Assembly Constituencies were countermanded due to death of the candidates.

Tenth General Elections: 27th February—1990

Orissa Assembly Seats

Janata Dal	—	123
Congress	—	10
CPI	—	3
BJP	—	2
Independents	—	6
		147

Biju Patnaik—Chief Minister

Eleventh Election: Feb.-March, 1995

Congress	—	
BJP	—	
CPI (M)	—	

J.B. Patnaik — Chief Minister

7

Local Self-Government in Orissa

In course of time, the indigenous Local self-Govt. of the past was doomed to death in India. The British Govt. had planted first the Corporation in September 1688 in Madras. A trial of Local self-Govt. in the Western lines began after the occupation of India in the Presidency towns because the indigenous self-governing institutions had already been decayed which could not serve as the models to set up during the course of their rule.

In 1726, the second attempt was made to set up the municipal Govt. in Calcutta and Bombay. Haphazardly, the Municipalities were established in different towns of India. Likewise a few municipalities were also established in Berhampur, Parlakhemundi, Cuttack, Puri, Balasore, Kendrapara and Jajpur. During the viceroylty of Lord Ripon (1880-1884) several municipal Acts and local self Govt. Acts of 1884 and 1985 were passed which made the local self-govt. broad-based and popular.

The British captured Orissa by conquest from the Marathas on 14th October, 1803. Before hand, they have ruled Ganjam, Koraput and Phulbani. They vivisected Orissa into four different administrative fragments. The districts of Cuttack, Puri and Balasore were tagged with the Bengal Presidency—Sambalpur was amalgamated with the Central Provinces Administrations. The districts of Ganjam, Koraput and the Agency area of Phulbani were kept under the control of

Madras Presidency. Besides, the Political Agents of the British Govt supervised the administration of the 26 Feudatory states.

After the repeated requests and criticism by the leaders of Orissa, Sambalpur was brought from Central Provinces and tagged with the districts of Cuttack, Puri and Balasore in July 1905.

George V—the king of England paid a royal visit to India and held a durbar in Delhi on 16th December 1911. There he declared the dissolution of the Bengal Presidency and created a new Province of Bihar and Orissa. And accordingly a Province of Bihar and Orissa was created on 1st April, 1912. But the Old Bengal Municipal Act III of 1884 and the Bengal Local Self Govt. of 1885 were still in vogue in Bihar and Orissa up to 1922. Mr. Madhu Sudan Das who became the Minister of Local Self-Govt. of the Province of Bihar and Orissa passed the Bihar and Orissa Municipal Act in the Provincial Council of Patna on 28th November, 1921 and it was finally adopted on 23rd August 1922. It was made effective from 1st January, 1923. Likewise the Bihar and Orissa Local Self Govt. Bill of 1922 and the Orissa Village Administration Bill were also passed. Once again all the municipalities and District Boards of Orissa were brought under the B and O Municipal Act and B and O Local Self Govt. Act in 1922.

Orissa remained with Bihar as a tail till the 31st March 1936. After a long period of Oriya Movement since 1882, Orissa was made a separate Province on 1st April, 1936. Although under the Govt. of India Act of 1935, elections were held in Orissa, the Ministries from 1936 to 15th August, 1947, did achieve absolutely nothing. The Governor of Orissa, Sir John Austin Hubback put Orissa under his direct administration from 4th November 1939 to 23rd November 1941. Out of total 11 years from 1936 to 1947—a period of 2 years basically wasted. And out of 9 years, there were 5 Ministries under Maharaja Krishna Chandra Gajapati (1-4-1937 to 19-7-1937), Biswanath Das (19-7-1937 to 4-11-1939),

Maharaja Krishna Chandra Gajapati (24-11-1941 to 29-6-1944), Governor's Rule (29-6-1944 to 23-4-1946), Harekrishna Mahtab (23-4-1946 to 11-5-1950.

Under such a circumstance, no developmental works of Orissa had been done. The spirit and enthusiasm of the Oriya people and the leaders who have displayed during the longest period of movement (1882-1936) for Orissa unification died and dried up. Orissa was awfully neglected by the Govt. and the leaders of Orissa. The cherished dream of Madhubabu, Maharaja Krishna Chandra Gajapati, Harihar Mardaraj, Fakir Mohan Senapati, Gopal Praharaj, Sri Ram Chandra Bhanj to see Orissa as a full-fledged flourishing state was shattered in to pieces.

India got Independence on 15th August 1947-but the old Municipal Act and local self Govt. Act of B and O of 1922 were also prevalent till 1950. The new Orissa Municipal Act of 1950 was made effective from the 1st April, 1951.

After Independence, all the old districts and 24 feudatory states were put together and created a full fledged Province with 13 districts on 1st January 1949 because Mayur Bhanj was the last feudatory state which merged with Orissa on 1st January 1949.

The size and spirit of the district Boards of Cuttack, Puri, Balasore, Sambalpur, Ganjam and Koraput were still maintained up to 25th January 1961. The Balbanta Roy Mehta .Committee in 1956 recommended to dissolve all the district and local Boards of all the Provinces in India and in its place the three-tier system of local self Govt. was established.

In the district level, the Zilla Parishad will function the Panchayat Samities in the Block level and the Panchayats in the village level. These 13 Zilla Parishads continued to function since 1961 to 1991. Biju Patnaik was elected as the Chief Minister of Orissa in February 1990 Assembly elections who formed the ministry on 5th March (1990) birthday. On the public demands, Biju Babu smashed 13 district into 30 small territorial segments or districts. Even a sub-division of Parlakhemundi in old Ganjam district was made a separate Gajapati district in honour of the Late Maharaja Krishna Chandra Gajapati of Parlakhemundi. This Gajapati district is the smallest of all the districts in Orissa . It not only fragmented the Province into several pieces but created crucial financial crises. Due to the paucity of funds, all the offices of the newly created districts Head Quarters are running in the rented house

There were three municipalities in the feudatory states of Mayur Bhanj and Balangir. The Municipality was established on 1-6-1905 in Baripada town of Mayur Bhanj during the reign of Maharaja Sri Sir Ramachandra Bhanj.

Two other municipalities were established at Sonepur and Binaka town before 1925.

The Zilla Parishads of the districts of Mayur Bhanj, Keonjhar, Bolangir, Kalahandi, Dhenkanal and Phulbani were constituted in January, 1961 under the Provisions of the Orissa Zilla Parishad Act of 1959. There were no District Boards in any of the districts which were previously ruled by the feudatory Chiefs.

Cuttack and Bhubaneswar Municipalities are converted into Municipal Corporation on 15th August 1994.

Zilla Parishads

At present, there are 30 Zilla Parishads for 30 districts in Orissa. The members of the Zilla Parishad directly elected by the adult voters from the different wards of the district. The chairman of Zilla Parishad is elected from among the elected members.

All the Zilla Parishads of Orissa are constituted on the

27th January 1961 and under the Provisions of the Zilla Parishad Act of 1959.

The Zilla Parishads were the Advisory Body, which suggested the different developmental works of the district. Zilla Parishads approved the programmes and budgets of the different Panchayat Samities.

The Zilla Parishads were replaced by the District Advisory Councils from the 1st November 1968. And it was to advise the Govt. regarding the developmental works of the district.

Again the State Govt. of Orissa in Planning and Coordination Dept. Resolutions No. 16636 dt. 14th November, 1970, superceded the District Advisory Councils and constituted the District Developmental Advisory Boards. The District Advisory Councils transferred all the works to the District Development Advisory Board.

But this District Development Advisory Board was also abolished on 8th July 1974 and the District Development Board was constituted on 9th July 1974.

The Collector became the Chairman. MPs, MLAs, Chairmen of the Panchayat Samities, Chairmen of the Municipal Boards, Presidents of the Central Cooperative Banks, and nominees of the Ministers, Ministers of the state, Deputy Ministers of that district.

The functions of the District Development Boards remained the same. To advise the Govt. in the developmental Programmes of the district and to review the developmental activities after the implementations.

A District Planning Board was also constituted to prepare Plans for development of the district in P and C Dept. Resolutions No 17070 dt. 31.8.1990.

Later on, the District Development Board and the District

Planning Board were also superceded in P and C Resolution No. 24336 dt. 21.12.1991 and in its place a District Planning and Development Board was constituted for each district by amalgamating the District Development Board: and the District Planning Board.

The aims and objectives of the District Planning and Development Board are the same as it were before of the District Development Board.

Membership is also the same. But the Chief Minister, Biju Patnaik once again liked to revive the old Zilla Parishads. So the Orissa Zilla Parishad Act of 1991 was passed in the Orissa Legislative Assembly, which came into force from 1st November 1993.

The provisions of the Zilla Parishad Act of 1991 are as follows:

1. Each Panchayat Samiti shall elect two persons on the basis of adult suffrage as members of the Zilla Parishad.
2. There shall be reservation of seats for S.C. and S.T. members on the basis of proportion of their population to the total population of the district.
3. One-third of the seats shall be reserved for women members including S.C. and S.T. women.
4. The President and Vice-President of the Zilla Parishad shall be elected from among the members.
5. All the Chairman of the Panchayat Samities of the district shall be ex-officio members of the Zilla Parishad.
6. All the members of the Legislative Assembly Parliament belonging to the district shall be members of the Zilla Parishad.
7. Chairman of the Municipalities and Notified Area Council and Cooperative Banks shall be ex-officio members.

8. District level officers of Health Education, Public Health, Agriculture, Forest Works, and Cooperative Depts. be ex-officio members.
9. Collector of the district shall be the Chief Executive Officer of the Parishad.
10. The tenure of the Parishad shall be five years from its first meeting.
11. Candidates contesting elections to this Parishad are allowed to use their Party symbol.

From the Provisions of the representation to the Zilla Parishads, it appears that the number of the members of the Zilla Parishad of each district is so large and variety that no important decision can be taken. Due to lack of Quroum, no meeting could be held at definite time. Too many cooks spoil the broth. Huge amount of expenditure will occur in paying T.A and D.A. to the members. More expenditure and no benefits. Political representation is more important here than any developmental works of the district. We make developmental works in resolutions—in pen and papers at a meeting—but no concrete work is being done in reality.

Panchayat Samiti

The second tier of the tier system of rural local self-Govt is the Panchayat Samiti. According to the Orissa Panchayat Samiti Act of 1959, several Panchayat Samities are constituted on 27th January 1961, along with the Zilla Parishads.

Each Panchayat Samiti is divided into several Gram Panchayats. Each Panchayat Samiti consists of official and non-official members.

The official members one Block Development Officer (B.D.O) and other officers of the Govt. posted in the Block Office. The non-official members are Sarpanchas of different Gram Panchayats under that Block Office. The women of S.T. and S.C are also the members. The Chairman of the

Panchayat Samiti is directly elected by the members of the Panchayat Samiti. Vice-Chairman is also elected from among the non-official members.

The Provisions of the Panchayat Samiti Act had been amended in 1991 and 1992 and incorporated the same Provisions of the Zilla Parishad (amended) into Panchayat Samiti.

The Block Development Officer is the Executive Officer of the Panchayat Samiti. The Panchayat Samiti mainly depends upon the grant-in-aid of the Govt. of Orissa.

Gram Panchayats

The Gram Panchayat is the third tier of the three-tier system of rural local self-Govt. and functions at the grass-root level of the villages. Before the introduction of the three-tier system of rural local self-Govt. in 1961, sufficiently before it, the Orissa Gram Panchayat Act was passed in 1948 to establish and develop the rural self-governing agencies. The Gram Panchayat is formed with a group of villages within — a definite jurisdiction.

The Gram Panchayat Act of 1948 was replaced by the Orissa Gram Panchayat Act of 1964 and was brought in the line of the three-tier system.

In 1991, several amendments were brought to provide representation to the members of the Scheduled Caste and Scheduled Tribe and one-third representation to the women. Further amendment was made in 1992 to provide the post of Sarpanch or Naib Sarpanch to a woman.

The Gram Panchayat has got its own sources of income. The funds are raised from the taxes, vehicle registration fees, rent from markets, income from cattle pounds, tanks, orchards, waste land, forest, ferry etc.

Panchayat Samitis and Gram Panchayats

Sl. No.	*Name of the Undivided districts*	*No. of Panchayat Samitis*	*No. of Gram Panchayats*	*Year*
1.	Mayur Bhanja	26	160	1967
2.	Balasore	19	337	1986
3.	Cuttack	41	890	1996
4.	Puri	29	368	1977
5.	Ganjam	29	467	1988
6.	Koraput	36	232	1963
7.	Boudh Kandhamala	15	132	1983
8.	Kalahandi	18	234	1980
9.	Balongir	20	152	1970
10.	Sambalpur	29	315	1971
11.	Sundargarh	16	139	1971
12.	Dhenkanal	16	231	1966
13.	Keonjhar	13	169	1986

Source: From the District Gazetteers of different districts published by the Govt. of Orissa.

Date of Establishment and Constitution of Old Municipality in Orissa

Sl No.	*Name of Municipality*	*Act under which constituted*	*Date of establishment*	*Population*
1.	Berhampur Municipality	Madras Municipal Act of 1867		
2.	Kendrapara Municipality		10-3-1869	15719
3.	Jajpur Municipality		1-4-1869	11233
4.	Cuttack Municipality	Bengal Municipal Act III	4-7-1876	38872
5.	Puri Municipality	(B.C.) of 1884	1-4-1881	24803
6.	Balasore Municipality		1-4-1877	20265
7.	Sambalpur Municipality	Act III of C.P. of 1903	9-4-1883	
8.	Parlakhemundi Municipality	Madras Municipal Act of 1885		
9.	Baripada Municipality	Imperial order of Maharaja of Mayur Bhanj	1-6-1905	

Constitution and Date of Establishment of Old District Boands in Orissa

Sl. No.	Name of the District Boards or Council	Act under which constituted	Date of establishment	Area in square Miles	Population
1.	Cuttack		1.4.1887	3628	2029257
2.	Puri	L.S.G. Act. of 1885	1.4.1887	2495	983716
3.	Balasore		1.4.1887	2079	1034206
4.	Sambalpur District Council	Act of C.D. of 1883	1883	3824	731212
5.	Ganjam	L.S.G. Act of Madras 1884	1884		
6.	Koraput		1905	10,498	1561051 (1961)

Constitution and Date of Establishment District Board in Orissa

Cuttack Dist.: Constitution of Municipality and NAC

SL No.	Name of Municipality & NAC	Date of establishment	Area in Sq. Kms. (1991-92)	No. of (1991-92)	Population wards	Act under which Constituted	Population 1991
1.	Cuttack Municipality	4.7.1876	81-91 Sq. Kms	30		Cuttack Munici-	402390
2.	Kendrapara (M)	10.3.1869	10.88 Sq. Kms	20		pality became a	35009
3.	Jajpur (M)	1.4.1869	11-65 Sq. Kms	15		corporation on	27310
4.	Choudwar (M)	4.10.1958	33.08 Sq. Kms.	16		15.8.1994	27310
5.	Jajpur Road (NAC)	12.6.1961	12.69 Sq. Kms	22	Constituted		25504
6.	Banki (NAC)	11.7.1966	6.22 Sq. Kms	17	under the Orissa	Came into force	14348
7.	Jagatsinghpur (NAC)	13.2.1972	18-25 Sq. Kms	19	Municipal	from 16. April 1951	25009
8.	Athagarh (NAC)	21.2.1973	10.36 Sq. Kms	14	Act of 1950		13664
9.	Paradip (NAC)	27.9.1979	22-65 Sq. Kms				48156
10.	Pattamundai (NAC)	8.12.1986		20			28908

Puri Dist.: Constitution of Municipality and NAC

Sl. No.	*Name of Municipality and NAC*	*Date of Establishment*	*Area in Sq. Kms.*	*No. of wards 1981*	*Population (1971)*	*Act under which constituted*
1.	Puri (M)	1.4.1881	16-84 sq. kms.	23 (1973)	72674	
2.	Bhubaneswar (NAC)	1.2.1948	10-07 sq. miles (1952)	23 (1974)	113095	Bihar & Orissa M Act of 1922, then OM Act of 1950
3.	Nayagarh (NAC)	13.7.1953	7.77 sq. kms	11	5209	
4.	Khurda (NAC)	12.7.1960	10 sq. miles	15	15879	
5.	Pipli (NAC)	17.4.1972	3.45 sq. miles	12	6152	
6.	Jatni (NAC)	13.3.1972	7.5 sq. miles	21	28965	Bhubaneswar became corporation on 15.8.1994
7.	Banapur (NAC)	15.3.1973	10.87 sq. kms	15	9664	
8.	Nimapara (NAC)	15.7.1973	14 sq. kms	11	8693	

Zilla Parishad came into existence on 26.01.1961.

Balasore Dist.: Constitution of Municipalities and NAC

Sl. No.	Name of the Municipalities ,and NAC	Date of establishment	Area in square KMs	No. of wards 1981	Population 1981
1.	Balasore (M)	1.4.1877	7½ sq miles (1981)	22	65771
2.	Bhadrak (NAC)	8.5.1960	9.80 sq miles (1961)	19	60573
3.	Jaleswar (NAC)	15.4.1964	17.09 sq kms	9	13147
4.	Soro (NAC)	12.2.1975	9.22 sq miles	15	18599
5.	Basudevpur (NAC)	24.11.1974	18.33 sq kms	17	20029
6.	Nilagiri (NAC)	23.2.1984	11-59 sq kms	16	10702

Bhadrak (NAC) became a municipality in 1989.

Zilla Parishad of Balasore was constituted on 1.9.1961.

Sambalpur Dist.: Constitution of Muncipalities and NAC

Sl. No.	Name of the Municipality & NAC	Date of establishment	Area in square KMs	No. of wards	Population (1961)	Act under which constituted
1.	Sambalpur (M)	9.4.1883	20=72 Sq. KMs (1961)	27	38915	Orissa Municipal Act of 1950 came into force from 1.4.1951
2.	Deogarh (M)	1912	7.5 Sq. Miles	9(1961)	6839	
3.	Bargarh (M)	1.5.1952	13-21 Sq. KMs	15	15375	
4.	Jharusuguda (M)	28.8.1951	10 Sq. Miles	13	19227	
5.	Burla (NAC)	23.6.1964	15.2 Sq. KMs	12	102370	
6.	Padmapur (NAC)	2.4.1965	8.03 Sq. Miles	11		
7.	Brajaraj Nagar (NAC)	Nov. 1968		17		
8.	Hirakund (NAC)	12.6.1964	8.81 Sq. KMs	12	8593	

Bolangir Dist.: Constitution of Municipalities and NAC

Sl. No.	*Name of the Municipality & NAC*	*Date of establishment*	*Area in square KMs*	*No. of wards*	*Population (1961)*	*Act under which constituted*
1.	Bolangir (M)	April-1938	6 Sq. Miles	12		Orissa Municipal Act of 1950 came in force from 16.4.1951
2.	Sonepur (M)	1951	3 Sq. Miles	15		
3.	Patnagarh (NAC)	6.1.1964	8 Sq. Miles	12		
4.	Titlagarh (NAC)	17.11.1951	5 Sq. Miles	9		
5.	Kantabanji (NAC)	17.11.1965	3 Sq. Miles			

Dhenkanal District: Constitution of Municipalities and NAC

Sl. No.	Name off the Municipality or NAC	Act under which constituted	Date of establishment	Area in square KMs	No of wards
1.	Dhenkanal Municipality		1.9.1933	5.18	12
2.	Talcher Municipality	Orissa Municipal	1913 Committee, 1.5.1954 Municipality	10.36	4
3.	Angul NAC/Committee	Act of 1950	1931 Committee, 1.8.1955 NAC	6.47	10

Mayur Bhanj Dist : Constitution off Municipalities or NAC

Sl. No.	Name off the Municipality or NAC	Act under which constituted	Date of establishment	Area in square KMs	No of wards
1.	Baripada Municipality	Orissa Municipal	1.6.1905	4 Sq. miles	15
2.	Rairangpur NAC	Act of 1950	8.4.1960	—	14
3.	Karanjia NAC		15.9.1973.		

Mayur Bhanj merged with Orissa on 1.1.1949

GANJAM DIST.: Constitution of Municipality and NAC

Sl. No.	*Name of the Municipality & NAC*	*Date of establishment*	*Area in square KMs*	*No. of wards*	*Population (1981)*
1.	Berhampur (M)	1867	76.15 Sq. kms.	27	162550
2.	Parlakhemundi (M)	1885	3.63 Sq. kms.	16	32317
3.	Bhanjanagar (NAC)	15-11-1957	6.06 Sq. kms.	15	15324
4.	Purusottampur (NAC)	1-1-1973	13.5 Sq. kms.	14	10739
5.	Chikiti (NAC)	15-3-1973	6.48 Sq. kms.	11	8177
6.	Chatrapur (NAC)	1-6-1955	4.40 Sq. kms.	11	14140
7.	Gopalpur (NAC)	20-5-1961	2.56 Sq. kms.	11	4503
8.	Aska (NAC)	15-11-1957	5.31 Sq. kms.	17	16394
9.	Rambha (NAC)	27-5-1964	7-77 Sq. kms.	13	8196
10.	Kodala(NAC)	20-10-1974	12-09 Sq. kms.	13	8537
11.	Hinjlicut (NAC)	2.6.1964	11.81 Sq.Kms	17	13761
12.	Buguda (NAC)	January 1973	7.45 Sq. Kms	11	8706
13.	Kabisuryanagar (NAC)	16.12.1960	18.13 Sq.Kms	15	11873
14.	Digapahandi (NAC)	1.3.1973	10-22 Sq. Kms	11	7853
15.	Sorada (NAC)	14.4.1962	4.92 Sq. Kms	11	11269
16.	Khallikote (NAC)	28.1.1973	28.49 Sq. Kms	12	8340
17.	Polasora (NAC)	29.3.1972	11-81 Sq. Kms	11	13039
18.	Kasinagar (NAC)	1.3.1975	10-36 Sq. Kms	13	9179
19.	Belaguntha (NAC)	7.4.1974	5-18 Sq.Kms	12	7915
20.	Ganjam (NAC)	13.9.1986	7.80 Sq. Kms	12	7580

Boudh- Kandhamal Dist.: Constitution of Municipality and NAC

Sl. No.	*Name of the Municipality or NAC*	*Act under which constituted*	*Date of establishment*	*Area in square KMs*	*No. of wards*	*Population*
1.	Phulbani NAC	Orissa Municipal	14.2.1963	7.77	9	4031
2.	Boudhagarh NAC	Act. Of 1950	14.10.1961	20.8	12	8884

Kalahandi Dist.: Constitution of Muncipalities and NAC

Sl. No.	*Name of the Municipality or NAC*	*Act under which constituted*	*Date of establishment*	*Area in square KMs*	*No. of wards*	*Population*
1.	Bhawanipatna Municipality	Orissa	16.4.1951	12-96	13	22808
2.	Khariar Road NAC	Municipal Act of 1950	11.8.1964	18-13	15	9226
3.	Kesinga NAC		2.6.1965	14-26	11	8536
4.	Khariar NAC		6.8.1972	23-82	11	7651
5.	Junagarh NAC		15.1.1970	12-95	9	7876

Keonjhar Dist.: Constitution of Municipalities and NAC

Sl. No.	*Name off the Municipality or NAC*	*Act under which constituted*	*Date of establishment*	*Area in square KMs*	*No of Wards*
1.	Keonjhar Garh Municipality		12.12.1947 before merger 3. 1.1951 (after)	15.54	13
2.	Barbil Notified Area Council	Constituted under Orissa Municipal Act of 1950	15.8.1957	17-30	9
3.	JODA NAC		16.6.1961	13	11
4.	Anandapur NAC		15.8.1974	9.32	13

Merged with Orissa on 1.1.1948.

Sundargarh Dist.: Constitution of Municipalities and NAC

Sl. No.	Name of the Municipalities and NAC	Date of establishment	Area in square KMs	No. of wards	Population
1.	Sundargarh (M)	1.11.1951	23.83 sq kms	10	
2.	Rajgangpur (M)	Oct. 1957	26.16 sq kms	12	
3.	Biramitrapur (M)	30.12.1969	35.22 sq kms	10	
4.	Rourkela (NAC) Civil Town	1.8.1955	7.2 sq miles	7	
5.	Rourkela (NAC) (Steel Township)	17.6.1963	38 sq miles	9	

Koraput Dist.: Constitution of Municipality and NAC

Sl. No.	Name of the Municipalities and NAC	Date of establishment	Area in square KMs	No. of wards	Population
1.	Jeypore (M)	1.7.1953			
2.	Rayagada (NAC)	15.5.1955	5 sq. miles		
3.	Koraput (NAC)	1.7.1953	5 sq. miles		
4.	Gunupur (NAC)	15.5.1955	4 % sq. miles		
5.	Nawarangpur (NAC)	1.4.1953	3 sq. miles		
6.	Kotpad (NAC)	1.5.1961	5 sq. miles		

8

Oriya Literature (1936-2000)

Kabi Samrat Upendra Bhanj, Kabi Surya Baladev Rath, Dhanajay Bhanj, Gopal Krishna Patnaik, Gangadhar Meher, Radhanath Roy, Fakir Mohon Senapati, Madhu Sudan Rao, Abhimanyu Samanta Singhar, Dinakrishna Das and Panchasakha (Balaram Das, Ananta Das, Yasowant Das, Jagannath Das and Achyuta Nanda Das)—the great literary stalwarts have strongly laid the foundation of the Oriya literature in the early part of 15th century to the second half of 19th century A.D. The twentieth century saw the emergence of five prominent poets in the Satyabadi yuga who contributed immensely to the Oriya literature. They are: Gopabandhu Das, Pandit Nilakantha Das, Godavarish Misra, Acharya Harihar Das and Krupasindhu Misra.

But it is no denying the fact that the ungrudging financial help and patronage of the Orissan Kings had strengthened the base of the Oriya literature. Dhananjay Bhanja, Kabi Samrat Upendra Bhanja, Vikram Dev, Padmanabh Narayan Dev of Parlakhemundi, Biswambar Rajendra Deva and Radha Mohan Rajendra Deva of Chikiti, Krishna Singh of Dharakote, Govinda Bhanja of Keonjhar and many other several royal houses of Orissa had themselves enriched the Oriya literature by their powerful writings. Otherwise the Oriya literature would have been a simple skeleton.

Gopabandhu Das died on 17th June 1928. Nilakantha Das and Godavarish Mishra continued to write different types of poems. Gopabandhu Das (1877-1928) wrote Abakash Chinta, Kara Kabita, Dharmapada, Bandira Atmakatha , Go Mahatmya, Nachiketa Upakhyan for which he remained an immortal figure in the world of Oriya literature. Nilakantha Das's poems were Konark, Mayadevi, Kharaveia and Rama Chandire Sandhya. Godavarish Misra Composed Kisalaya, Kalika, Gitayan, Alekhika, Chayanika and Kalijai etc.

From 1936 onwards, Oriya literature has flourished in different dimensions in Prose, Poetry, Novels, Drama, Literary-Criticism, Travelogue, Biography and autobiography, Science literature etc. The bright luminaries who dazzled the readers of Orissa and India are Kantakabi Lakhmikanta Mohapatro (1888-1953), Godavarish Mohapatro (1898-1965), Padma Charan Patnaik (1885-1955), Narikabi Kuntala Kumari Sabat (1900-1938), Harekrishna Mahtab(1899-1987), Baikunth Nath Patnaik (1901-1991), Mayadhar Mansingh (1905-1973), Radha Mohan Godnaik (1911-2000), Annada Shankar Roy (1904-) and Bhagabati Charan Panigrahi.

A new era of progressive thoughts in Oriya Poems started in 1936. The poets aspired a revolting attitude against the exploitations of the Kings and Zamidars. This period lasted up to the year-1960. During this period the prolific poets who wrote different revolutionary poems are Ananta Patnaik (1914-1987), who was the Secretary of the Nabayuga Sahitya Sansad formed on 29-11-1935. He was a Leftist. Raghunath Das who wrote "August-15" and Man Mohan Misra who wrote basically on the principle of socialism condemned the exploitation of the Zamindars and declared social equality and justice.

Here is a long list of the Oriya poets who contributed to enrich the Oriya Poetry and literature.

Sachi Routroy (1915-)

During his youthful days, he was a nationalist composed so many patriotic songs. Later on he became a revolutionary poet. He published the poetry- Baji Rout, Pandulipi, Patheya,

Bhanumatira Desa, Pallisri and poems of 1962. He is awarded the most coveted literary prize of India—"Jyanapitha Award" in 1989.

Rabi Singh (1932-)

He is the undisputed poet of the progressive thoughts in Orissa. He is direct and true to his approach to the problems and realities of life. He leaves no stone unturned and a fire-brand speaker. In 1959 he published his first poetry: "Patha Prantara Kabita". He is fearless as a critic and exposes all the vices of Oriya literature or the exploitations of the royal and democratic administration. Out of his many poetry books: Charam Patra Sithila Bolga, Lal Pagodar Bhuta are important.

Krishan Charan Behera (1931)

He is against the social injustice and exploitation of the society. He takes pity to see the degeneration, corruption and greed of the modern men. Men have destroyed the value of life., peace, fraternity and love in the modern days and lives a lonely life. This is the theme of his poems.

Brajanath Rath (1936)

His approach to poems is also revolutionary. He is a man of Leftist attitude. His collections of poems are —Moru Golap, Tinoti Niswasar Akash, Nijaswa Somlapa.

Prasanna Kumar Patasani (1947-)

During his early days as a poet he exhibited the progressive ideas in his poems, but later on he became a humanist with enormous consciousness to society. His poems are — Sapa Gatare Sakaala, Raktapatha and Barsa.

Nirmala Devi (1907-1989)

Nirmala Devi was very sensitive and delicate as a poet. Having the soft heart as a woman, she loved the God of her heart, the man of the earth. She used very beautiful allegory and words in her poems.

Guru Prasad Mohanty (1924-)

As a student of English literature Guru Mohanty had adopted the style of writing of T.S Eliot and his valuable poetry: "The Waste Land". His poetry "Kalo Puruso" is a unique creation though lengthy.

The Samudra Snana of Guru Mohanty is the reflection of the utter disappointment, sins and corruption of the modern men. All his poems are acceptable and appreciated by the countless readers of Orissa.

Durga Madhab Misra (1929-1997)

As the highest police officer: I.G. of Orissa, Durga Madhab Mishra though contrasts in his profession and poetry has occupied a very important position in Oriya literature. He is a humanist. His universality of thoughts is exhibited in his poems of " Mutha-e-Maati O' Chena'e Akash", "Bruto Abruto", and "Mouna Mukhora". He was a great sympathiser of mankind.

Bhanuji Rao (1926-)

His poems are "Nutan Kabita", "Kathajodi and Bishad Eka Rutu" which reflect the versatility of his mind and the realistic picture of life.

Binod Nayak (1919-)

He is famous for his poems 'Chandra O' Tara', 'Sarisrupa' and "Haimanti Nila Chandra Upakatha."

Dr. Kunja Behari Dash (1914-1994)

He is a great literary genius of Oriya literature. His poems are- "Chhinnamasta", "Prabhati Birasri", "Naba Malik", Mati O' lathi" and 'Kankalara luha' etc.

Jnanindra Burma (1917-1989)

His poems are "Bole Huunti", "Prarnilar Smruti" and "Swarna Jugar Sandhya."

Dr. Gopal Chandra Misra (1925-1990)

Poems—"Bidrahi Dibakar" and "Patasani" etc.

Janaki Ballav Patnaik (1927-)

Poem—"Sindhu Upatyaka".

Dr. Janaki Ballav Mohanty (1925-)

Poems-"Tirjak" and "Bichitrabarna".

Benudhar Rout (1927)

Poem-"Pingalar Surya".

Chintamani Behera (1928)

Poems-"Swetapadma", "Swastika" and "Nutan Swakhar" etc.

Bidyut Prabha (1926-1927)

Poems-"Sabita Kanakanjali", "Marichika", "Bandanika" and "Swapnadwipa" etc.

Bibhudutta Mishra (1936-)

He is a very emotional poet. His poems are-"Urbasra Chithi", "Saheti Sonnet" and "Smruti Bismruti" etc.

Sarat Chandra Pradhan (1934)

His poems are—"Nai Aou Machha" (River and Fish), "Hansa O' Sarasa."

Ramakanta Rath (1934-)

His style of writing poems is completely untraditional. His poems are "Sandigdha Mrugaya", "Saptam Rutu", "Sachitra Andhara". His monumental creation is "Radha" which fetched " Saraswati Award" from the Center to him. A retired I.A.S. officer is the President of Kendra Sahitya Academy.

Sitakante Mohapatro (1937-)

He is also a retired I.A.S. officer, awarded the "Kendra Sahitya Academy Award.' His poems are: "Astapadi", "Dipti O' Dyuti", "Sabdar Akash", "Samudra", "Chitranadi" etc. He worked on the Santali language of Mayur Bhanj and brought out Anthology on it.

Kamala Kanta Lenka (1935-)

His poems are—"Suna Phasal", "Priti O' Pratiti," "Uttarana", "Kabitara", "Meenhasrator Naam Rutu".

Jagannath Prasad Das (1936)

Poems—"Pratham Puraso", "Je Jahar" and "Nirjanata," 'Anya Sabu Mrutyu' etc.

Nrusingh Prasad Rath (1935-)

His poems are "Sruyatam", "Chhabi O' Chhaya", "Utkanthar Mratyu".

Dipak Misra (1935-)

Poems—"Asamapika ', Nisidha Hrada (Prohibited lake), "Madhyanhar Chhai" (Shadow of the noon), "Saptama Prithvi" etc. He got Orissa Sahitya Academy Award.

Rajendra Prasad Panda (1944-)

Poems—"Gouna Devata", "Nijapain Nanabaya", "Shaila Kalpa" etc. An I.A.S. Officer.

Dr. Saubhagya Kumar Misra (1941-)

Poems—"Atmanepadi", "Madhya Padalap Bajrajana". He exposes vices, corruption, alienation and helplessness of the modern men in his poems. Got the Kendra Sahitya Academy Award.

Saroj Ranjan Mohanty (1942-)

Poems—"Kagaz dangar Soka", "Boigeni Rutu" etc. He is the co-editor of the leading Oriya magazine—"Jhankar".

Lakhmi Narayan Mohapatro (1942-1995)

A Philosopher poet got the Lenin Award from Soviet Russia. Poems: "Anya Dwipa"," Stthiti Gotia Atmara", "Tara Saptaka Bhuma" etc.

Debdas Chhotroy (1946-)

An I.A.S Officer. Poems-"Neela Saraswati", "Katak". He is the lyricist of an Oriya film—"Kia Kahara", "Paradesi Bandhu Tume Jiba Udi Udiki"—the most popular among the Oriya cine-goers.

Phani Mohanty (1944-)

Poems—"Manachitra", "Swayambar", "Ruchira Nagar", "Priyatama" etc.

Praharaj Satya Narayan Nanda (1943-)

Poems-"Raj Hansara jwala", "Adhapatanar Chhanda", "Jianta Shalagram" etc.

Sourindra Barik (1938)

Poems—"Samanya Kathan", "Upabharat", "Aksha Pari Nibida" etc. got the Kendra Sahitya Academy Award.

Srinibash Udgata (1936-)

Poems — "Pratima Apratim", " Apanara Geet".

Sudhansu Mohan Routroy (1932-1990)

Poems-"Pakhyahina Kapot', "Sanja Sakala" and "Sesha Basanta".

Manorama Biswal (1948-)

A poetess of eminence. Poems "Thare Khali Dakidele", "Swapnare Biwhala etc. She got Orissa Sahitya Academy Award.

Prativa Satapathy

She is a realist in her approach to poems and also a

romantic. Poems-"Sahada Sundari", "Asta Janhar Aligi", "Nimise Akhyara".

Dilip Das (1942-)

An eminent poet of Oriya literature. His poems are Bilupta Samrajya", "Pakhi Basichhi Dalaare Chhai Padichhi Jalare", "Sudararu Anek Dura"-and "Budi Jauthiba Desa".

Gopal Krishan Rath (1945-)

Poems-"EKL Manisa"

Hara Prasad Das (1945)

Alokita Banabas awarded Orissa Sahitya

Dr. Giribala Mohanty

A poetess of eminence.

Many more young poets emerged during the last quarter of 20th Century. It-is difficult to mention their names-Hrushikesh Mallick, Haraprasad Parichha Patnaik, Prafulla Das, Nityananda Pati are some of them.

ORIYA NOVELS

The foundation of writing Oriya Novels has already been laid by Ramesh Chandra Sarkar, Umesh Chandra Sarkar, Rama Sankar Roy and Fakir Mohan Senapati in the last part of the 19th Century. In the beginning of the 20th Century, Gopal Ballav Das, Chintamani Mohanty, Nandakishore Bal, Baishnab Charan Das, Padma Charan Acharya, Godavarish Misra, Godavarish Mohapatro, Lakhmikant Mohapatro, Govind Tripathy, Kuntala Kumari Sabat, Upendra Kishore, Kamala Kanta *and* Chakradhar Mohapatro maintained the spirit of writing novels and enriched the Oriya Novels.

After 1936, many more Novelists devoted their time, energy and talent in writing new Novels and made them popular among the countless readers in Orissa. They are:

Rama Chandra Acharya

Novels—"Piyush Prabah" (1935), "Birangana" (1936).

Tarini Charan

Wrote "Annapurna" in 1934.

Godavarish Misra

Ghatantar", 1917 (a novel), "Abhagini."

Godavarish Mohapatro

Novels—"Rajdroha" (1925), "Raktapat" (1930), "Bandira Maya" (1934), "Veer Jubak" (1936) and "Bidroh" (1938).

Lakhmikanta Mohapatro

Lakhmikanta Mohapatro wrote "Kana mamu".

Govind Tripathy

This novels are "Pramad" (1925), "Mayabi" (1941), "Guinda Gadadhar" (1949), "Chatura Gadadhar" (1951).

Harekrishna Mahatab (1899-1987), Kalindi Charan Panigrahy, Nityananda Mohapatro, Rama Prasad Singh, Raj Kishore Patnaik, Lakhmidhar Nayak, Gopinath Mohanty, Sachidananda Routroy, Dibyasingh Panigrahy, Jagabandu Mohapatro, Bata Krishna Praharaj, Mayadhar Mansingh, Pranakrishna Samal, Faturananda (Rama Chandra Misra) and Ananta Prasad Panda are the novelists of eminence during the period from 1936 to 1960.

Harekrishna Mahtab (1899-1887)

He was a personality of different dimensions. He combined in himself the best qualities of a historian, a politician, a literatuier, a critic and a statesman. It was an astonishing point to all that how could he succeed in all his enterprises in life.

His notable novels are "Prativa O'byapar", "Nutan

Dharma", "Toutor", "Trutiya Parva". In all his novel he portrayed the social and political life of the Indians and Orissa.

Kalindi Charan Panigrahy

The novel ' Matira Manisa' made him immortal in Orissa a deep impression upon the minds of the readers.

To his credit, he wrote so many other novels like "Luhar Manisa", "Ajira Manisa" etc.

Nityananda Mohapatro

As a Gadhianite, he wrote many Oriya novels like "I "Bhangahad", "Heedamati", "Jalanta Nian" (Burning Fire), "Jianta Manisa", "Jibanar Lakhya" (Aim of life), "Sukhar Sandhan" (In search of happiness).

Rama Prasad Singh

Novels-"Hemasikha", "Sampati", "Marichika", "Poojar bali" "Marura Sathi", "Agni Pathe" and "Pratihimsa" (Revenge).

Rajkishore Patnaik

Novels-"Panjuri Pakhi", "Premar Niyati", "Sindura Gar", "Premikara Diary", "Chalabaat", "Kajalagara", "Astami Chanda", "Sapan Kuhudi", "Kala Parada", "Sanjabati", "Bhasamegha", "Pritira Baniza", "Pritira Kazala," etc.

Lakhmidhar Nayak

He is also a believer in the socialistic thoughts of the time and wrote so many novels such as "Oodbhranta", "Charitrahinar Chithi", "Haire Durbhaga Desa", "Bhulila Sate Sakhi", "Sarbahara", "Asiba Kebe Priya" etc.

Basanta Kumari Devi

Wrote the novel "Amadabata", which has been made a popular Oriya film and earned a great reputation.

Sitadevi Khadanga

Novel "Agraja" and "Poshyaputra" a native of Aska.

Kanhu Charan Mohanty (1906-1994)

He made the Oriya novels broad based and made them popular among the countless readers. Kanhu Charan Mohanty is the pillar of the Oriya novels. His novels are "Palatak", "Baliraja", "Nispati", "Haa Anna", "Parakiya" Jhanza", "Kaa", "Sasti", "Pani, "Bajrabahu", "Abhinetri", "Aruna", "Parichaya", "Bhooli Huena", "Mamatar Maya", "Mana Manthan", "Apa", "Sharbani", "Angana", "Namati Tara Champa", "Tapasa", "Swapna", "Adekha hata", "Prikhya", "Satyabati", "Baga bagula", "Tamasa Tire" etc. He has written nearly 60 novels in Oriya. He has presented a real serial scenario of the Oriya society-the sins, corruption, miseries due to machine civilization and focussed on the life of the tribal people.

Gopinath Mohanty

As a brother of Kanhu Charan Mohanty, Gopinath Mohanty too set an unprecedented record of his literary achievements. He was awarded the "Jyanapitha Award" for his literary genius for "Mati Matal". His novels are "Paraja", "Harijan", "Amrutar Santan", "Danapani", "Diga dihundi", "Sapan Mati", "Shivabhai", "Laya Bilaya", "Pahanta", "Tantrikar".

His works are lovely-governed by appropriate objectives. The message of his characters in different novels is to stand firmly on your legs by fighting against the odds of your life.

Surendra Mohanty

He is a notable novelist of Oriya literature. He combined Oriya literature and history in most of his novels. They are-"Neela Shailo", "Satbdira Surya", "Niladri Bijoy", "Krishna Benire Sandhya", "Andha Diganta", "Kulabrudha", "Kalantar", "Bodhu O' Priya", "Phatamati" etc.

He is also a veteran short story writer—"O'Calcutta" is his creation.

Another period of Oriya Novels began after 1960. The novels are characterized by the conflicts of life, alienation, the impact of industrial civilization and the ultra modernity-the people began to lead. And those reputed novels who have flooded the Oriya markets by their powerful writings are Santanu Kumar Acharya, Mahapatro Nilamani Sahu, Sri Krishna Prasad Misra, Chandra Sekhar Rath, Dr. Nrusingh Charan Panda, Bibhuti Patinaik, Satakodi Hota, Govind Das and Prativa Roy.

Prativa Roy

As a novelist, she flooded the Oriya novels in the Orissa market. The novels are: Ashabari, Aarichita, Silapadma, Jagyanseni, Megha Medura, Gangasiuli.

Shantnanu Kumar Achariya (1933-)

Novels-"Satabdira Nachiketa", "Nara Kinnar", "Dakhinabarta", "Shakuntala", "The Share of Minister", "Anya Ek Samay Anya Ek Bharat".

Mahapatro Neelamani Sahu

Novels—"Tamasi Radha", "Dhara O' Dharaa". Translated the 'Savitri" of Sri Aurobind into Oriya.

Krishna Prasad Misra

Novels—"Mruga Trusna", "Singhakati".

Chandra Sekhar Rath

Novels—"Nabajatak", "Jantraraddha", and "Asurya Upanibesh"

Nursing Charan Panda: (1933-)

Novels—"Chandaoka", "Dharmasoka"

Bibhuti Patnaik: (1939-)

A most successful Oriya novelist. He attracts the attention and interests of the readers to his characters, lover and beloved by his style of writing and magic words. He has written nearly 45 novels. They are "Prema O' Prithvi", "Nayikara Naam Shrabani", "Gare Kajwal Dhare luho", "Poro Puraso", "Grahana", "Eeiman Brundaman", Chapala Chhanda". "Eei man Akanta Adim", "Priya Bandhavi", ' "Andhakarar Sidi", "Ranganati", "Sesa Abhinaya", "Paapa Punya", "Pratham Sakala", "Bandi Jajabar", "Ujaani Jamuna", "Badhu Nirupama" "Vitamati", "Keshabati", "Bidayabela".

Satokodi Hota: (1930-)

Most of his novels deal mainly with the stories of the alienation, loneliness, tears and laughters, hopes and despair of modern life. His novels are—"Madhu Chhanda",' "Swapana Seuli", "Aneka Diganta", "Ashanta Aranya", "Rajadhanira Ranga", "Pratham Adhyaya" etc.

Govind Das

His novel "Amabasyara Chandra" is the most popular among the Oriya readers.

Ganeswar Misra

Novels—"Samudrika", "Arohi", "Neta" and "Sakalar Muhan".

Jadunath Das Mohapatro

Novels—"Luhar Phoola", "Rahumukti", "Needara Sandhane", "Magha Sesa Megha Sesa", "Gramya Nadira Tire".

Besides this, there are a host of noted novelists who have enriched the Oriya novels immensely. They are Dasarath Samal, Braja Mohan Mohanty. Jameswar Misra, Gokulananda Mohapatra, Bikram Das, Harihar Das, Prafulla Tripathy, Debraj Lenka, Balaram Patnaik, Jagannath Mallick etc.

Short-Story Writers

In Oriya literature, Fakir Mohan Senapati is the pioneer of the short story writing, who made a substantial contribution. Out of his many short stories "Rebati", "Sunababu", "Patent Medicine", "Garadi Mantra", "Dhuliababa" and "Dak Munsi" are most conspicuous. All the short stories are reformative in character. All the short stories carry the message of change in the nature, character and thoughts of men. There is sufficient humour, satire and scientific approach in his short stories.

Next to him, Chandra Sekhar Nanda, Dayanidhi Misra, Bankanidhi Patnaik, Dibyasingh Panigrahy, Lakhmikant Mohapatro, Kamapala Misra, Chintamani Mohanty, Basanta Kumar Kar, Godavarish Misra, Kalindi Charan Panigrahy, Bhagabati Charan Panigrahy contributed immensely to the growth and enrichment of the short story in Orissa.

The style of writing of short stories was also changed after the Second World War. The traditional themes of the society were dropped. And a new idea of modernity crept in to the mind of the writers. Sachidananda Routroy, Ananta Prasad Panda, Godavarish Mohapatro, Raj Kishore Roy wrote the short stories like "Andharua", "Manara Bhuta", "Mu Dine Mantri Thili", "Neela Lahari" respectively where they have added a new dimension of thoughts.

Pranabandhu Kar wrote "Suo Muhanre Patara", "Bhranti". Rajkishore Patnaik's "Pathika", "Tutho Pathar", "Kalpanar Phoola", "Hata and Souda", Nityananda Mohapatro's "Dholagaar Kalagaar" are important.

After the Indian Independence, many new short story writers emerged in Orissa and they made Oriya literature rich and varied. They are-Surendra Mohanty, Manoj Das, Kishore Charan Das, Bama Charan Mitra. Dr. Krishna Prasad Misra, Akhil Mohan Patnaik, Shantanu Kumar Acharya, Rabi Patnaik, Satakodi Hota, Mahapatro Nilamani Sahu, Bibhuti Bhusan Tripathy, Achyuta Nanda Pati, Chandra Sekhar Rath,

Basanta Kumar Satapathy, Dr. Bhubaneswar Behera, Yasodhara Misra, Durga Madhab Misra, Tarunkanti Misra, Hrusikesh Panda (I.A.S.), Jagdish Mohanty, Phaturananda, Uma Shankar Misra, Harihar Das, Binapani Mohanty, Nemai Patnaik, Barendra Krashna Dhal, Niru Mohanty, Arun Patnaik and many others.

Surendra Mohanty

"Rooti O' Chandra", "Maralar Mratyu", "O" Calcutta "Mahanirvan".

Kishore Chandra Das

"Bhanga Khelana", "Gaman", "Ghara Bahuda", "Thakur Ghar".

Manoj Das

"Manoj Dasanka Kath O' Kahani", "Abu Puraso", "Aranya Ullasa" and other stories.

Bama Charan Mitra

"Mitrakalpa", "Kirtabirja".

Dr. Krishna Prasad Misra

"Aranya O' Upabana", "Paschima", "Bichitra Chadar"

Achyutananda Pati

'Ugrasena Ubach, Asubha Putrara Kahani" etc.

Mahapatro Nilamani Sahu

"Sumitrar Hasa", "Bishnu,' Maya", "Akash O' Patalo", "Andha Ratrira Surya", "Abhisapta Gandharba".

Bibhuti Bhusana Tripathy

Setu", "Nishanta", "Chandana".

Akhil Mohan Patnaik

"Jhadara Eagle", "Dharanira Krushna Sara", "Andhagli".

Rabi Patnaik

The presentation of facts and the message of the short story are unique. "Andhagalir Andhakar", "Bahurapi", "Hiranya garva" Bichitrabarna."

Satakodi Hota

"Madhu lagna", "Mo Golpara Nayak", "Neela Chala Ku Rasta", "Begum Saheba" etc.

"Katha O' latha", "Ansari Chacha".

Harihar Das

'Sesa Sanlap", "Krantikari Jibanava Oopakatha".

Choudhury Hemakanta Misra

"Nisidha Pustak", "Hasakura Kathamaan", "Kurulia Galpa".

Umashankar Misra

"Sweta Anuta", "Trishanku", "Bohu Bohuka".

Chandra Sekhar Rath

"Aswarohira Galpa", "Samrat" *and* Other Stories, "Aneka Banya Pare."

Bijoy Krishna Mohanty

"Mlana Jyotsna", "Pagla Saheb".

Binapani Mohanty

"Kasturi Mruga O' Sabuja Aranya", "Madhyantar", 'Patadei."

Nemai Patnaik

"Padmatola," "Andharara Muhan."

Ramchandra Behera

Diwitiya Smasan", "Abasista Piyusa", "Onkar Dhwani"

Jagdish Mohanty

"Dakhina Duari Ghar", "Irsa Ek Rutu," "Album."

Barendra Krishna Dhala

"Paanigar", "Klanta Nakhyatra."

Besides, many more short story writers wrote innumerable stories in their own style. The most important among them are—Naru Mohanty, Tushar Kanti Misra. Yasodhara Misra, Gaur Patnaik Hrushikesh Panda (I.A.S.), Souribandhu Kar, Arun Patnaik, Shyam Prasad Choudhury and Amulya Krishna Misra.

Meanwhile a group of youngsters have also written the short stories.

LITERARY PROSE OR "PRABANDH"

During the post-Independence era, a good number of prose writers emerged to focus upon the different aspects of life. Aurobind Philosophy, Gandhianism, Five Year Plans, Socialism, animals, politics and Bhoodan Movement etc. The prolific writers of "Prose Classic" who flooded this aspects of Oriya literature are Krishna Chandra Panigrahy, Hare Krishna Mahtab, Golak Behari Dhal, Bama Charan Mitra, Sri Rama Chandra Dash Sadasiv Misra, Dr. Baidya Nath Misra, Dr. Ghanashyam Samal, Nityananda Mohapatro, Dr. Gokulananda Mohapatra, Dr. Radhanath Rath, Krishna Prasad Basu, Dr. Suryakanta Das, Dr. Kulamani Samal, Bhubaneswar Behera. Mahapatra Nilamani Sahu, Debakanta Misra, Dr. Nrashingh Charan Panda, Sarat Kumar Mohanty. Dr. Krishna Prasad Misra etc.

Ratnakar Pati is the pioneer of the writing of the "Prose Classic" after 1936. His writings are exhaustive, incomparable pieces. He wrote on "Titikhya" very difficult to analyze the elements of virtues. But he has lucidly presented them.

Krupasindhu Basu: "Akhada Ghare Baithak"

Golak Behari Dhol: "Odia Kebe", "Bichar Alochana

Bama Charan Mitra: "Jeevan" "Sahitya O' Kala"

Dr. Krishna Chandra Panigrahy: "History of Legends", " Prabadh Manas".

Mayadhar mansing: "Jeevan Path", " Odiya Samaj O' Sahitya" "Sikhya."

Hare Krishna Mahtab: "Gan Mazlis" through which he pointed out the mistakes and suggested constructive idea.

Hrusikesh Roy: "The Married life of Gandhi", "Test Tube Baby", "Mu Asili Keunthu", "Bibaha Pare" etc.

Surendra Mohanty: He analysed the facts and sequences taking some mythological characters and historical characters. "Odiara Nida", "Kagaz Danga", "Mahisasura Badha", "Madya O' Banya", "Matira Darsanika" etc.

Dr. Baidyanath Misra: "The future of Communism", "Unemployment Problems."

Dr. Ghanshyam Samal: "Calender Mangal', "December Pachis","Budha."

Sri Rama Chandra Das: "Rajanaitika Chintadhara"

Nityananda Mohapatro: "Patra O' Pratima"

Dr. Gokulananda Mohapatro: "Bigyanar Diga," "Hydrogen Bomb," "Jibanu Boma" etc.

Dr. Basant Kumar Behura: "Kankalar Bhasa," "Santana Utpadan," "Bharatar Sabutharu Puruna Manisa," "Uii", "Manyusara Janmakatha."

Dr. Bidyadhar Padhi: "Byakti", "Bigyana Bichara O' Janasukha," "Bhoga O' Rog", "Bigyan Parikrama"

Dr. Radhanath Rath: "Buddhi," "Bicharar Manastatika Diga" etc.

Dr. Suryakanta Das: "The Echo of the Kremlin", "Point for Jojona," "Soviet Rajyare Bazar Dar"

Hundred of feature articles are published in daily newspapers Samaj, Prajatantra, Anupam Bharat, Sambad and Samay.

Dr. Bhubaneswar Behera: "Suna Parikhya"

Dr. Kurshna Charan Behera: "Agony of a Lecturer" (Adhyakar Bedana)

Chittaranjan Das: "Sila O' Salagram," "Jeeban Bidyalaya," "Jatire Mu Jaban', "Samaj" etc.

Chandra Sekher Rath: "Man Aranya", "Drusti O' Darsan", Asruta Swar", "Mu Satyadharma Kahuchhi", "Madhu Sandhan" etc.

Mahapatro Nilamani Sahu: "Swapna Aneka Swapna", "Ame Odia Odia Kia"

Dr. Basudev Sahu: "Samaj Jingyasa" and "Samaj O' Sanhati"

Debakanta Misra: "Science, Democracy, Socialism," "Jibanara Chhanda", "Satabdira Ahwan"

Sarat Kumar Mohanty: "Bigyana Drusti", "Socrates Plato"

Dr. Nursingh Charan Panda: "Bigyana O' Prakruti", "Bigyana O'

Dr. Kulamani Samal: "Srestha Jiba"

Dr. Krishna Prasad Misra: "Darsan O' Samalochana", "Religion, Philosophy and Humanitarianism" (in Oriya).

AUTOBIOGRAPHY

It is the most interesting point to read the lives of great men in the world. A man of abscure origin has also ascended the highest position of the state. The gradual development of their personality is determined by their ceaseless efforts, perseverance, honesty, sincerity and hard works "From the Log-Cabin to the White House" is an unprecedented record and achievements of Abraham Lincoln of U.S.A.

Likewise many such books of Autobiography are written by some noted educationists and politicians of Orissa. Here is a catalogue of such books.

Dr. Prana Krishna Parija:- "Akinchanara Jiban Smruti"

Dr. Manmath Nath Das: "Jibanara Patha Prante Digantara Drushya"

Rabi Singh:- "Nishanga Padatika"

Surender Mohanty:- "Patha O' Prithvi"

Dr. Krishna Chandra Panigrahy:- "Mo Samayara Odissa"

Manoranjan Das:- "Smruti Sainlapa"

Godavarish Misra:- "Ardha Satabdira Orissa O' Tahin re Mo Sthana"

Dr. Harekrishna Mahtab:- "Sadhanara Pathe"

Pabitra Mohan Pradhan :- "Mukti Pathe Sainika"

Manoj Das: "Samudra Kulare ek Grama"

Nilamani Routroy:- "Smruti O' Anubhuti"

Surendera Dwevedy:- "Mo Jibana Sangram"

Beni Madhab Padhi:- "Ashi Varsara Smruti"

Ananta Prasad Panda:- "Mo Jiban Smruti"

Kali Charan Patnaik:- "Kumbhar Chaka"

Kalindi Charan Panigrahy:- "Mu Ange Jaha Livaichi"

Dr. Kunja Behari Das: "Mo Kahani"

Nanda Kishore Das: "Mo Jiban O' Janjala."

TRAVELOGUE

Men travel to different places for several reasons. And during his visits, he comes across different events, see different persons and places, monuments etc. and out of curiosity, he writes and narrates his experiences, which excites the interests of the readers. Likewise many educationists and politicians of Orissa have visited different foreign countries and brought forth their experiences in the form of books.

There is a list of foreign visitors who have written down books-travelogue.

Sriharsa Misra: "Paschima Diganta," "Bipula Cho Prithivi"

Sri Rama Chandra Dash: went to Berlin for research works and wrote a book "Europe re Mo Anubhuti." Gokulananda Mohapatra ("Nilachakra Para Pare"), Chittaranjan Das (Denmark), Surendra Mohanty ("Peking Diary"), Mayadhar Mansingh ("Paschima Pathika"), Shatrughna Nath ("Bilat Katha"), Dr. Gopal Chandra Misra (Russia), Sradhakar Supakar (Russo Bhraman), Dr. Suryakanta Das (Moscow Darshan, Alakapuri America) Dr. Krushna Prasad Misra (Canada), Sitakanta Mohapatro ("Aneka Sarata"),

Dr. Baidyanath Misra (England and Europe), Golak Behari Dhal (London Chithi), Dr. Kunja Bihari Dash (Germany), Kalindi Charan Panigrahy (Russia *and* Germany), Dr. Bhubaneswar Behera ("Paschima Africa re Odia Dhinki"), Manoj Das ("Dura Durantara"), Dr. Ganeswar Misra ("Kantara Bari Kahani"), Govinda Das ("Dese Dese"), Dr. Basudeb Sahu ("Bombay Ru Nairobi"), Dr. Radhanath Rath (America Diary), Gorachand Misra ("Siriduri Puttapatti"), Dr. Bidyadhar Misra (Developing western Countries) have immensely contributed to the study of foreign culture and history of different countries of the world to the Oriya readers.

DETECTIVE NOVELS

Keeping everything in thrills and suspense, many authors written mysterious detective novels in Oriya. In one time, these books have captured the imagination of the readers.

Those who have written the thrilling detective novels *in* Oriya are: Dwaraka Nath Das, Bhupen Mohapatro, Kanduri Charan Das, Jameswar Tripathy.

TRANSLATION WORKS

Translation works are the most popular techniques of the translators. Translation abundantly helps to understand the mutual culture, literature and thought process of different people. As India is a land of multi-languages, translation works are carried out mostly by the National Book Trust of India. Books of famous authors, novelists and poets of different languages are being translated. Oriya, Telugu, Tamil, Bengali, Konkoni, Hindi, Assamese, Kannada books are translated and being widely circulated in all the states of India.

The noted Oriya writers have also translated many books of different languages into Oriya. The important books are:

1. Uncle Tom's Cabin of by Uday Nath Sadangi as Tom Kakanka Kutira

2. Lajja (Bengali)—Tasalima by Mrs Nandini Satapathy
3. Sri Kanta (Bengali)-Sarat Chatterjee by Gorachand Misra
4. Gopinath Mohanty translated the Novel "War and Peace" of Leo Tolstoy in to Oriya.
5. Golak Behari Dhol rendered the Novels of the famous Hindi Novelist Prem Chand, Godan, Gaban and Premasran in to Oriya.
6. "The Wasteland" of T.S Eliot was translated in to Oriya by Gyanendra Burma as "Padabhuin".
7. Kalidas's Meghadoot is translated by Radha Mohan Godnayak
8. Rubayat-e-Omar Khayam has been translated by Gopal Kanungo

9

Oriya Theatre, Dance and Cinema

In the most ancient period, the dramas were staged on the roadsides without scene and screens. The characters of the drama simply enacted the role and conveyed the message and the theme of the drama to the audience. Sariputra became a Buddhist monk after having seen the scene of Nirvana on the road side drama. Many such dramas were being staged in the stages of Khandagiri-Udaygiri during Kharavela and even during the Gupta Emperors.

But during the modern age, the concept of such drama did not ordinarily strike to the mind of Oriyas. And until 1877, there was no Oriya play to be staged though the different theatre groups of Bengal and Bombay have staged the non-Oriya plays in different places of Cuttack, Balasore on different occasions in Orissa during the middle of 19th century.

The first Oriya Play-"Babaji" written by Jagamohan Lal of Mahanga in Cuttack district was staged in 1877. After that, scarcely the Oriya plays were staged till 1940. But with the emergence of two dramatic stalwarts in play writing and acting, Mr Kali Charan Patnaik and Mr Aswini Kumar Ghose, the Oriya plays took a dramatic turn. Not only these two wrote innumerable Oriya plays but staged their own plays on stage uninterruptedly in Cuttack town under the banner of "Orissa Theatre". Thus started the First Theatre Movement in Orissa in 1940-41.

Kali Charan Patnaik was a versatile genius—a musician, a dramatist, an actor, a writer and a director. He had to his credit nearly 30 plays. They are—Raktamati, Girl School, Abhijan, Jayadev, Bhata, Chakri, Sarala Das, Rakta Mandir, Atibadi Jagannath Das.

Likewise, Aswini Kumar Ghose was also an eminent writer of dramas and a good stage actor. His immortal creations are Konark, Bandhu Mohanty, Raghu Arakhita., Salabeg, Kala Pahar, Hindu Ramani, Bhisma, Kapilendra Deva, Govind Bidyadhar, Master Babu, Chandaluni.

These dramas were regularly staged at Cuttack by some selected actors and actresses.

Thereafter, a group of play writers began to write different plays because there were famous permanent Theatre Parties in Cuttack and Puri towns, which staged regular Plays. They are Rupasri Theatre, Annapurna 'A' and 'B' Groups, Kalasri Theatre and Janata Theatres. Actors Dukhiram Swain, Priyanath Misra, Master Mania, Rama Padhiary, Samuel Sahu (Babi), Byomokesh Tripathy, Niranjan Satapathy, Durlabh Singh, Netrananda Misra, Sarat Mohanty, Tima, Mani Mala Krishnamani, Bhanumati, Leela Dulali etc.

Annapurna 'A' Group toured to different parts of Orissa and presented spectacular shows of Lakhyahira, Bhai Bhauja, Kansa Kabat Chandaluni, Bhata, Jahar, Jayamalya, Chakri, Ghara Sansar, Para Kalam, Mulia, Bairagira Sansar, Saanta Ghar, etc. Annapurna 'A' Group not only acquainted itself with the general audience of Orissa but also created an indescribable zeal in the heart of the young generations to stage more dramas in their own locality.

On the other hand, 'Annapurna' 'B' Group staged different Plays in Puri town for days and months together. It attracted unlimited audience to its fold. These theatre groups made the Oriya drama most popular in Orissa and lift the indelible impression upon the mind of the people.

Besides, the Amatuer Artistes also staged different dramas in their local towns and villages, which made the Oriya drama widespread in Orissa. Under the banner of the Dramatic Societies almost all the Colleges of Orissa state stage their dramas in their College premises. Especially in the P.C.M. Club of Rairangpur in the district of Mayur Bhanj, we have staged Saant Ghar, Luha Sikuli, Kapat Pasha, Bandita, Janani, Bhai Bhouja, Bairagir Sansar Chakri, Timira Tirtha, Aparajita, Suryasnana, Buxi Jagabandhu, Suna Sujane, Mu Saitan Kahuchi during the period from 1959 to 1971. It was a golden period in the cultural history of Rairangpur.

Lakhmi Narayan Achari—the doyen of Stagecraft made the stage so spectacular, attractive and lively that enhanced the gravity and spirit of the drama and the show. The audience felt spell-bound to visualize the stage craft of Lakhmi Narayan Achari.

Apart from the traditional sets of village, town, palace or houses, rivers, streams, trees etc., different stage crafts also developed. They substituted one set and the entire drama is staged there. Unconventional and absurd books are gradually written which facilitated the change of Stagecraft. The books Banahansi, Aranya phasal, of Mano Ranjan Das and the Saba Bahak Mane of Bijoy Misra forced the organizers to set the stage in a different order and style.

The glorious period of Oriya Drama lasted so uninterruptedly and so successfully from 1950 to 1975. This period of 25 years was the climax of stage show and performance of the veteran actors and actresses in Orissa. New books of drama were written by the dramatists keeping in view of the actors and actresses. But thereafter the Oriya Cinemas attracted the large audience to the talkies and the production of Oriya films was also catapulted. And later on the Televisions discouraged audience to visit Oriya films in the halls. So the focal point of audience to the Oriya drama was abruptly diverted.

The notable play writers who flooded the Orissa theatres and audience with their spectacular play books and would remain immortal and glittering in the arena of the Oriya dramas are: Kabi Chandra Kali Charan Patnaik and Aswini Kumar Ghose etc.

1. Bhanja Kishore Patnaik

Manika Jodi, Ashok Stambh, Jhadarati, Prema Puspa, Jahar, Devi, Benaami, Sikari, Topan, Gariba, Jeevan Jua, Alok, Bairagir Sansar, Jayamalya, Atithi, Pahili Raza, Kuli Bohu, Prataprudra, Raj Gotia Maa Gotia Santan, Debabhumi etc.

2. Rama Chandra Misra

Mulia, Kumbhar Chaka, Manager, Kabisurya, Ghara Sansar, Sai Podisa, Bhai Bhouja, Sebika, Mamata, Chabuk, Puani Ghar, Paro Puruso, Godhuli Lagna, Narottam Das Kahe.

3. Gopal Chhatroy

Phari-a, Bharasa, Para Kalam, Sankha Sindur, Ardhangini, Abhaginira Swarg, Ghatak (1961), Sadhana (1964), Dala Behera. He has also dramatized so many novels such as Amadabata of Basanta Patnaik, Mala Janha and Prativa, Badhu Nirupama. Besides, he had innumerable One-Act Plays.

4. Kamal Lochan Mohanty

Samadhana, Dak Bungla, Matru Mangala Kendra, Jahar, Pipasa, Papa *and* Punya, Sumitrar Sansar, Ghara Bahuda. Kirani, Ram Rahim, Azadi, Mani Kanchan, Suvarna Pur.

5. Ananda Shankar Das

Kapat Pasha, Luha Sikuli, Bulu Ostat, Chandra Bhanu, Joutuka, Chaka Bhounri, Peta Patana, Phoola Sajya, Bhanu Matira Khel, Chidiakhana, Samadhi.

6. Bhubaneswar Mohapatro

Baduo Jhia, Aparajita, Bata Baran, Kacha Kanchan.

7. Kartik Kumar Ghose

Matrupooja, Mir Kasim, Lakhyahira, Bichaar, Raktara Dak, Emiti Be Hue, Mahapathara Jatri, Ka Puruso, Dukho Karibaar Kichhi Nahin, Yaa Pare Kaan, Apana Kuhantu, Dhritarastra and Gandhari.

8. Aditya Chandra Mohanty

Radhika Sadhab Jhia, Parichaya, Tipu Sultan, Urvasi.

9. Pranabandhu Kar

Swetapadma, Ashanta, Snayu Sanhar, Dukha-bataran. He has written so many One-Act Plays *and* Radio Plays.

10. Biswajit Das

Pratap Gadre Duidin , Suna Sujane Banhi Sujane, Banhi, Nalipaan Rani Kalapaan Tika, Samrat, Mrugaya.

11. Bijoy Chandra Misra

Janani, Timira Tirtha, Tataa Niranjana, Ashanta Graha, Pratikhya, Asatya Sahar, Jajabar, Saba Bahak Maane, Jadukar, Ethi Sethi Sabuthi, He Swarga Biday.

12. Prafulla Kumar Rath

Saba Padichhi, Sindur Topa, Sangharsha, Aji O Kali', Purna Champa, Interview, Dharam Puo, Chari Chhak, Di-Pat chudi, Jahakahibi.

13. Kartik Chandra Rath

Jivan Jagyan, Swargadwar, Anya Akash, Jaughar, Chaiti Ghoda, Samudrar Ranga, Jantrana, Ajira Raja etc.

14. Ramesh Chandra Panigrahy

Mu, Ambhe O' Ambhemane, Hathiku Hameopathy, Mukti Mandap, Dhrutarastra Akhi, Atmalipi, Shilar Swapna, He Prithvi Biday, Timira Trusha.

15. Byomokesh Tripathy

Raaj Mukuta Jagarana, Matira Swarga, Akhhanda Jyoti, Sati Parikhya, Ek Dui Tin, Kansa Kabaat, Tolakonia.

16. Manoranjan Das

Kathaghada, Aranya Phasal, Buxi Jagabandhu, August Naa, Kabi Samrat Upendra Bhanja, Agaami, Abarodh, Banahansi, Amratasya Putro, Sagar Manthan, Klant Prajapati, Sabda Lipi, Bhadralok, Mahododhi, Nandika Keswari.

17. Dr. Basanta Mohapatro

Jhara Boula, Monalisar Hasa, Kachaghar, Jwala Pasana Kabya, Mukti Mashal, Suryasnan, Sesa Srabana.

18. Chintamni Jena

Sandhyatara, Rakta Tilak, Srusti O' Pralaya, Krushna Chuda, Dhumaketu.

19. Purna Chandra Kanungo

Mu Saitan Kahuchi, Abhisapta Ghungur, Palasa Kanya, Krushnachudar Hasa, Dola Mukuta, Jeevan Sangram, Ranga Taranga, Andha Jamuna, Maru Jharana etc.

Beside these dedicated dramatists, there are innumerable authors of famous Oriya dramas. They are: Manmath Kumar Satapathy, Prafulla Kumar Mohanty, Rajat Kumar Kar, Ratnakar Chaini, Himansu Bhusan Sabat, Harihar Misra, Narasingh Mohapatro, Suren Mohanty, Bana Behari Panda. Raghunath Misra, Nilakahtha Misra, Jadunath Das Mohapatro, Kulamani Mohapatro, Bijoy Kumar Nanda. Niladri Bhusan Hari Chandan, Nikunja Kishore Das, Lakhmidhar Nayak, Narayan Satapathy, Janaki Ballav Mohanty, Prafulla Chandra Das.

These dramatists have profusely enriched the dramatic aspect of the Oriya literature.

Innumerable One-Act Plays and Radio Plays are also written by Harekrishna Mahtab, Pranabandhu Kar, Gopal Chhotray, Kulamani Mahapatra, Kartik Chandra Rout Suren Mohanty, Himanshy Bhusan Sabat and Ratnakar Chairi.

Harekrishna Mahtab, Pranabandhu Kar, Gopal Chhatroy, Kulamani, Mohapatro, Suven Mohanty, Himansu Bhusan Sabat and Dr. Ratnakar Chaini.

In addition to it, the Oriya writer Baishnab Pani evolved a drama, "Geetinatya"—diologue with music and action. He wrote countless books on mythologies and fictions.

"Gotipuo", "Das Kathia", "Suango Pala", "Krishna Leela", "Prahallad Natak", "Rama Leela", "Debadasi System," "Bharat Leela", have also immensely contributed to the growth and popularization of Oriya literature and provide entertainment to all sections of the people.

Opera Theatres: Open air Theatre)—have now gather rapid momentum in Orissa. There is a great deviation from the style, stage management, dialogues, dance, acting and lighting arrangement of the opera parties of the yester years. The old opera parties put emphasis upon the dialogues and superb acting and the dramatic personnel were so skilled and veteran, that they kept the audience spell-bound.

But the modern Opera parties have adopted brake dance, duet of males and females, erratic dances acting and dialogues. Like the Hindi films, the Opera party exhibits the rape cases on the stage. The women actively enact the roles in the Opera and dance with the male counter parts, which was absent in the past. The brake and vulgar dances attract thousands of onlookers.

DANCES OF ORISSA

Dances are the most important performing art of all the people of different periods in history. And these are the prime sources of entertainment of the people-rural or urban. The movements of the legs, heads, eyes, hands and the entire body are regulated by the tunes of different songs and musical instruments of Dhol, Mrudanga, Mahuri, Chad Chadi, Casio, Bongo, Kongo and Triango etc.

ODISSI DANCE

The earliest classical dance of Orissa is the Odissi dance. We can date back the origin and history of the Odissi dance to 700 years or more than that because this dance form was practised by the Debadasis of the Jagannath Temple at Puri. As Dr. Charles Fabri, an authority on Indian culture describes "Odissi is one of the most perfect classical systems of Indian dance surviving. Odissi is a more pristine, a more carefully preserved primitive form of natya and is nearer to the ancient classical temple dancing as it was known 700 or more years ago".

They used Pakhouja, Gini *and* flutes etc. as the musical instruments. Violin is also added.

Among the different items, Mangala Charan, Batu Nrutya, Pallavi, Abhinaya and Mokhyanata are the main. Many beautiful songs of (Champu) of Kabi Surya Baladev Rath relating of Radha-Krishna are associated with this dance.

This Odissi dance is the most popular dance in Orissa and is one of the assets of the Orissan culture. Late Sanjukta Panigrahy and her husband pandit Raghunath have made the Odissi international. She danced in a most lucid style in all the Capitals of Moscow, Washington, Paris, Berlin and London. The celebrated Odissi dancers and Gurus are Padmabhusan Sri Kelucharan Mahapatro. Late Sanjukta Panigrahy, Mayadhar Rout, Dayanidhi Das, Minati Das, Kum Kum Das, Kabita Dwevedy, Sonal Mansing, Pankaj Charan Das, Deba Prasad Das and Raghunath Dutt.

Even the Odissi dance attract the foreign lady to Orissa and they have learned it. Training classes at BBSR and Delhi are being held to institutionally make the dancers skilled.

GHUMURA DANCE

Although the Tribals used to adopt the Ghumura dance in the early period of Kalahandi subsequently it became the most popular dance form in the district and irrespective of everything, the youths dance the Ghumura with most enthusiasm and devotion in all the occasions of Indian festivals in the temples, marriages, Dussera, Sivaratri, Nuakhai.

Ghumura is so named after a typical eastern drum 'Ghumura'. It is made of burnt clay with the long neck and covered by a skin of some animals. The dancers hang it by a rope from their neck across the shoulders on their chest. And during the time of dancing they beat it by their fingers with the spirit of tune of the songs and other musical instruments. They move their legs and body accordingly.

Ordinarily 15 to 20 male dancers perform it in a group. They use coloured dhotis and beautiful embroided jackets. They use a turban on their head fitted with peacock feathers. They also fasten 'Ghangudi' (a chain of brass bells) on their wrists and the Ghoongroos (a chain of small brass bells) on their feet which produce a spectacular and enchanting sound during dancing.

The dance is accompanied by beautiful devotional songs of Chhanda, Choupadi and songs relating to Ramayan *and* Mahabharat *and* Puranas. They sing in the Sambalpuri dialects of different beautiful songs. The Ghumura is the most popular and attractive dance form in the districts of Kalahandi, Balangir and Sambalpur.

Beside this, the people of Kalahandi use to dance the Dhap dance, Mandal dance, Dhangada—Dhangidi dance and keep themselves happy throughout the year. The dances are connected with the different social festivals of the district.

CHHOU DANCE

The Chhou dance is the most popular among the people of district of Mayur Bhanj. The name Chhou is derived from the word 'Chhouni' means the military camps. The approximate year of the origin of the Chhou dance is not ascertained yet, but it has formed a part of the culture of the people. The movements of hands, legs, and body symbolise that it is basically a war dance. Previously the dance was practised by the male dancers only, but recently the women of Baripada too take active role in the Chhou performances.

This dance has got a very serious Abhinaya, Mudras, music and rhythm with the facial and eye expressions.

As the patterns of Chhou dance designed particularly to the war-events, the people in general did not like it in the past. Later on the Guru (Teachers) introduced the events and characters of Ramayan, Mahabharat, Puranas, Folk tales and legends, which made the dance more popular and attractive.

The musical accompaniments are Mahuri (Sahnei), drums (called Dhumsa), Nagara, Dhol and a Chad Chads beaten by two small sticks.

They introduced different types of dance performances as solo, duet and group dance. Siva, Parvati, Nataraj, Sovara, Srikrishna and Arjuna (Gita), Tamudi Krishna and Gopi, Characters of Meghadut of Kalidas is introduced.

Maharaja Sri Krishna Chandra Bhanj Deo (1867-1892) of Mayur Bhanj codified the Manuscripts, techniques and grammar of the Chhou dance. And later on his son, Sri Rama Chandra Bhanj made it national and international when he presented a spectacular Chhou dance before the King George

V. of England during his royal visit to Calcutta in January 1912.

At Baripada and Rairangpur, during the Chaitra festival in the middle of the month of April, Baisakha—a mega show of Chhou dance is performed. Different teams of Chhou dance from different villages of Mayur Bhanj district participate in it every year throughout the nights, which make the festival colourful and alluring. Dance critics and the lovers of folk culture of India and abroad flock together to undertake research works. The present different mythological and fictitious themes with beautiful dramatic characters, customs, dresses of embroidery brocade, of gold and silver swords, Tridents, Shields, flutes dazzle in the most illuminations *and* spectrum of light of the nights.

Chhou dance is also prevalent in Sareikala and Kharsuan-the two Oriya speaking territories of Bihar. Even the King of Sareikala used to dance the Chhou. The difference of Chhou dance between the two areas is that while the Chhou dancers of Sareikala and Kharsuan extensively use mask whereas the dancers of Mayur Bhanj do not use as a result of which they exhibit fully their facial and eye expressions to the public.

The Chhou dance was flourished due to the active patronage of the Maharajas of Mayur Bhanj but after independence of India and the accession of Mayur Bhanj with Indian Union, the financial condition of the Maharajas was deplorable for which they could not extend any financial assistance to the Chhou dancers. As a result of which the Chhou dance of Mayur Bhanj was enlivened by the rural people and the local contributions of the local men. The future of the Chhou is bleak.

After the introduction of T.V., the Govt. of Orissa and India tried to encourage this neglected art, Recently two training centers of Chhou dance at Baripada and Rairangpur are opened by the Natak Academy of the Central Govt. in 2001, April.

In Baripada town, the royal Palace of Bhanj a Maharjas is flanked by two "Sahi"-"Uttara Sahi " and "Dakhina Sahi". The young and old characters of Chhou dance have enriched and perfected this performing art of Mayur Bhanj district.

KARAMA DANCE

This dance is ordinarily performed in the district of Sambalpur. "Karam Rani" is the presiding deity of the Binjhal, Kharia, Oraon, Kisan and Kol tribes of Sambalpur whose blessings adore children and good fortune to the people. So they perform this dance in honour of this Goddess.

On the 11th day of Bhadrav Month, the young boys and girls go to the jungle in group singing the devotional songs and beating the drams. They bring with them the branches of 'Karam' or 'Sal' tree with them to the village and place them in a place of worship. The village Priest recites the mantras and worship the branch by pouring liquor, rice and sweets. A fowl is also sacrificed and the blood is offered to the branch.

The boys and girls dance in different lines and poses with the rhythms of the musical instruments and songs. The female dancers bend their bodies left and right-front and backside crossing the hands of each other maidens through the backside and clap each other. They use beautiful Sambalpuri sarees and on their head they put different short branches and flowers while the male dancers use coloured jackets and dhoti and on the turban peacock feathers. They hold a small mirror in their hand.

In a most emotional mood of ecstasy and enthusiasm, the young girls and boys dance in turn the entire night. Next day in the morning, the performance is over and the people take the branch in a procession and throw the branch into a tank or river.

DALKHAI DANCE

Besides this dance, the Dalkhai is also a very colourful dance performed by the tribes of Binjhal, Soura, Kuda and Mirdha during the Dussera, Bhai Jiuntia, Phagun Punei and other social functions.

The maidens use beautiful sarees with small branches in their dressed hair on head. They stand in a semicircular way to start the dance with beautifully Sambalpuri Songs. The enchanting songs thrill the heart and the postures and gestures of body and the movement of legs excite wonder.

Different types of musical instruments like Dhol, nisan, tamki, Mahuri and flutes are extensively used to produce rhythm in the hearts.

Besides these two leading dances, people have adopted the Sua dance, Ghumura dance, Kalasahandi dance, Dandanata etc.

DASAKATHIA

Dasakathia is the indigenous form of dance and ballads. It is more a recitation of the poems of Upendra Bhanja, Kabisurya Baladev Rath, Abhimanyu Samanta Sinhar, Gangadhar Mehar, Gopalkrishna Patnaik and other noted poets in a beautiful tone by a singer and accompanied by his companion.

Dasakathia is displayed by two persons—a singer and his companion. These two persons are dressed themselves with beautiful lose pyjama, and overcoat size with embroidery and turban over head. They use to sets of solid wooden clappers in the left hand fore finger open and thrashed by right hand while singing and dancing. They sing the songs with utmost rhythms. The singer explains every word and stanza lucidly. The Palia or assistant creates humour by his comic songs and dialogues. During their singing, they too both slightly dance and present dramatic actions.

Thereby they keep the audience absorbed and happy. They usually stage this show in the temples, courtyard or in a premises of a landlord or in any place the organisers please on different occasion of any temple festivals or marriages etc.

Dances of Ganjam-Daskathia, Chadheya Nacha, Dandanach, Ghodanach, Ghoomra nacha, Ghuduki nacha, Kandhei Nacha, Kela Nacha, Paika Nacha, Ranapa nacha, Sakhi Nacha, Soara dance, Bagha Nacha.

Prevalent Dance Forms in Different Districts of Orissa

1. Mayur Bhanj dist-Chhou dance, Kharia dance, Jhoomar dance, Karma Dance, Santal dance, Chadeya-Chadeyani dance, Thus dance.
2. Koraput dist. Koya dance, Paraja dance, Gadaba dance.
3. Sundargarh dist. Oraon dance, Kisan dance, Changu dance, Bandi Butal dance.
4. Sambalpur dist. Dalkhai dance, Kisanbadi dance, Changu dance, Karama dance, Humo and Bouli dance.
5. Bolangir dist.-Ghoomara dance.
6. Cuttack, puri, Balasore dist. Pakia dance, Kela-Keluni dance, Odissi dance,

Dhangda-Dhangdi dance, Sabar-Sabari dance, Dhuduki dance, Horse dance etc. are performed in different villages on different marriages or religious functions.

Among the renowned "Gurus" who have taught the Odissi dance to the girls and boys in Orissa are :—

1. Kelu Charan Mohapatro
2. Pankaj Charan Das
3. Mayadhar Rout
4. Dhirendar Patnaik

5. Hare Krishna Pradhan
6. Gangadhar Pradhan
7. Deba Prasad Das.

Odissi Dancers

Sanjukta Panigrahy, Sonal Mansingh, Minati Das, Kum Kum Das, Kabita Dwevedi, Alok Kanungo. Kukumina Mohanty.

ORIYA CINEMA

Like the other states of India, Oriya cinema also made its first appearance in 1936-When Mohan Sundar Deb Goswami made his first Oriya film "Sita Bibaha". This film was first released and screened in the Lakhmi Talkies of Puri Town on 28th April 1936. Mohan Sundar Goswami himself was the producer and director of the film.

Since that day to 2000 A.D. the destiny of Oriya films has passed through different vicissitudes and adversities of Time-but still it has not completely buried in the oblivion. On the road of ups and down the Oriya cinema still retains its identity in the national and international sphere.

The entire period of the progress of Oriya films from 1936 to 2000 AD can broadly be divided into two phases (1) 1936-1976 and (2) 1976-2000 AD.

1936-1976

These two phases have been divided on the issue of the production of the Oriya films. The first phase that covered the four decades in the history of Oriya cinema has seen the scarcity of adequate production of Oriya films. Leaving aside the "Sita Bibha", Lalita, Sri Jagannath, Sri Lokanath, Amadabata, Naba Janma, Ka Sadhana, Bhai Bhouja, Dasyu Ratnakar, Parinam, Stree, Arundhati, Jiban Sathi, Kia Kahar and some other films were produced. The number of films produced during the 40 years could be counted in fingers-only 26 films.

Although the number of the Oriya films was limited during the first phase, some Oriya films were excellent and became very popular in those days Especially, Sri Lokanath, Amadabata, Naba Janma, Suryamukhi, Matira Manisa, Bhai Bhauja and Arundhati were outstanding in story and melodious songs. The songs of Sri Lokanath and Amadabata directed by renowned Balakrishan Das and of the film "Arundhati" directed by Shantanu Mohapatro of Baripada still echoed in the heart of countless cine-goers till to-day. "Mayuri go Tuma Akashe Mu dine Malhare Megha Sajili" of Arundhati was the exquisite creation of the unchallenged lyricist-Late Jibanananda Pani of Baripada.

The old novels and Playbooks were converted into screenplay and dialogues and the Oriya films were made. "Amadabata"—a novel of Basanta Kumari Patnaik, "Nabajanma"—a drama of Bhanja Kishore Patnaik, "Ka"—a novel of Kanhu Charan Mohanty, "Malajanha"—a novel of Upendra Kishore Das were picturerised into films. The noted actors and actresses who have played the lead roles in the above films were Soumendra Misra. Minati Das, Umakanta Misra, Jharana Das, Gita Dutta, Akhaya Mohanty (not singer), Dukhiram Swain, Urvashi Priyanath Misra, Byamokesh Tripathy, Babi, Parvati Ghose, Ramachandra Padhiary, Sarat Pujari, Prashanta Nanda, Bhanumati, Radharani, Sujata, Master Mania, Gitisudha Jena, Gloria Rout, Gopal Ghose, Kartik Ghose, Manimala, Lila Dulali.

As the Music Directors-Balakrishna Das (Sri Lokanath, Amadabata), Shantanu Mohapatro (Arundhati, Suryamukhi), Bhubaneswar Misra (Matira Manisa), Nachiketa Ghose (Mahalaxmi Puja) were famous.

The lyricists-Jibanananda Pani (Arundhati, Suryamukhi),

Jitendra Patnaik (Naba Janma), Debadas Chhotroy (Kia Kahar) are excellent in their composition of wordings and emotions.

Babulal Doshi of Cuttack being a Gujarati rendered immense services to the Oriya films. He formed the "Chhayabani Pratisthan" at Cuttack and under this banner, he produced "Amadabata", "Ambhinetri", "Matira Manisa" and "Adina Megha", which were proved as the best films and "Matira Manisa" was the outstanding of all. Which begged the national award.

Kabiraj Sri Krishna Chandar Tripathy of Aska is another patron of Oriya cinema. He displayed his unusual courage and determination to produce oriya films and under the banner of Utkal Chalachitra Pratisthan, he produced "Mahalakshmi Puja", "Parinam" and "Dasyu Ratnakar".

During the first phase of the Progress of Oriya cinema (1936-1976) as many as 26 films were produced.

1976-2000 AD

During the second phase of the history of Oriya cinema, many producers came forward to produce more Oriya films. The Govt. of Orissa established the Kalinga studio in Bhubaneswar in the year 1981 which lessened the financial burden of the producers. In the first phase, the producers moved with the team of actors, actresses, directors, music directors, lyricists and a host of other assistants to Prasad Studio, Madras, Calcutta or Bombay for shooting and recording songs.

During this period of assessment (1976-2000), as many as 300 Oriya films were produced within these 25 years. The Govt. of Orissa also declared to pay subsidy to the non-Oriya producers who would produce Oriya films. The Orissa film Development Corporation was founded in 1976.

Besides, many Oriya boys and girls opted to enact the

different roles in the films. The cameramen brought the most sophisticated cameras to take shots in the shooting places. The stage craft, the technique of sets, make-up, the technique of recording the songs became easier due to unexpected scientific know how. Many young and beautiful girls destroyed the barriers of social conservatism and played the roles of heroines. The horizon of outlook was changed. The parents also take pride for their daughters as the heroines of the films. The Western Culture engulfed and dominated the life of the Oriyas. The nakedness, the errotic scenes and some vulgar dialogues in films were cordially accepted.

It is extremely difficult to prepare a list of all the Oriya films during this period of 1976-2000 AD. But some of the outstanding films like "Mamata" of Prasad Nanda *and* Byomokesh Tripathy, "Gapa Hele bi Sata" of Nagen Roy, "Shesa Shrabana" of Prasanta Nanda were memorable in the early part of 1976. Mahesweta Roy made her first debut in this film and left a deep impression in the mind of the people. Dr. Basant Mahapatro was the writer of "Shesa Srabana", while Prafulla Kar rendered music direction.

"Abhiman" was produced by the Baripada Patrons and directed by Sadhu Meher. Radhakrishna Bhanja was the Music director. Uttam Mohanty though made his first appearance in this film but laid the foundation of his future filmic career, which is still continuing.

Among all the Oriya films like "Mrugaya", "Sasti", "Hakim Babu", "Suvarna Sita", "Bhagya Hate Dori", "Kaberi", the "Maya Miriga" of Nirod Mohapatro (1984) marked a distinctive position in the national level of selection. It was adjudged as the second best regional film and Nirod Babu got the laurel. It was a story of a lower middle class family, a retired teacher heads the family and a few sons of his behave in a peculiar way of their style, which hampers the unity, and happiness of the family. The dialogue sequences and the presentation of the Characters were unique which enticed the audience.

There was no cock-tail party, no swimming pool, no cabaret dance, no romantic pair with sensual songs, still it was admired and appreciated. After so many years of film making in Orissa the audience got such a rare film-"Maya Miriga".

Other than this art film the audience of Orissa got innumerable commercial and entertainment films like "Abhilasa", "Samay Bada Balaban" of Sisir Misra, "Hisab Nikash", "Swapna Sagar", "Katha Kahiba Mo Sankha Sindur", "Suna Chadhei", "Dharitri", "Chaka Akhi Sabu Dekhuchhi", "Janani", "Paka Kamal Pot Chhota", "Phoola Chandan", "Jajabar", "Kurukhetra", "School Master", "Nagaphasa", "Suna Sansar", "Ram Rahim", "Babula", "Klanta Aparanha", "Nirab Jhoda", "Sita rati", "Dhira Aluo", "Gouri", "Rajani Gandha", "Sindur Bindu", "To Poie",Gouri, Kanak Lata,

Music Directors:—Balakrishna Das, Bhubaneswar, Rakhal Mohanty, Akshaya Mohanty, Shantanu Mohapatro, Prafulla Kar, Radha Krishna Bhanja, Saroj Patnaik, Swarup Nayak, Basudev Rath, Amarendra Mohanty.

Lyricts: Madhu Sudan Rao, Ramakrishna Nanda, Guru Krishna Goswami, Debadas Chhotroy, Sirsananda Das Kanungo, Jiten Patnaik, Jibanananda Pani, Prafulla Kar, Akshaya Mohanty, Gour Patnaik,

Male Singers: Balakrishna Das, Mohmmed Sikandar Alam, Prafuila Kar, Akhaya Mohanty, Pranab Patnaik, Mohammad Rafi, Manna Dey, Hemanta Kumar Mukherjee, Mukesh, Raghunath Panigrahy, Chitta Jena, Subash Das, Bhikari Bal, Radha Krishna Bhanj, Arjun Samal, Nemain Bhusan Hari Chandan, Debasish Mohapatra, Shantanu Mohapatra, Fakir Patnaik.

Those who have produced the Oriya films in Orissa are : Mohan Sundar Dev Goswami, Kabiraj Krishna Chandra Tripathy (Aska), Babulal Doshi (Cuttack), Dhirendra Biswal (Cuttack), Prasanta Nanda (Cuttack) ,Raghunath Misra

(Berhampur), Subash Rout (Cuttack), Basanta Kumar Nayak (Cuttack), Ganesh production (Baripada), Govinda Tej, Subodh Samal, Kedar Guru, Prafulla Kr. Rath, Nitai Palit, Puspa Samal, Durga Nanda, Subash Misra, Sarat Pujari, Subimal Mallick, Chittaranjan Mohanty Keshab Rout, Batakrishna Nayak, Gour prasad Ghose, Rabe Kinnagi, Raju Misra, Biplab Roy Choudhury, A.K. Bir, Sabyasachi Mahapatro,

Odissi Dancers: Minati Das, Sanjukta Panigrahi, Kum Kum Das, Priyambada Mohanty Hejmadi, Kukumina Mohanty, Kabita Dwibedy, Sonal Mansingh, Alok Kanungo, Susama Tej.

Female Singers: Shyamamani Devi, Nirmala Misra, Trupti Das, Gita Patnaik, Kabita Barik, Namita Agrawalla, Lata Mangeshkar, Usha Mangeshkar.

Male Actors: Dukhiram Swain, Priyanath Misra, Ramchandra Padhiary, Samuel Sahu (Babi), Govind Tej, Byamokesh Tripathy, Gour Chandra Ghose, Soumendra .Misra, Sarat Pujari, Dhira Biswal, Prasanta Nanda, Netrananda Misra, Uttam Mohanty, Bijoy Mohanty, Ajit Das, Sri Rama Panda, Debu Bose, Prithivi Raj, Mihir Das, Sidhanta Mohapatro, Sritam, Uma Kanta Misra, Pradyumna Lenka, Mahasin, Sisir Misra, Sadhu Meher, Ashrumochan Mohanty, Niranjan Satapathy, Biren Routroy, Hemant Das, Natabar Sena, Bimal Ghose, Asit Pati, Gopal Ghose, Nari, Shyamalendu, Radha Panda, George Tiadi, Hara Patnaik, Rai Mohan Parida, Ananta Mohapatra, Hemanta Das, Akshaya Mohanty, Raju Sadangi, Bibeka Satapathy, Bibhuti Padhi, Sompad Mohapatro, Pravanjan Parida, Batakrishna Mohanty.

Villian Roles: Dukhiram Swain, Hara Patnaik, Rai Mohan Parida, Asit Pati.

Female Actress: Urvashi Manimala, Gloria Rout, Parvati Ghose, Minati Misra, Lila Dulali, Krishnamani, Bhanumati, Mahasweta Roy, Malabika Roy, Aparajita, Sujata Anand,

Rachana Benerjee, Baisali Panda, Susmita Pradhan, Niharika Sahu, Tripura Misra, Isha Bebarta, Jharana Das, Jayi, Rekha Rao, Sadhana Das, Jyoti Misra, Priyanka Mohapatro, Nandita Das, Dali Jena, Gita Dutta (Rao), Banaja Mohanty, Anita Das, Usasi Misra, Tandra Mohanty, Subhra Pati, Manaswini Mohanty, Sangeeta, Dipti Pati, Mamina, Lakhmi Devi, Subhra.

Comedians: Tima, Sarat Mohanty, Nari, Shyamalendu, Radha Charan Panda, Jayi Samal, Debu Bramha.

Oriya artists and Painters: Binod Kanungo, Jatin Das (Baripada), Dinanath Pathy, Chandra Sekhar Rao, Rama Hari Jena, Asit Mukherjee, Siba Panigrahi, Rajendra Burma, Udaya Nath Jena, Hari Saran Mahapatra. Basant Patnaik.

Oriya Chief Justice of The Supreme Court of India

1. Ranganath Mishra
2. Gopal Ballav Patnaik

Oriya Judges of The Supreme Court

1. Deba Priya Mahapatra
2. Radha Charan Patnaik
3. Abhijeet Pashayat.

10

Science and Technology in Orissa

Throughout the 19th century, there was no industry in Orissa except the famous Sugar Factory at Aska in the district of Ganjam. This factory was the first great Sugar Industry in India and Asia. This Sugar factory was founded by the British with some local entrepreneurs probably in. 1841. Frederick Vivian Minchin joined in 1852 as a member of the Board of Directors and later on purchased it.

Next to it, Madhusudan Das of Orissa established two factories at Cuttack-Utkal Artware (Filigree Works) and Utkal Tannery at the cost of Rs. 180000/ in the early part of 20th century, 1904 to create an awareness and idea in the minds of the Oriyas to establish industry in Orissa. But his mission was not fulfilled. No Oriya learnt anything from his brightest examples.

There was a long way in the history of Orissa up to 1956. No industry worth its name was visible in Orissa. The Rourkela Steel Plant is the first and greatest enterprise of the Govt. of India, which was established in Rourkela in 1956 with the collaboration of German Govt.

Aska Sugar Factory

Aska is famous in the history of the world for its Sugar Factory. When the world was experiencing the infant stage of the Sugar factory, Aska was fortunate to have a noted Sugar Industry in the first half of the 19th century probably in 1841. The credit, the name and the fame of such spectacular Sugar Industry would go to the renowned organizer-Vivian Frederick Minchin, who was an English by birth.

Long before Mr. Minchin took over the administration and management of the factory in 1872, the Sugar Industry was started by the English with the local Co-operation. In 1852, Minchin joined as one of the shareholders and Board of directors of the Sugar Factory. In 1872,

Frederick Minchin purchased the entire Sugar Factory and became the owner and the Managing Director.

Frederick Minchin was born on 4th February 1829 in the Kampti of Madras where his father Colonel F. Minchin was the Army Officer of the East India Company. Minchin is known as Frederick James Vivian Minchin. Minchin went to London and finished his education there during the period—1836 to 1847. Then he joined in the British Indian Army. But he was not happy as a soldier. He left the service and came to Aska to join in the Aska Sugar Factory.

The old Aska Sugar Factory was located in Aska Town (now Vani Vihar) and the present Harihar High School was the bunglow of Frederick Minchin.

Minchin had devoted his energy, attention and wealth to the Sugar Factory and enriched, perfected it day by day. It was astonishing and crowning glory of Mr. Minchin and Aska Sugar Factory that Minchin got the Silver Medal by displaying the Aska Sugar in the International Sugar Exhibition in Paris in 1878.

Mr. Minchin got married to a daughter of an Oriya woman who was serving in his bunglow. The bride was Suna who was later on changed into Sona Minchin. Minchin took Sona to England for her education. She was made a full-fledged English woman with all her Western style and etiquettes and lived with Minchin at Aska.

The entire working Capital of the Aska Sugar Factory in 1872 was 60,000 dollars. It was run by the steam power. The method, which was adopted to squeeze the juice from the Sugar cane, was the "Diffusion Process". By this process, 80% of sugar was being manufactured. Along with it, he also prepared the "rum". The sugar was being sold in the Hyderabad State, Madras and in the entire South Indian territories. He also exported the Sugar to Burma, Java, Borneo, Sumatra and Cambodia from the Gopalpur Port in sea-route where Minchin had set up a great "Godown".

Mr. Minchin passed away on 3-4-1908 at Gopalpur-on-sea in Ganjam district and his dead body was cremated in the premises of Aska Sugar Factory. His wife managed the Sugar Factory up to 1910 and sold it to one-Paramananda Sahu of Nimakhandi near Berhampur town. Sona also died on 25-10-1916 in Calcutta. Her dead body was brought to Aska and buried near the Samadhi of Minchin on 27th October 1916. Frederick Minchin and Sona-an unprecedented couple in the world of it more dignified than Shah Jahan and Mumtaz Mahal.

Minchin was regarded as the "Father of Aska Sugar" in history. But nobody of this locality is aware of preserving his memory. Even the bust size bronze statue of Mr. Minchin, which was installed in the old Sugar Factory at Aska, was stolen away in 1992 by some miscreants. The fairie-like marble statue of Sona Minchin is taken away to the Orissa Museum, which was kept under the scorching heat of the sun in the Museum Premises.

A very small village near Rambha is named after Mr. Minchin as "Minchin Patna". This small village bears the eloquent testimony of the greatness of Mr. Minchin.

After the death of Sona, the Aska Sugar Factory was managed by Paramananda Sahu who continued the administration till his death in 1933. And then it was managed by his sons' up to 1946. Due to various reasons, the Sugar Factory was closed down from 1949 to Dec. 1963.

The new Aska Sugar Factory was inaugurated by Biju Patnaik the Chairman of Orissa Planning Commission on 16-12-1963. Since then the present Sugar Factory has been functioning under the direct supervision of an I.A.S. Officer as the Managing Director at Nuagan- 3 K.Ms away from old Sugar Factory.

Kalinga Prize

Kalinga was the ancient name of Orissa. Ashok, the third ruler of the Mouryan dynasty of Pataliputra, invaded Kalinga in 261 BC. The Kalinga War with Ashok was the bloodiest war in history, which took away the lives of one lakh of soldiers. Realising the horror and holocaust of Kalinga war, Ashok abandoned warfare forever. H.G Wells writes, "Ashok was the only military monarch on record who abandoned warfare after victory".

Biju Patnaik was the worthy son of that Kalinga, now Orissa, who in commemoration of the old glory of Kalinga, instituted the Kalinga Prize in 1955. He formed the Kalinga Foundation Trust and became the Founder-Chairman of that Trust.

He entrusted the work of selecting the best scientist of the world for their distinguished contributions to the arena of Science and mankind to UNESCO (United National Educational Scientific and Cultural Organisation).

Kalinga Prize is the annual award given to such scientists which worth one thousand pounds sterling and an Albert Einstein Silver medal.

The selection of the distinguished scientist of the world is made by a jury of four members-three of them are from different Countries and one is recommended by the Kalinga Foundation Trust.

The venue of awards given is Paris in every odd years and New Delhi in every even year.

Biju Patnaik established the Oriya identity in the durbar of world through this spectacular Kalinga Prize.

Rourkela Steel Plant

Rourkela is situated on 22°12° N latitude and 84°53' E longitude on the Howarh-Bombay Railway line under South Eastern Railway zone. The distance from Sundargarh town to Rourkela is 67 miles. Rourkela is one of the important Steel plants of India, situated in the district of Sundargarh in the Orissa state.

The Selection of Rourkela for a Steel Town is made in 1955 among three-Rourkela, Durgapur and Bhilai. And the construction of Steel Plant and Township Started in October, 1956 in collaboration with the Federal Republic of Germany at the initial capital of Rs. 764 crores. Production from the plant was started in 1958.

The Township covers an area of 95.31 Square kilometers. The Township in divided into 20 sectors and contained 18,000 residential quarters.

Area of the plant is 33.38 Square kilometers.

The utilized capacities of Plant in 1982 are 18,00,000 tonnes of ingot Steel and 12,25,000 tonnes of saleable Steel per annum.

In 1982, nearly 39,676 employs of different categories work in the Plant.

It is one of the biggest Steel Plants in the Public Sector of India.

The Orissa University of Agriculture and Technology

It was established under the OUAT Act of 1961 in 1961

only. Previously a College of Agriculture was established in 1954 under Utkal University and worked till 1962. Then it was transferred to OUAT.

The OUAT has got three faculties, the faculty of Agriculture, faculty of Veterinary Science and Animal Husbandry and the faculty of Agricultural Engineering and Technology.

It performs three types of functions-Teaching, Research and Extension.

Thousands of students from all over India read in this institution.

Regional Research Laboratory—Bhubaneswar

This Laboratory was set up in 1964 at Bhubaneswar to under take Scientific and Industrial research works in India. It is a premier and outstanding Research Center to widen the scope for utilization of natural resources.

This Laboratory works under six major Divisions and prepares the feasibility reports after testing and analysis.

1. Chemical Metallurgy Divisions

(a) Hydrometallurgy
(b) Electrometallurgy
(c) Engineering services

2. Materials Technology Division

(a) Advanced Materials Technology
(b) Design and Project Engineering
(c) Rural Technology Development

3. Energies and Environment Division

(a) Environment Management and Inorganic Chemicals

(b) Energy Technology
(c) Bio-Minerals and Biotechnology

4. Natural Resources Division

(a) Forest and Marine Products.
(b) Aromatic and Medicinal plants.
(c) Control Physico-Chemical Analytical Facilities.

5. Minerals Engineering Division

(a) Mineral Processing Technology
(b) Mineralogy and Metallography
(c) Pyrometallurgy

6. Resource Planning and Information Division

(a) Information and Technology and Process Engineering
(b) Library / Documentation
(c) Project Monitoring and Evaluation.

Paradip Port

Paradip is situated on 20°15' N latitude and 86°42′ E longitude on the Sea-Coast of Bay of Bengal. The distance from Cuttack town to Paradip is 95 Km by road and Rail.

As legends reveal, the name of Paradip is derived from the ancient Sage of Parasara. Roughly the place is known by the present name in the 10th century AD.

In 1960, the Preliminary idea to develop Paradip into a port was conceived. In the third five-year plan, which commenced in 1962-63, it was decided to make it an all weather intermediate port. Mr. Biju Patnaik, the then Chief Minister of Orissa in 1962 invited Jawaharlal Nehru, the Prime Minister of India to lay the foundation stone of the port in Paradip on 3-January 1962. Messers Rondel Palmer and Tritton of United Kingdom prepared the report with a Provision of one iron berth to accommodate 60,000 D.W.T. ore carriers, 2 dry locks, a slipway and a marine workshop.

The project, which started in November 1962, was opened to traffic in November 1966 within a period of 4 years.

The volume of Cargo handled through this port in the year 1989-90 was 61.84 lakh tonnes.

The entrance Channel is 500 meters long and 160 meters wide and 12.8 meters deep.

Loading and unloading of Chrome ore, Pig iron, Sugar, Coal, Steel structures, food grains, fertilizer, Cooking, Steel billets, Sraps etc. are the daily works in the port.

The Govt. of India took over the management of the port on 1st, June 1965 and declared the eighth major port in India on 8th, April 1966. Many ancillary industries developed there- Paradip Phosphates Ltd. (major fertilizer Plant) and Dia monia Phosphate Plant (DAP) have been commissioned on 1st March 1986.

Fishing Industry started with 254 small-mechanized boats.

There are many Govt. offices, Post office, Banks, SBI, Colleges, High Schools, English Medium Schools, Govt. Hospitals, Port Hospitals, Recreation Clubs, Bars, Cinema Halls, Bunglow, Guest House, Telephone Exchange. A N.A.C. is there. Population in 1981 was 33042.

Nalco Damonjodi and Anugul (National Aluminium Company Ltd.)

NALCO is one of the major public sector enterprises of the Govt. of India. The discovery of huge amount of Bauxites in 1975 in the East Coast of India and particularly in the district of Koraput in Orissa necessitated the Govt. of India to form the National Aluminium Company Ltd. It is estimated roughly that at the place, Panchpatmali (Koraput), there is a vast of deposits of 370 million tonnes of Bauxites covering a distance of nearly 14.6 kilometers.

Keeping a view the vast deposits of Bauxite at one place, the Govt. of India prepared a feasibility report in July 1979 to explore the Bauxite.

The Govt. of India also took a final decision to invest the original project cost of Rs. 2408 Crores, out of which 980 million dollars will be financed by U.S.A.

Due to the lack of the technological know-how in India to explore such a big project, the Govt. of India concluded an Agreement as Indo-French Collaboration Agreement in January 1981. And on January 7, 1981, this NALCO was founded as the company.

Mrs. Indira Gandhi who was keen to establish Industry, as the Prime Minister of India, was kind enough to lay down the Foundation stone in March 1981.

The civil works were under taken in February 1982 and the different plants, mines were established as follows.

Port facilities-September 1985
Bauxite Mines-November 1986
Alumina Refinery-September 1986
Captive Power Plant-September 1986
Smelter Plant-March 1987

Now the NALCO has got a planned and beautiful Township at Damanjodi and Angul. Schools, Colleges, Clubs, Public gardens, Hospitals, Market places are provided to the employees. The people are leading the most urbanized and luxurious life with all facilities.

By 1998, the NALCO has got an investment with expansion plan of Rs 3700 Crores of rupees.

The Company exports Alumina and other products to England, U.S.A., and other European Countries. The dream came to a reality.

IMF A—Indian Metals and Ferro Alloys Limited Theruveli—Koraput

All men see dreams in life. But a handful of men materialize it, because many factors shape the dreams into reality. One such dream is of Dr. Bansidhar Panda-a metallurgist by Profession. He was employed abroad as a scientist. There he cherished a dream to set up a Plant of Ferro Alloys in Orissa-his motherland.

He has given up all the dreams of a scientist abroad, the luxuries, comforts, crores of rupees, prestige and position, name and fame and came down to Orissa. He established the limited Company as the Indian Metals and Ferro Alloys limited popularity known as IMFA as registered it in the sixties of the 20th Century.

The foremost objective of this company is to manufacture Ferro Silicon, which is an essential ingredient for the preparation of special Steels. Ferro Silicon is a rare material in the world. The Govt. of India also depends very much on the imports of the Ferro Silicon from abroad. So Dr. Panda made Ferro Silicon an asset to people of India.

On 3rd May 1967 the Ferro Silicon Plant at Theruveli was inaugurated by the then Deputy Prime Minister of India Sri Morarji Desai.

Dr. Bansidhar Panda invited the Elkem Spigerverket A/s Olso-Norway to utilize their technical know-how and finally the first Ferro Silicon unit of IMFA having the capacity of 10,000 KVA smelting furnace was set up in Theruveli. The construction and installation of this Plant was so rapid and the labour of the Indian Scientists was so honest that the

Plant area was completed within a shortest period of 21 months only.

The manufacture of Ferro Silicon at Theruveli Plant in the district of Koraput, Orissa minimized the import of Ferro Silicon from abroad-rather made India self-sufficient in Ferro-Silicon.

In 1974, IMFA developed its technology and established the Second product line of Silicon Metal. The utility of Silicon metal is vital and is used in the production of aluminium castings for automobiles, scooters, fans, aero-engines, Defence equipment and Space exploration. It not only fed abundantly to the Indian' industries, but also enormously supply to the world markets. Thereby earning adequate foreign exchange.

Besides this, two other Units of IMFA are established—they are the Kalinga Tubes Ltd. and Indian Metals and Carbide Ltd. in 1955 and 1973 respectively.

Institute of Physics—Bhubaneswar

To promote the study and research works in the arena of Physics, the institute of Physics was established in Bhubaneswar on 4th, September 1974.

The entire management of the Institute is looked after by a full-time Director.

The objectives of the Institute are multifarious: 1) To promote research activities in different branches of physics 2) To provide training in advanced physics 3) To provide technical know-how to different industries etc.

Here is a long list of the Industries, small and major, founded in different districts of Orissa.

1. Iron and Steel — Rourkela (SAIL) - 1956

2. Iron Industry — Barbil (Keonjhar)

Kalinga Iron Works (1-4-1963)

2. Cement — Rajgangpur (Sudargarh)

Investment (1647)-29 lakhs (1948)

Bargarh-Sambalpur

Hira Cement Works -1964

Investment-Rs 933 lakhs

3. Ferro-Manganese—Joda (Keonjhar)-1957

Investment 260 lakhs

Rayagada-1958

4. Fertiliser—Rourkela (Sundargarh) -1958

2729 lakhs

Talcher (Dhenkanal)-1980

Paradeep (Cuttack)-1986

Bargarh (1981)- Rs 36 lakhs

5. Aeronautic Industry—Sunabeda (Koraput) Collaboration with USSR (1981-82)

6. ALUMINIUM—Largest deposits of Bauxites at Angul and Damanjodi (Koraput) exploited (Dhenkanal) with the Collaboration of the French Govt (1986-1989) Construction of Plant and the production *and* sale started in 1989 23-May. Investment Rs 2408 Crores. Another Aluminium Plant was established at Hirakund in 1959 with the working Capital of Rs 760 Lakhs.

Paper—Brajaraj Nagar (Sambalpur) in 1939. Investment 1619-63 lakhs of rupees.

Rayagada (Koraput) in 1962. Investment Rs 6.5 Crores-Chouduar (Cuttack) in 1960

Sugar— Aska (the old Sugar Factory was closed from 1946 to 1963) and a new Sugar Factory was inaugurated on 16.12.1963 in Ganjam dist Investment Rs 75-74 lakhs

Rayagada (Koraput) -1937

Investment -Rs 87 lakhs

Bargarh (1971)

Investment-Rs 220 lakhs

Nayagarh in puri District and Baramba in Cuttack have got two other Sugar Factories. Ferro-Silicon This Plant has been founded at Theruveli in Koraput dist in 1981.

Investment -Rs 557 lakhs. It also produced Silicon Carbide. The different handcrafts are prepared by the skilled workers in Orissa. They are :-

Applique Work-Pipli (Puri) like multi-coloured garden umbrella, Canopies and Wall-hangings.

Silver filigrees-Cuttack

Dye Sarees or "Patto" -Berhampur (Ganjam) and Sambalpur,

Nuapatna (Cuttack)

Patta Chitra-Sakhigopal (Puri)

Dhokra and Clay toys- Mayur Bhanj, Keonjhar and Cuttack

Horn work-Parlakhemundi (Ganjam) and Cuttack (Prawn, Crane, Palm, Dali trees, dancing girls, Moon, Fish etc.)

Brass art-Belaguntha (Ganjam), Balakati (Puri)

Bell-Metals-Kantilo (Puri)

Lacquer Works-Nabarangpur (Koraput)

Stone and Wood Carving-Lalit giri (Puri), Bhubaneswar, Puri Town.

Wooden painted toys: Cuttack, Puri, wooden carpets and other ordinary carpets are woven by many people in their localities.

Sericulture-(Matha fabrics) in Mayur Bhanj, Keonjhar and Sundargarh.

Cotton Textiles— Textile mill was founded at Chouduar in Cuttack district in 1949 at the total cost of Rs 362 lakhs. Besides this, there are Spinning Mills at Bhagatpur (Cuttack), Jharsugada and Tora (Sambalpur) Govindapur (Dhenkanal), Rajggangpur (Sundargarh), Aska (Ganjam), Baripada (Mayur Bhanj) and Bolangir.

Mineral Sand—The Indian Rare Earth Ltd. was established at Aryapalli (Chatrapur) in the dist of Ganjam at the total investment of Rs 183 Crores. It started production in October 1986.

Apart from this, the Govt. of Orissa has provided loans to the skilled craftsmen and the educated youths to start a small scale or cottage Industry which facilitated the growth of production of several usable commodities like PVC pipes, nails, tarpaulins, polythene bags, ropes. Pilot Project Schemes, Rural Industries Project and Panchayat Industries Programmes of the Govt. of Orissa have immensely helped the persons to earn their livelihood. Leather works are done at Titlagarh (Bolangir), Boudh (Phulbani), Rourkela (Sundargarh) and at Cuttack they manufacture shoes, safety boots, money purses, horse-jins, bags etc.

11

Tourism in Orissa

In the vast panorama of Indian culture, Orissa occupies a very enviable and important position. It substantially contributes to the growth and variety of Indian culture through ages. Orissa has a very rich and spectacular cultural heritage of its own Situated on the Eastern side of the Indian peninsula and in between the longitude 70° E to 97° E and latitude 8° N to 37° N, the greatness of Orissa lies in its immortal historical monuments and in the cult of Jagannath at Puri.

Orissa is the Paradise of the Tourists—the Eldorado of Archealogists. Orissa unfolds itself in the beauty and elegance of the sun temple of Konark—the Rajarani Temple, Lingaraj Temple and the Mukteswar Temple of Bhubaneswar, the Jagannath Temple of Puri—the scintillating golden beach of Puri and Gopalpur, the Flora, Fauna and the fountains of Mayur Bhanj, Phulbani and Koraput districts.

BHUBANESWAR

Among all the sensitive spots of Orissa, Bhubaneswar presents a unique canvas of historical legacies. It bears the eloquent testimony of the earliest historical writings in the Dhouli Mountains by Ashok and Hathigumpha of Khandagiri and Udayagiri Hills by Kharavela of Chedi dynasty. These Inscriptions throw a flood of light upon the career and achievements of Ashok and Kharavela more than two thousand years ago. Kharavela became a great saint of Jain Faith who spent his last days in the imperial castle of Kalinga Nagar but in the Kumari Hills amidst the Jain Monks. The Ranigumpha, Baghagumpha, Ganeshgumpha, Hathi Gumpha have been hewn from the rocks and they still stand superb against the ravages of time.

Kalinga war was fought in 261 BC on the bank of the river, Daya—a few miles away from the modern Bhubaneswar between the Ashok and Kalinga soldiers. Although Kalinga War brought a trail of tragedies to its people, it rendered a metamorphic change to victorious Ashok who abandoned warfare after victory. There after in 259 BC, Ashok engraved the Inscriptions and we find the two Ashokan Inscriptions at Dhouli in Puri district and at Jaugarh in Ganjam district. These inscriptions directed the state officials of Kalinga to treat the Kalingans as the children of Ashok and rendered immense material and moral services to them.

Bhubaneswar is a city of temples—big or small and in different sculptural richness, have sustained through the passage of Time. Bhubaneswar is an abode of Saivism and hundreds of Saiva temples dotted here and there, so it is called the "Saiva Khetra" some have been damaged and some were ruined to its foundation. Lingaraj Temple, Rajarani Temple, Mukteswar Temple are a few of those which speak the cultural grendure and greatness of its builders of Kalinga and its kings. All these temples which were built at Bhubaneswar in different times were mainly of Kalinga style of architecture. It is difficult to provide a list of all the Siva temples of Bhubaneswar—to record a few, Tribhuneswar, Siddheswar Temple, Bhaskareswar Temple, Kapileswar Temple, Sisireswar, Parasurameswar, Shatrughneswar, Kedareswar and Uttareswar etc. All these temples crowd the Bhubaneswar Town. To observe so many temples in one place, it is said, "It is indeed rare to find any where in India such a large number of ancient monuments at one place as we have at Bhubaneswar and covering such a long period and so well representing the dynastic changes in History".

A great "Shanti-stupa" (Tower of peace) is built at Dhouli to propagate the messages of peace—the Doctrines of Goutam Buddha.

At the Bhubaneswar itself, the Pathani Samanta planetarium is built which focuss the origin and evolution of the sun-moon-planets, satellites, Earth and the research results of Pathani Samanta, Copernicus, Galelio etc.

In the Orissa Museum, many rare and rich specimen of Orissan sculptures, coins, copper plates, stone Inscriptions, armoury objects, palm-leaf manuscripts, lithic and bronze age tools, paintings, anthropological elements, filigree works, brass-castings are carefully preserved.

Ratnagiri, Lalitgiri and Puspagiri are the three major complexes, which are the abode of Buddhism in ancient times. Many sculptured Buddhist statues, Bricks, Stupas, entrance styles are unearthed. Hieun Tsang pointed it during his journey in Kalinga that Puspagiri was a Buddhist University like the University of Nalanda in Bihar.

KONARK

Konark is another attractive spot for the tourists of the world. The Sun Temple or the Black Pagoda is situated on the sandy-bed of the Bay of Bengal - 65 Kms away from Bhubaneswar. According to Silpasastra the main temple is built on the Colossal Chariot of 24 big wheels—drawn by a set of 7 horses. The main sanctum where the presiding Sun-god was placed was destroyed. As the legacy of the ancient Orissa sculpture, only the Bhoga Mandap and NataMandir of the Konark Temple exist. This fragments of iconography exhibits the splendour, grendure, elegance and style of Orissan art. The Alasa Kanya, the celestial nymphs, the errotic pictures of women developed bodies, swelling busts, rounded hips, rhythmic movements of the body, the dancing poses with different mudras, the horses, elephants, procession of elephants, and soldiers, the horses trampled the enemies, depict the wonderful realism in architecture and sculpture. These pictures of the Iconography of the Sun temple attract the tourists in crowd and they, after visiting it, become mesmerized, stunned. In recognition and appreciation of the Iconography of Konark temple, a lover of Orissan sculpture, commented." One must visit Konark Temple in his life time at least once and he can go by aeroplane, or by a vehicle—if not he should visit Konark by a bullock cart, but he must visit it".

Nandan Kanan

It is famous for its attractive zoological and botanical gardens. The Nandan Kanan was inaugurated on 29th December 1960. It claims to be one of the most enchanting centres because here in itself, we come across a great number of white tigers, hippopotamus, and many other rare species of birds and animals. They have built the big artificial sizes of Dinosaur. There is a Children's railway, boat-racing in the pool, and the hanging rope tolley in the sky for entertainment. Hundreds and thousands of tourists flock round the place everyday. Nandan Kanan is situated only 20 Kms away from Bhubaneswar either by bus or train.

PURI TOWN

Puri is renowned in the world for the Jagannath Temple. The Lord Jagannath reigns supreme. The sculpture of the Jagannath Temple is also exquisitely majestic. The Jagannath, Balabhadra and Subhadra are seated on the Jewel Pedastal in the main sanctum of the temple. Every year, the Car Festival is being celebrated in the month of June or July with much pomp and grendure. Lakhs of devotees and spectators from India and abroad swarm round the place to witness the colourful function at Puri. Besides, everyday thousands of devotees visit the God and pray for prosperity. They take "Abadha"—the Sacred Mahaprasad of the God and are satisfied.

The extensive Sea-beach with countless Casurina trees offers opportunity for relaxation and amusement. In the queue, shopkeepers sell beautiful stationery commodities of Jagannath Photo, Conch-shells, garlands of Oysters, terracotta and wooden toys.

On the Sea-shore, innumerable Govt. and Private Guest Houses, Panthasalas, luxurious hotels and lodging houses are built to accommodate the crowd of tourists throughout the year.

Chilika Lake

In the districts of Puri and Ganjam itself, we come across Chilika lake—the vast expanse of Sea-water. The natural beauty of the Chilika lake is raped and destroyed by the fishermen and Mafias. Birds of different species migrate in thousands from the Caspian sea, Dal lake of Kashmir and from the Siberian belts to Chilika during the winter season. The Orinthologists of different countries crowd there to study the movements and behaviour of the birds.

Besides, the Goddess Kalijai temple is also situated on a small rocky island in the waters of the Chilika lake. The tourists derive immense pleasure from boating and enjoy the scenic beauty of the lake.

Jougarh

To the southern part of Orissa and particularly in the Ganjam district, there are a few pockets of tourist importance. Jaugarh - 35 Kms away from Berhampur Town is famous for the Ashokan Inscriptions which are engraved in the rock in 259 B.C. in eastern Bramhi script. They are now in a very miserable condition.

Taptapani

This place attracts the tourists because of its natural flow of phosphorus water, oozing out ceaselessly from the bottom of the earth. It is situated 60 Kms away from Berhampur Town on a hilltop surrounded by the big stones and leafy trees. There is also a small deer garden.

Gopalpur-on-sea

It is the most lovable and attractive resort for the tourists of India and abroad. The extensive Sea-beach with wild waves attract the people and most of the tourists love to take bath in the Sea-water. The colossal waves of the sea (Bay of Bengal) are cast a shore every bit of the clock.

There is a big light House on the shore.

Many beautiful and luxurious lodges and hotels are there to accommodate the tourists of different parts of India.

In the four distant district of Koraput, the Gupteswar Siva temple is a worth-visiting place. It is beyond imagination that how did the Siva Lingam originate in the cave of a hill top.

Mahendragiri in the extreme South Orissa of Koraput district is another centre of tourist importance, which attracts thousands'of devotees.

The Siva temple, the natural beauty and the flora and fauna of the district of Koraput is famous in India. Many tribal people of Kandha, Paraja, Bonda now live in the deep forests of the district.

In the western Orissa of Sambalpur, Bolangir and Kalahandi districts, there are many tourist spots of interests. The Chief Places are the Narasingh Temple, Ushakothi wild life Sanctuary (Sambalpur district), Vedavyas and Khandadhar Water fall (Sundargarh district), Ranipur-Jharial of historical importance (Bolangir district), Asurgarh—a fort and Junagarh (Kalahandi).

In the extreme North of Orissa lies the district of Mayur Bhanj -Most of the areas of the district were once upon a time was full of deep forests and mountains. And one of the deep mountaineous area is the Similipal National Park. More than one hundred tigers live in that area -Besides, the wild animals like leopards, elephants, reptiles and different species of birds. The green natural scenic beauties of the countless trees and mountains, pools are the main attractive spots.

Besides—a Waterfall named the Barehipani Water fall is the chief spot for the tourists. The water is poured down from the height of 400 meters—creating the spectrum of the rainbow.

In the Central district of Dhenkanal, the Kapilash Mountain, famous for the Chandra Sekhar Siva—Jaronda—a seat of the Mahima Dharm Cult—SaptaSajya—a hill divided by a river, are the chief centre of tourism.

In the Balasore district, the Chandipur Sea-beach is also a beautiful tourist spot. More than two miles into the Sea of Bay of Bengal, we find the shallow depth—And it is easy to take bath there with much pomp.

Orissa is the most ancient in history. People of different races and religious, cultures and customs had lived here and passed away. So the different art and architecture, sculpture, religious sects, temples of different Gods and Goddesses—Siva, Vaishnab, Shakti, Buddha Vihar co-exist here. The cultural heritage of the last several centuries is the property of Orissa—the legacy of the land of Lord Jagannath.

12

Oriya Newspapers and Magazines

ASHA

The "ASHA" as a weekly newspaper was first published on 13.4.1913 from Berhampur near Venkateswar Temple in Ganjam. The editor of the Asha was Sashi Bhusan Rath. It became a daily newspaper on 30.4.1928. Sashi Bhusan Rath died on 20-3-1943. It continued to be published as a daily newspaper up to 1951 by Madanlal Jajodia, the owner of the Barang Glass Factory who purchased it. But on all a sudden, the publication was discontinued till 9th February 1982. On 10th February 1982, Sri Brundaban Nayak—the noted philanthropist of the Ganjam district revived it. The publication of the Asha is continuing till today. Sri Sriharsha Misra was the first editor of the Asha in 1982. He died on 8,4.1984. Chandrasekhar Mohapatro succeeded him. After him Sri. Pramod Kumar Panda is still continuing as its Editor.

SAMAJ

In the present Orissa, "Samaj" is the leading daily newspaper being circulated more than one lakh paper daily.

The founder of the Samaj as a weekly newspaper was Sri Gopabandhu Das of Puri. It was first published on 4th, October 1919 from Sakhigopal, Puri. Then it was shifted to Cuttack in 1927. From 6th April 1930, the Samaj became a daily newspaper.

Gopabandhu Das was a great freedom Fighter-a versatile

poet a Philanthropist. For his outstanding contributions, he was awarded the title "Utkalamani" in 1924 by the Congress leader of Calcutta Sri Prafulla Chandra Roy.

During his campaign in the freedom movement, he came *in* close contact with Mahatma Gandhi and Lala Lajapat Roy of Punjab. Lala Lajapat Roy formed the "Lok Sevak Mandal" and Gopabandhu Das became the Vice President of Lok Sevak Mandal in 1927. Later on, Gopabandhu Das pledged the responsibility of the Samaj, the Press—Satyabadi to Lok Sevak Mandal Since that day, the Samaj is being published under the banner of Lok Sevak Mandal till today.

Lingaraj Misra, Sriharsa Misra were the editor of the Samaj many years.

Radhanath Rath there after became the editor. The Samaj brought out all the vices of the Govt. and rendered immense services to make Oriya literature more popular and broad-based. Under the column of the "Jhitipiti Kahe" in the Samaj it focussed with floodlight on the misdeed, irregularities and corruption of the leaders and the Govt. of Orissa and ultimately suggested ways and means.

Smt. Manorama Mohapatro, the daughter of Radhanath Rath is the editor of "SAMAJ". Today Samaj also brings one weekly magazine highlighting the events, personalities of the last weeks.

PRAJATANTRA

The Prajatantra was first published as a weekly newspaper in 1923 from Bihari Bag—Cuttack by Harekrishna Mahtab. Then it was shifted to Balasore. In 1930, it was made a daily newspaper, Because of the objectionable publication of news, views and articles against the Govt., the Govt. banned the publication of the paper for 17 years from 28th December 1930.

On 8th August 1947, the Prajatantra was published again under the editorship of Harekrishna Mahtab. Dr. Mahtab formed the Prajatantra Prachar Samiti to run the administration of the Press and publication of different literary magazines. It highlighted the socio-political and economic problems of the Oriya people and of India.

Sriharsa Misra and Mr. Janaki Ballav Patnaik were the editors of Prajatantra for several years.

Dr. Mahtab through the Gan-Mazlis in Prajatantra column every week suggested advice and guidelines to the innumerable socio-political cultural and economic problems of Orissa. He also started "Mina Bazar" in Prajatantra to include the adolescent boys and girls and to encourage them for team works. He also patronized the members of the Mina Bazar with their writings and social works.

The greatest and undying contribution of Dr. Mahtab of Oriya literature is the monthly literary magazine—JHANKAR—the unchallenged creative and research oriented Oriya monthly magazine. The Jhankar is the measuring rod of the standard of the writers who write literary Oriya criticism, short stories or poetry. Not only the writers derive immense pleasure to see their articles/poem published in Jhankar- but they are recognised and awarded prizes in the Bishub Milan held every year on 14th, April. The Bishub Milan has been celebrated since 1950—a spectacular get together of the Oriya literary elites.

Mahtab was born on 21.11.1899 and died on 2.1.1987.

GANATANTRA

This was published as a weekly newspaper by Rajendra Narayan Singhdeo, the Maharaja of Bolangir in 1956 from Cuttack. Later on it became a daily edition. It highlighted the activities of the Ganatantra Parishad as a political party of R

N Singhdeo. Sri Surendra Mohanty was the editor of the paper. It was stopped in 1961.

KURUKEHTRA

It was published as a daily news paper from Badambadi. Cuttack Chittaranjan Misra was the editor.

AJI O' KALI

This daily newspaper was published from Bhubaneswar.

NAVEEN

It was first published from Berhampur on 13.5.1930 as a weekly news and literary paper by Krapasindhu Narendra Dev, the king of Mahuri Kalua in the fond memory of his father—Naveen Chandra Narendra Dev. This Naveen weekly paper has made Sri. Sachi Routroy, Kishori Chandra Das and Pathani Patnaik the great literary genius in the subsequent period.

This "Naveen" as a weekly newspaper is still being published and circulated under the editorship of Sri. Rabi Rath of Engineering School Road-Berhampur.

KALINGA

Sri. Biju Patnaik sponsored the Kalinga News Paper as a daily published from Cuttack in 1960. Biju Patnaik was the Chief Minister of Orissa in 1960. Man Mohan Misra and Surendra Mohanty became the Editors of the daily newspaper. Even Sriharsa Misra had also edited the paper for a few years.

In 1973, the publication of the newspaper stopped forever.

JANASAKTI

It was published as a daily news paper in 1966 by Biren

Mitra one-time the Chief Minister of Orissa after Biju Patnaik. Biren Mitra and his wife were involved in many other corruption cases and could not repay the loan of Orissa State Financial Corporation. So it was stopped after years.

PRAGATIBADI

The publication of Pragatibadi newspaper was started by Sri. Pradyummna Kumar Bal as a weekly, edition in 1972 from Cuttack. And later on it became a daily newspaper and shifted from Cuttack to Bhubaneswar. Pradyumna Kumar Bal died in 2000 A.D. but the paper is still published and circulated under the editor ship of Sri. Samahita Bal.

MATRUBHUMI

Matrabhumi was first published as a weekly in 1947 by Bala Krishna Kar. In 1951, it became a daily newspaper. It has exhibited tremendous courage and freedom to criticize the illegal affairs of the Govt. and made the people of Orissa aware of their rights. Later on it was ceased for sometimes.

'Sahakar' was another sister publication of Matrabhumi under the editorship of Balakrishna Kar.

SAMBAD

The "SAMBAD" as a daily newspaper was first published on 4.10.1984 from Bhubaneswar under the editorship of Sri Soumya Ranjan Patnaik. He went to London for his higher studies in printing technology. After his return, he formed the Eastern Media limited and by an improved method of photo type off set printing, he published the "SAMBAD".

The noted short-story writer and one of the literary genius, Surendra Mohanty, was also the Editor.

Soumya Babu also published one daily English as "Sun-Times".

To make the "SAMBAD" broad based he simultaneously started publishing the different editions of it from Berhampur, Sambalpur, Rourkela

MATRUBHASA

Matrabhasa is the new incarnation of the old Matrabhumi edited by Ananda Shankar Ray and Chandra Sekhar Mohapatra. The publisher and patron is Bikash Kar.

DHRITRI

Dharitri made its first appearance on 24 November 1974. Nandini Satapathy during her regime as the Chief Minister of Orissa from 1972-1975 nourished a desire to present her views and the achievements of her Govt. to the public. It was published under the banker of "Samajbadi Society" under the Chairman ship of Sri Kalindi Charan Panigrahy the noted Oriya Novelist and the father of Nandini Satapathy.

Ramanath Panda was the first editor of Dharitri. Later on Tathagata Satapathy, the son of Nandini Satapathy became its editor.

UTKALIKA

It was first published as a Magazine some 35 years ago by Sri Ramahari Misra. It was discontinued. It was revived in 1996 under the editorship of Sri Krishna Mohan Rao as a daily edition from Bhubaneswar.

SAMAYA

To mark the august birthday of Mahatma Gandhi, the 'SAMAY' was first published on 2-10-1996 as a daily newspaper from Bhubaneswar. Sri Basanta Biswal who was then the Deputy Chief Minister of Orissa in the Cabinet of Janaki Ballau Patnaik, patronised the Sambad with a view to drawing the attention of the Orissa public to the advertisement and achievements of the Govt. and of himself.

By using the process of modern Printing technique, he published the first coloured pictures of the events and persons of the world and made it attractive to the readers.

Mr. Satakodi Hota—another noted short- story writer of Orissa is the Editor of Samaya till today. They also publish a weekly book-let highlighting the different events of the past week, which is very popular in Orissa.

SWARAJ

It was first published as a weekly paper by Raj Krishna Bose a prominent freedom fighter from Cuttack in 1930. Later on it became a daily news paper in 1966 and highlighted the activities of the freedom Movement. Ultimately it was stopped.

JANATA

Pandit Godavarish Misra brought out this newspaper, as a daily edition is 1940. It focussed the important issues of the National Movement and the problems of the Oriya people. Ultimately the publication was ceased.

ANUPAMA BHARAT

The "Anupama Bharat" as a daily edition was first published on 26-9-1996 from Berhampur under the editorship of Sri Sarat Misra. The financial patronage was rendered by one of the most enterprising young men Kali Charan Panda and the brain behind the publication of this newspaper is Sri Manoj Das- undisputed short—story writer in Oriya and English.

Anupama Bharat excelled many Oriya dailies in contents, design and subject matters. It created a sensation among the readers of especially in south Orissa but not less in other parts of Orissa.

The founder of the Anupam Bharat, Kali Charan Panda, died in a road accident on 12-11-2001.

Anupama Bharat- Industrial Estate- Berhampur- Ganjam- Orissa.

HIRAKHAND

As a news paper, it was first published in 1981 from Sambalpur town under the banner of Prajatanta by Dr. Harekrishna Mahtab.

ORIYA MAGAZINES AND JOURNALS

There was no dearth of Oriya magazines in the early part of 20th centuries—'Mukura' Magazine made it first appearance in 1906, April.

But the earliest magazine that came out to light was the "Prajabandhu" the weekly edition from Rambha under the editorship of Nilamani Vidyaratna. Maharaja Harihar Mardaraj of Khallikote made all arrangements to publish it in 1902.

"Satyabadi" was published in March 1915 by Gopabandhu Das.

"Sahakar" was edited by Lakhmi Narayan Sahu and was published in 1919 from Puri

"Nababharat" was published in June 1934 under Nilakantha Das.

Like wise "Adhunika" in 1935 was published.

"Sankha" an Oriya magazine was published in 1945 by the patronage of the Maharaja of Bamanda from Deogarh. Important articles of Krishna Chandra Panigrahy, Gyanenda Burma, Sradhakar Supakar were published.

Mayadhar Mansingh was the editor of the magazine.

CHATURANGA: This magazine was published under the patronage of Maharaja Sri Rajendra Narayan Singhdeo of Balangir on 14-5-1946. The editor of the magazine was the Yubraj Sri Brajendra Narayan Singhdeo.

In 1951 the publication was completely stopped.

JHANKAR: It was published in the month of April 1949 under the care and editorship of Dr. Harekrishna Mahatab from Cuttack. Jhankar and Prajatantra are closely associated. And Dr. Mahatab was the patron.

The 'Jhankar' is the only leading monthly Oriya magazine, which has maintained its style, standard and sanctity of the Oriya literature since April 1949 to till to-day. Poems research articles, literary criticism, short stories, satire, One-Act plays fictions are regularly published in Jhankar. The established poets of Orissa like Ramakanta Rath Sitakanta Mohapatro., Sachi Routroy. Kishori Charan Das, Soubhagya Kumar Misra, Hara Prasad Das, Sourindra Barik, Dipak Misra, Dilip Das, Smt. Monorama Biswal, Smt. Giribala Mohanty, Srinibas Udgata, Bansidhar Sadangi, are the honoured patrons of Jhankar,

To encourage the poets and writers of Jhankar, Dr. Mahatab organized the "Annual Get-Together on the day of the "Visuba Sankranti 14th April, of every year. An outstanding literacy genius of Sahitya Academy or any other Indian languages of any state is invited to grace the "Visuba Milan" and he gives away the Visuba Prizes to the Poets, writers and artists. It is an uncommon tradition of the Jhankar to honour the literary elites. This "Visuba Milan function" has been celebrated since the 14th April 1950 (the first Visuba Milan).

Asantalali: It was the next important monthly Oriya magazine than Jhankar. It was published first in 1950 from Prem Chand Baral Street, Calcutta. It was edited by different persons in different times. They were Sri Kanta Panda,

Jadumani Parija, Shyam Sundar Mahapatro, Kanduri Charan Das, Kali Charan Das.

This magazine has also maintained the spirit and style of the writers for so many years and earned a good reputation but on all a sudden Asantakali was collapsed like a house of cards.

Once again the Asantakali has been revived.

KONARK: This Magazine has been published by the Orissa Sahity Academy since 1958, September. Four issues are published in a year.

This magazine contained the research articles regarding the Oriya literature, culture, art and sculpture.

Pandit Binayak Misra, Dr. Nabeen Kumar Sahu, Dr. Ḳunja Behari Tripathy, Kalindi Charan Panigrahy, Satya Narayan Rajgura, Debi Prasanna Patnaik, Dhirendra Nath Patnaik, Artaballav Mohanty have contributed articles for publication.

The noted literary genius, who have edited "Konark" in different times are Binod Chandra Nayak, Manoranjan Das, Rai Charan Das, Chintamani Behera, Radha Mohan Godnayak. Srinivash Udgata The first editor of Konark was Sri Gouri Kumar Bramha.

POURUSO: It is completely a different type of magazine in Oriya. No poem is published here. It is a magazine to rejuvenate the spiritual sense of men. Articles on Veda, Upanishad, philosophy, Indian culture, mythology and history are mostly written.

The lives and philosophy of Ramakrishna Paramahansa, Swami Vivekananda, Swami Dayananda Saraswati Chidananda, Raja Ram Mohan Roy, Shankaraeharya, Sri Krishna, the chapters of Gita are mostly discussed.

This magazine was first published in July 1967 under the

of Sri. Janaki Ballav Pattnaik. Later on Smt. Jayanti Patnaik. Editor and Smt. Sudatta Patnaik the working editor.

NABARABI: This Oriya magazine made its first appearance in July 1970 from Calcutta. The owner and editor was Sri Rabindra Kumar Parija.

Nabarabi has lighted and delighted the Orissan culture and literature and the people. The publication of Nabarabi in 1970 really created a new era of resurregence in Oriya literature. Those writers and poets who have enriched the pages of Nabarabi are Manoj Das, Sachi Routroy, Surendra Mohanty, Kalindi Charan Panigrahy, Krishna Chandra Tripathy, Radha Mohan Godnayak, Sitakanta Mohapatro, Shantanu Acharya, Ramakant Rath, Rajendra Kishore Panda, Rabi Singh.

But on all a sudden, the Nabarabi—the rising sun was set forever in 1976.

Manas: Manas as monthly Oriya magazine was first published in November 1972 from Bhubaneswar. Sri Ananta Misra was the founder. Dr. Krishna Prasad Misra was the editor of the magazine.

Manas has also strove hard to make the Oriya literature and culture most popular among the readers of Orissa.

Many prolific authors have contributed valuable articles and poems to Manas. They are: Chandra Sekhar Rath, Mahapatro Nilamani Sahu, Ramakant Rath, Bama Charan Mitra, Dr. Nrusingh Charan Panda, Rajendra Kishore Panda, Dr. Khageswar Mohapatro, Harihar Das, Lakhmi Narayan Mohapatra, Srinivas Udgata, Phani Mohanty, Dr. Surya Kanta Das, Sri Ram Chandra Dash, Dr. Ganeswar Misra, Dr. Sadasiv Misra, Bidhu Bhusan Das.

Manas was stopped in March 1981.

Amrutayan: It is a monthly literary Oriya magazine

published and edited by Sri Satakodi Hotta from Bhubaneswar. Geeta Hota is the Co-editor.

Nian Khunta: It was published in 1938 by a public-spirited man-Sri Godabarish Mohapatra—a man of Banapur, Dist, Puri. This monthly magazine was really a burning fire which brought to the limelight all the vices, corruption irregularities in the sphere of economy, politics, society or culture. It scathingly satired all the loopholes of the Govt. of Orissa and Ministers and their nature and character and tried to set right the behaviour of the persons and the administrative machinery.

It served uninterruptedly for a period from 1938 to 1965 to the needs of the Orissa people. And the fire of criticism was extinguished with the death of Godavarish Mohapatro in 1965 September.

After his death the daughter of Godavarish Mohapatra managed to publish it a few years and thereafter it was stopped forever.

Durmukha: Was also monthly magazine publisehd from Cuttack. Sir Achyutananda Kar was the Editor of it. This magazine also vehemently criticised the irregularities, corruption of the Orissa Government.

Different Oriya magazines have been published spontaneously by the zeal and will of a group of persons who have got an inclination to Oriya literature. There are many:

Arati — 1940

Kunkuma — 1948 - (Bombay) Deba Mohapatro

Bina — (1950) Tekkali

Diganta — (1950) Cuttack - Sachi Routroy

Dagar — (1936) - Lakhmi Kanta Mohapatro

Chandrika — (1953) Mahesh Pr. Mahapatro

Mehera Pradip — (1955) - Sambalpur

Pragyan —(1960)

Nabapatra — (1962) Rourkela - Rajanikanta Das

Sammikhya — (1963) Dr. Radhanath Rath

Suchitra — Shankuntala Panda - Bhubaneswar

Pancharanga — (1970) Bolangir, Durga Charan Kuanar

Galpa — (1970) Bibhuti Patnaik

Saptarsi — (1972) Sambalpur University

Adhuna — (1973) - Raghunath Mahapatro

Baisi Pahach — (1976) Berhampur - Dr. Prafulla Ku. Mohanty

Galpajhara — (1977) Bhadrak - Balaram Sahu

Istahaar - (1975) Nityanamda Satpathy

Mulyayan — (1979) Prafulla Ku. Jagdev

Esaana — (1980) Cuttack - K.B. Nayak

Gokornika — (1982) Ramakanta Jena

Panchajanya — (1981) - Bhubaneswar - Durga Charan Kuanar

Basundhara — (1981) Dr. Gopal Ch. Misra

Phalgu — (1984) Berhampur

Sourava — Bina Mohapatra- Cuttack

Sri Jagannath — Dr. Bansidhar Mohanty

Alok — (1968) Aska - Dilip Das

Samabesa — Jagdish Pani

Nabalipi — N.C.Tripathy

Suryasnan — (1983) Edited by Smt. Madhulita Biswal (Rourkela)

Vijaya — Sunil Kumar Prusty (Pondicherry - Madras)

Utkal Prasanga: It is a magazine owned and edited by the Govt.of Orissa. This magazine reflects the achievements of the Govt. and variety of articles on Orissa economy; temples, culture, freedom movement, religion and personalities are published.

With illustrations *and* photo of the Chief Minister and other Ministers are published every month.

Orissa Review: It is also the magazine of the Govt. of Orissa published in English every month with the same objectives of Utkal Prasanga.

1. *The "New Orissa"* as a first English daily of Orissa was published in 1933 from Berhampur-Ganjam under the editorship of Sashi Bhusan Rath the founder of "Dainika Asha". In course of time, it was stopped after the death of Sashi Bhusan Rath in 194 .
2. *The Eastern Times*—It was published from Cuttack in 1949 under the editorship of Harekrishna Mahtab.
3. *The Sun Times* and the *Orissa Times* from Bhubaneswar and the News of the World from Cuttack and "The Bharat—my Nation" from Sambalpur are being published.

(a) There are innumerable English periodicals published in Orissa from different places. Some of them are totally stopped. The periodicals which are in circulation in Orissa are: The Oriyas, The Cuttack Law Times, The Adventure, The Observer, The Current Affairs, The Orissa Law Journal, The Games and Sports, The New Life, The Orissa Historical Research Journal, The Puri Express, The Community, The Chariot, The Orissa -Past and Present.

13

Profile of Important Personalities and Landmarks of Orissa

MAHARAJA KRISHNA CHANDRA GAJAPATI NARAYAN DEO (1892-1974)

Maharaja Krishna Chandra Gajapati Narayan Deo was the most familiar name in Orissa. Had there been no Maharaja, the process of Orissa unification would have been incomplete. He has given a final touch to the portrait of Orissa state in the canvas.

He was born in a royal family of Parlakhemundi on 26 April, 1892. Father was Gour Chandra Gajapati Deo and mother was Vishnu Priya Devi.

He received his early education at the Palace. The eminent scholar and a writer, Sri Apana Panda was his private tutor who has diversified his outlook. Likewise. Shyam Sundar Rajguru, the first graduate of Ganjam district, also taught the Prince about the different aspects of Orissa and India. Mr. W. Taylor, the manager of the Paralakhemundi Estate was also engaged in teaching the English and their ettiquettes.

As unfortunate he was, he lost his father at the very early age of years only in 1904. The British Govt. took over the administration.

Gajapati was admitted into the Maharaja High School of Paralakhemundi.

After that he took admission into the Newington Residential College of Madras. Mr. Cameroon Morrison and Dela Hay—Two British scholars taught him there.

He returned home and was coronated on 26.4.1913 as the Raja of Parlakhemundi. Next year on 28th January, 1914 he got married the Princess Nalini Devi, the daughter of Mahendra Narayan Singh Deo—the King of Kharsuan.

He did not forget Orissa. As a staunch Oriya nationalist, he organized the 10th session of the Utkal Sammilani at his capital Parlakhemundi on 26th and 27th December of 1914. It was a mammoth gathering of all Oriya elites from all parts of Orissa and outside Orissa Vikram Dev Verma—the king of Jeypore of Koraput presided over the meeting and Madhusudan Das was the Secretary. Besides, Fakir Mohan Senapati, Gopabandhu Dash, Sashi Bhusan Rath, Braja Sundar Das, Jagabandhu Singh, Gopal Chandra Praharaj, Godavarish Misra, Sri Batsa Panda, Neelamani Vidyaratna, Biswanath Kar were the prominent who attended the session.

Madhusudan Das was overwhelmed to see the organisation and management of the meeting and lavishly praised Maharaja for his undauntable spirit to organize the Oriyas into a homogenous unit. The King alone had spent Rs. 10,000/- from his royal treasury.

In the wake of the First World War, in July 1914, he donated a huge amount of money nearly Rs. 3 lakhs to the Defence of the British Govt. The Govt. out of gratefulness conferred on him the title of KCIE (Knight Commander of the Indian Empire).

In consultation with Madhu Babu, the Maharaja represented the case of Oriya problems and separate electorate for the Oriyas to Montegu-Chelmsford in January 1919 in Madras.

Madhusudan Das took oath as the Minister of local self-Govt. in the Province of Bihar and Orissa on 6th January 1921 at Patna. A resolution for the amalgamation of the Oriya-speaking areas of different neighbouring Provinces was passed and accordingly the Govt. of India appointed the Philip-Duff committee in 1924. The Committee collected the opinions of the people of Jeypore, Tekkali, Jalantara, Ganjam, Aska, Russelkonda etc. who expressed their desire to merge themselves with Orissa. Maharaja also convinced the Committee of the outstanding problems the Oriyas were facing in two different areas. This Committee recommended for the annexation of Ganjam and Koraput with Orissa but the British officers and the Telugu-Tamils of Ganjam resisted. The proposals were dropped.

Maharaja was elected to the Madras Legislative Council in 1930.

As a delegate of the Bihar and Orissa Govt. Maharaja was selected to participate in the First Round Table Conference in London to be held from 12th November, 1930 to 19th January 1931. Maharaja was permitted to speak on 16 January 1931. Gajapati delivered the most inspiring and convincing speech in favour of the unification of all the fragmented Oriya-speaking areas which were laying in Madhya Pradesh, Bihar, Bengal and Andhra Pradesh. By the magic of his voice and the representation of his problems, he drew the rapt attention of all the dignitaries present there.

Having been convinced by the illuminating speech of Maharaja, the British Govt. appointed the Orissa Boundary Committee consisting of Samuel O'Donnel as the Chairman H.M Mehta of Maharastra and T. Phokan of Assam as the members. The two Indian members whole-heartedly supported the amalgamation of all the areas of Ganjam, Koraput and Phulbani—but O' Donnel excluded the two estates of Jeypore and Parlakhemundi.

Maharaja was extremely shocked to see the final report of the O' Donnel Committee but was not disappointed. He went to meet the viceroy Lord Willington at Simla with a group of Bhubananda Das, Madhu Sudan Panigrahy, Lingaraj Panigrahy, Biswanath Misra, Lakhmi Narayan Sahu, Shyam Sundar Gantayet and Kings of Madhupur and Parikud. They explained the process of works they have done so far. And then he went to London and met Mr. Samuel Hoare—the Secretary of Indian affairs and other dignitaries of the Govt. and demanded the inclusion of Jeypore and Parlakhemundi with Orissa.

Later on the Joint Select Committee under Mr. Linlithgow was formed. On March 3, 1936, His Majestry gave his consent to form the separate Orissa state and a new Orissa was formed on 1st April 1936 with Jeypore and Parlakhemundi. Sir John Austin Hubback become the first Governor of Orissa.

The tireless efforts, the indefatigable determination and the selfless dedication of Maharaja made Orissa unification a reality.

Orissa after Unification

Elections for 60 seats in Orissa Assembly was held in January, 1937. Congress won 36 seats and other Parties got 24 seats. The Governor invited Biswanath Das to take oath as the Prime Minister of Orissa, but he asked for an assurance that the Governor would not interfere unreasonably in the affairs of the administration of the state: But Mr. Hubback refused to accept his request. Then Maharaja Krishna Chandra Gajapati took oath as the first Prime Minister of Orissa on 1st April 1937 with two other Ministers of Mandhata Gorachand Patnaik (Revenue) and Moulavi Mohmmed Latif Rehman (Education), Maharaja retained Law, Commerce and Finance. He knew that he could not prove his majority on the Assembly floor. So he resigned from the office on 13th, July 1937.

Meanwhile, Biswanath took oath as the Prime Minister of Orissa on 9th July 1939. He resigned on 4.11.1939 because the All India Congress decided not to Cooperate the British Govt. in anyway.

On 24.11.1941, the Maharaja once again formed the Coalition Ministry with two other Ministers—Godavarish Misra (Education) and Moulavi Shovan Khan (Law). During this period, the Orissa University Bill was passed and the Utkal University was founded on 27th November, 1943. It was one of the crowning achievements of Maharaja and his Govt.

During his tenure, the Central Rice Research Institute at Bidyadharpur, Cuttack was established.

He encouraged the female education in Orissa and established a Sanskrit College at Paralakhemundi. He contributed Rs. 5000/- to the publication of Purna Chandra Bhasakosh in Oriya by Gopal Chandra Praharaj. Many important books of Gopinath Nanda—the lexicographer of Parlakhemundi were published.

He formed a Flood Committee in Orissa to tackle the problems of the flood situations and spent huge amount of money for irrigation projects.

He was nominated as the member of the Constituent Assembly in 1947 to draft the Indian Constitution.

In his personal sphere, he set up the Gajapati Salt and Steel factory at Srikakulam. He created a great Agricultural Farm and a garden a few miles away from Parlakhemundi. He took care of the farm and livestock.

To encourage the poor and meritorious students of the district he maintained the free hostels.

He donated money to the Food Nutrition Factory at Conoor.

Despite his family misfortune, he has rendered valuable services to the people of Orissa. A man of integrity and selfless dedication, Maharaja Krishna Chandra Gajapati would remain as an immortal and indelible figure in the memory of the Oriya people.

He passed away on 25th, May 1974 at the age of 82.

SUBHASH CHANDRA BOSE (1897-1945)

Very few persons in history have left their indelible footprints on the sands of time. Subash Chandra Bose was one of them who left behind him the lengthening shadow of his incomparable achievements for India. His sense of Patriotism was limitless. The techniques of works were extraordinary. His genius was exceptional in history. The name of Subash Chandra Bose as the freedom fighter and the first-rate Patriot of India has been written down in golden letters in the annals of Indian history.

He was born on 23rd, January, 1897 at Oriya Bazar—Cuttack in Orissa. His father was the leading advocate of Cuttack and was the public—spirited man—Janaki Nath Bose. He was the student of law classes of Madhu Sudan Das in the Ravenshaw College. The mother of Subash Bose was Prabhavati Devi—a Pious lady. Subash Bose was an ardent student of Ravenshaw Collegiate School, Cuttack. During his school days he formed a volunteer organisation and rendered useful services to the down-trodden or to the cholera affected villages of Cuttack. After his school education in 1913, he went to Calcutta to prosecute higher studies in the Presidency College of Calcutta. He graduated himself from that University. His father sincerely wanted to see Subash Bose as the ICS officer. So he sent him to London to take admission into M.A classes in the Cambridge University and to prepare for the ICS examinations. He landed on England in the month of October 1919. He got hardly 8 months for the ICS exams and appeared the toughest exams in July, 1920 along with other English aspirants. To our surprise, Subash Bose secured the 4th position in order of merit. It was a rare achievement in British Indian history. But he did not like the post as the ICS officer in India. He resigned in April, 1921. Mr. Redway—the Censor Officer in England commented, "No Indian within my knowledge had ever done so before".

Subash Bose returned to India and joined as the Executive Officer in the Calcutta Corporation Mr. Chitta Ranjan Das who was the Mayor of Calcutta Corporation remarked to see the process of works of Subash Bose as "Subash is young old man"—means he is young in age but old in wisdom.

Subhash Bose jumped into the main stream of the movement of India and was courted arrest in 1924 December. He was sent to the Mandalay Jail in Burma and was released in May, 1927. In the same year he was elected as one of the Secretaries of the Indian National Congress.

On 5th, January 1932 he was arrested for the second time and was cast into a jail of Madhya Pradesh. He fell seriously ill and was taken to Switzerland for treatment. There he wrote a book "Indian Straggle".

In April 1936, he was imprisoned for the third time.

In 1938, at Haripur Session of Indian National Congress, Subash Bose was elected as the President of Indian National Congress worked to his satisfaction but some of the leaders of the Congress were not happy.

In 1939, once again the election took place to select the President of Indian National Congress. Subash Bose filed nomination for the second term—Mahatma Gandhi set Pattavi Sitaramaya as the rival candidate of Subash Bose. Sitaramaya was defeated. Gandhi remarked "The defeat of Pattavi Sitaramaya was my defeat". This clearly manifested the intolerant attitude of the Mahatma. If the aim of Indian National Congress was to achieve the freedom of India, it was immaterial whether Subash Bose became the President or Pattavi Sitaramaya. The statement of Gandhiji was evident that he wanted to perpetuate his interest and his supremacy in Indian National Congress through Sitaramaya-Anyhow Subash Bose could not successfully discharge his normal duties as the President because of the opposition of some Congress leaders. Ultimately he resigned not only from the post, but also from the Congress Party. There after he formed the Forward Bloc in Bengal.

Subash Bose was again arrested in 1940 for the fourth time. And under the Act of Sedition, he was to appear before the Magistrate Court on 27th January 1941.

But instead of appearing in the Court, Subash Bose prepared an extraordinary plan to fly away from India to Berlin. In order to carry out the plan most successfully, he employed his nephew (brother's son), Sisir Kumar Bose to drive the car from the Eligin House, Calcutta to the railway station of Gomoh—210 miles away from Calcutta. Sisir was asked to submit a report of his Journey—the nos, of railway crossings, nos of Police Stations-Police checking, impediments in the way—rivers villages etc. Sisir kumar Bose did as Subash desired. And ultimately, he dressed himself as a Pathan-keeping beards, a cap and the loose pant overcoat He kept his name Moulavi Zia-udin. On the appointed date of 17-1-1941, Subash Chandra Bose set for a non-return Journey to his mother land-India.

At Gomoh railway station, he boarded into the train and Sisir Kumar Bose weaved his hand for the last see-off with tears in his eyes. The train entered into the pitched darkness of the night.

He met according to the previous Plan, Mr. Bhagat Ram at Peswar Railway Station. Bhagat Ram's is nickname was Rehmat Khan who acted as the elder brother of Subash Bose. Both of them gave impression to others that Zia-udin is deaf and dumb and Rehmat Khan is taking him to the Western country for medical treatment. But this forged story was also doubted by some people here and there, but they escaped from the crises by paying them cash or watch. Rehmat Khan returned to India and Subash Bose reached Berlin through Kabul and Moscow in disguise of an Italian passport Orlando Mazzota in April, 1941.

The dramatic disappearance of Subash Bose from the Eligin house of Calcutta puzzled the British Govt in India. The Govt. made a thorough investigation in Calcutta and India but failed to trace out his whereabouts. Ultimately the Govt. announced the death of Subash Bose. The unwise declaration of Subash's death shocked the Indian leaders and the people. Meanwhile Subash Bose after his arrival in Berlin wanted to meet Hitler—the Military dictator of Nazi Germany. When the thickest dark clouds of the Second World War were looming large in the European sky, and the British Govt. was the die-hard enemy of Hitler and the entire populace of India sided with the British Govt. to fight against the Axis Powers of the world, Subash Bose's visit to Berlin was awfully surprising. Hitler bluntly refused to meet Subash Bose. But Subash Bose knew the art of diplomacy. He chalked out a vivid Programme of his action in Germany against the Allied Powers. Hitler himself was flabbergasted to see it and allowed Subash Bose for military actions in Germany. He allowed Subash to broadcast through the Azad Hind Radio from Berlin—and handed over the British Indian soldiers to Subash Bose who were captured in Europe as the prisoners of war. Subash Bose arrested the attention of the entire world on the day when his brilliant speech was broadcast from the Azad Hind Radio of Berlin in 1941.

The Indian students of Engineering, medicine reading in Germany and the businessman extended unequivocal support to Subash Bose in his enterprises. The Indian community in a meeting at Berlin passed four important resolutions: (1)

Jaihind—(Victory to India) (2) Janagana Mana adhinayak Jay he—the song of Rabindra Tagore was adopted as the national song. (3) The title Netaji was conferred on Subash Bose and (4) Hindi was adopted as the national language. These were the major contributions of the Indians of Germany and Subash Bose to the Indian nation.

Subash Bose spent the most hectic period of nearly two years in Germany. Then he decided to leave Germany for Japan. By a German submarine U-Boat, Subash Bose left Kiel, Gemany on 8th February 1943 and in a hazardous voyage under the waves of the Atlantic, Indian Ocean and Pacific Ocean. He landed on the Japanese seacoast on 13th June 1943. Life of Subash in the fathomless waters amidst the Sharks, Whales, the British war-ships and submarines was safe by the bounty of the God.

In Japan, Subash Bose met Mr. Tojo—the Prime Minister who assured him all military help. Subash Bose was cordially welcomed by an another royal Bengal tiger—Mr. Rash Behari Bose. Rash Behari Bose had left India long before in 1915 when the British Govt. tried to punish him for his revolutionary activities with the Extremist group. Since that day, Rash Behari Bose had been living in Japan with his Japanese wife and had organized the Indian National Army in the South-East Asia. Rash Behari Bose handed over all the crucial charges of the INA to Subash Chandra Bose.

On 21st October, 1943 at the Cathey Cinema Hall of Singapore, Subash Bose declared the establishment of the Provisional Indian Govt. in exile. He was made the Head of the Govt. and the Commander-in-Chief. He took official oath. Jana-gana-Mana-adhi-nayak-Jay-hai... was sung as the national anthem. After the formation of the Provisional Govt. Subash Bose officially declared war against England in the midnight on 23rd October, 1943.

A new spirit of Indian nationalism was surcharged among the countless Indians living in Malayasia, Burma and Siam. In Malayasia—8 lakhs in Burma—6 lakhs and in Siam—55 thousand Indians lived. They paid utmost reverence to Subash Bose and donated lakhs of rupees to the Defence Fund of the Provisional Govt. The Indians weighed Subash Bose in terms of money. The garlands of Subash Bose were publicly auctioned in lakhs of rupees. It was a tremendous response of the people to Subash Bose the world has never seen before. A Muslim of Rangoon, Mr. Habib donated his entire properties-lands, houses and Jewelleries which was valued nearly more than one crore of rupees.

Subash Bose organized the entire INA into several military divisions. The important divisions were Gandhi Division, Nehru Division, Subash Division, Patel Division, Rani of Jhansi Division and each division was placed under the Lt. Colonel. Shah Nawaz Khan. Mohan Kumar Lakhmibai, G.S. Dhilon were the top military officers of Indian National Army. Subash Bose gave a clarion call to all the INA soldiers "Delhi Challo".

The first shot the INA soldier had started against the enemies on February 4, 1944 at the Arakon front. On March 18,1944, they crossed the border of Jayanta, Garo hills and reached Indian soil. The INA soldiers had fought in eight sectors on the Indo-Burma border on the plains of Imphal and Kohima. On April 14 ,1944, Colonel S.A. Malik first planted the tricolour flag at Moirang in Manipur. It was the greatest military victory of INA to do in the teeth of stiff Allied forces. Major General A.C Chatterjee was appointed as the Governor designate of all the liberated territories. Netaji set up the National Bank of Azad Hind at Rangoon. There was an agreement between the Japanese Govt. and INA that INA would be given priority to exercise powers in the liberated areas.

Netaji made a thrilling speech in the Rangoon Radio on 4, August 1944 especially meant for Mahatma Gandhi.

"India's last war of Independence has begun. Troops of the Azad Hind Fauj are now fighting bravely on the soil of India and in spite of all difficulty and hardship they are pushing forward slowly but steadily. The armed struggle will go on until the last Britisher is thrown out of India and until our tricolour flag floats over the Viceroy's house in New Delhi.

Father of our nation—In this holy war for India's liberation we ask for your blessings and good wishes—Jaihind."

Had there been no natural calamities of torrential rains, slush and in the uneven lands, they could have pushed themselves to Bengal through Assam, but the Nature Played adversely against the fortune of the INA soldiers and their advancement. The incessant rain, quag, torrential flow of rain water, lack of food, medicines and arms and ammunitions coupled with the terrible cholera, dysentery and malaria took away the lives of the countless INA soldiers. And those survived were impatient of taking medicine and food but were killed in the battlefield.

At 2 P.M on August, 12, 1945, Netaji received the sad news from his own men, Dr. Lakshunniyah and Ganapathy that Japan had surrendered. This news upset all the dreams of Netaji.

America dropped two Atom bombs on Hirosima on 6.8.1945 and on Nagasaki on 9.8.1945, which completely shattered the military backbone of Japan.

Netaji decided to leave for Japan from Taipei of Formosa on 18th August 1945. A few minutes after the take off of the plane, the engine of the plane was ablaze and fell down. Netaji died of severe burn in his body.

The Second World War came to a close after the catastrophic bombardment on Hirosima and Nagasaki—but the war with the British Imperialism did not end in India. The Anglo-American soldiers capitulated the entire East Asia and the British rounded nearly 17 thousand INA soldiers and three military stalwarts. Major General Shah Nawaz, Colonel Sehgal and Colonel Dhilon as the prisoners of war. They were packed in Red fort, New Delhi Cantonment in October 1945.

The court martial started from November 5 to December 1945. The British framed charges against three INA officers that they had waged war against the British King. In the Red fort itself, Jawaharlal Nehru who had almost left practice as a barrister for last 30 years, once again donned his barrister's robe to defend the INA officers-a spectacular heart bleeding for the fellow Indians.

Along with Nehru were Sir Tej Bahadur Sapru and Bulabhai Desai. It was a historical trial-a travesty of truth to punish the worthy sons of India who were fighting for their motherland. Bulabhai concluded the trial and released all the prisoners of war on 3rd January 1946. It was the day of the delirious exuberance of the leaders and the people of India. And eighteen months later, India got independence in the mid-night of 14th August 1947.

Regarding the mystery of Netaji's death, the Govt. of India set up a Commission of enquiry in April 1956 under the headship of Shah Nawaz Khan, Suresh Chandra Bose (elder brother of Netaji) and S.N. Maitra I.C.S. (Chief Commissioner of Andaman and Nicobar islands). This Commission took witness of 67 persons in Delhi, Calcutta, Bangok, Sigon, and Tokyo. They examined all the facts and Shah Nawaz and A.C Maitra were convinced that Netaji was killed in an air crash. But Suresh Chandra Bose did not accept the truth of Netaji's death. The people of India loved

Netaji so intimately that they also ordinarily did not believe the death of Subash Bose.

Likewise a period of few years passed away. Once again, the question of Netaji's death arose. So having been forced by some of the M.Ps of West Bengal, the Govt. of India set up another Enquiry Commission in 1970 which collected a variety of facts, opinion and witness from Singapore, Rangoon, Formosa and Tokyo and concluded that Netaji is dead in a plane-crash on 18th, August 1945. Still then some of the leaders of West Bengal clamoured that Netaji is still alive. But the death of Netaji is true because a leader of such public spirited and ardent patriot of India can never hid himself in cognito.

Subash Bose's conjugal life was as romantic as tragic it was. Because he did not marry any Indian bride—but married a very beautiful Viennese lady, Miss Emilie Schenkl who was her closest worker since 1934 at Badgastein in Europe. The marriage took place in December 1937. Since that day till 1943 January, Subash Bose did not disclose his secret wedding with Schenkl but in February, 1943, whenever he was to leave for Japan from Berlin, he divulged his marriage with Schenkl by writing a letter to his brother—Sarat Chandra Bose that they should take care of Schenkl and his daughter if he dies in the hazardous journey during the thick of the Second World War.

Schenkl died in 1995 and their daughter Anita Bose became an eminent economist and is a Professor at Augsburg University in Germany. She married to Martin Pfoff who is a member of German Parliament and is also an economist. They are blessed with two sons and a daughter.

It is beyond any point to estimate the sense of bravery of Subash Bose who secretly escaped in cognito as Ziauddin to Berlin—then his hair escape perilious sea-voyage to Japan and his wars with the Allied powers across the torrential rain, quagmare and wild mosquitoes in the Burmese border.

He was the immortal son of the Indian soil and an unforgettable character in Indian history.

BIJU PATNAIK (1916-1997)

As a man of dauntless courage and indefatigable zeal, the name of Biju Patnaik has been written down in the golden letters in the history of Orissa and India. He could have rendered more spectacular services to Orissa during his tenure of Chief Ministership in 1961-1963, had he not resigned under the Kamraj Plan. Because it was the period of rapid construction of Indian economy and developments in India. The departure of Biju Patnaik as Chief Minister was a colossal loss to Orissa. Kamraj Plan did not boost the image of the Congress Party in India rather negatived the progress of Orissa.

The life history of Biju Patnaik is an unending epic. His life was short but his achievements had lengthened the span of his life to an indefinite. He was born on 5 March 1916 at Tulasipur-Cuttack Town to the parents of Lakhmi Narayan Patnaik and mother Ashalata Devi. His father Lakhmi Narayan Patnaik was the Magistrate under the British Govt, so he worked in different places. The forefathers of Biju Patnaik were the inhabitants of Nuagam village near Bhanjanagar in the dist. of Ganjam. Lakhmi Narayan Patnaik built a house "Ananda Bhavan" at Tulasipur, Cuttack town where Biju was born.

He was a student of Ravenshaw Collegiate school and Ravenshaw College of Cuttack. As a science student of Ravenshaw College, he has proved his merit and became the most successful Pilot. From the childhood, Biju Babu was extremely courageous. He has done the impossible in life. The cycle journey from Cuttack to Pathankot (Jammu) with his friends was an impossible task to do—but he has done it.

The release of Sukarna and Hotta Mohmmed in 1949 from the clutches of the Dutch Govt. from Indonesia to Delhi by a helicopter driven by Biju Patnaik is a sensational and spectacular feat in history. After Independence, Dr. Sukarna awarded Biju Patnaik the highest title of Indonesia—the "Bhumiputra" 1973 and "Bintong Jaso Uttam" (1995) with a luxurious castle and one hundred fifty acres of land in Indonesia. But Biju Babu magnanimously returned the castle and land to the Indonesian Govt.

Biju Babu as a pilot entered into the most hazardous area of battle fronts to supply food to the Indian soldiers who were fighting against the Pakistani and Chinese soldiers.

He fought against the British imperialism for freedom and was arrested on 13 January 1943 during the thick of the Quit India Movement.

He chose ultimately Politics as a career leaving aside the job of a Pilot. In the first general election of India, which was held during the month of January 1952, Biju Babu was elected as a member of Orissa Assembly from Jagannath Prasad Constituency in the dist of Ganjam. In 1957, he was elected to Orissa Assembly from Sorada Constituency, in 1961; he was elected to Assembly from Choudwar Constituency and became the Chief Minister of Orissa. His tenure as Chief Minister of Orissa from 1961-1963 was a memorable period in Orissa Political history—invited Nehru to lay the foundation of the Paradip Port on 3 January 1962—established the Regional Engineering College at Rourkela.

He was elected several times to Orissa Assembly and to the Lok Sabha. In 1977 he was given the Cabinet rank of Steel Minister in Centre in the Coalition ministry of Morarji Desai as the Prime Minister (1977-1980).

In 1990 February elections, Biju Babu was once again elected to the Orissa Assembly from Bhubaneswar Constituency and became the Chief Minister of Orissa for the second time. But he could not prove his might and political wisdom to redesign the State administration for developmental works. The entire administrative system of Orissa was rust and the employees from top to bottom were corrupted. As an octogenarian, he has lost his vitality and dynamism. He promulgated the theory of beating the officers of the state who are not doing their duties sincerely. Anyhow he completed the full term of five years as the Chief Minister in the Political doldrums and in the administrative inefficiency of the Orissa state. Nothing tangible is achieved during this period of 1990-1995 in Orissa.

Another notable contribution of Biju Patnaik was the creation of Kalinga Prize to be awarded to the scientists of the world for their outstanding contributions to mankind. He has deposited huge amount of money and the Kalinga Prize is being awarded to the scientists of all nationalities since 1955. Therefore Biju Patnaik established the Oriya identity in the world.

Biju Babu combined in himself all the qualities of a Political leader, Pilot, Administrator, Industrialist, Philanthropist and a herbinger of peace.

After an eventful career of long 54 years in the history of Orissa and India, Biju Patnaik passed away on 7.4.1997 at the age of 81.

DR. SHYAM CHANDRA TRIPATHY (1893-1951)

It was a rare moment in History that Mayur Bhanj Estate has given birth to such a great man like Dr. Shyam Chandra Tripathy. He was the jewel of Orissa and an imperishable character in the history of education in Orissa.

Shyam Chandra Tripathy was born at Madhapur in the Estate of Mayur Bhanj on 1st March 1893 in a conservative family of the Brahmins. His father was Chintamani Tripathy—an employee of Mayur Bhanj.

After his village education, he took admission into the Maharaja Krishna Chandra High School—Baripada and passed matriculation in 1910 with 1st division. then he was admitted in to I.Sc classes of Ravenshaw College—Cuttack and passed it in 1912. Keeping the 2nd position in the Calcutta University.

Then he went to Presidency College-Calcutta for B.Sc. examinations and secured the 2nd position in the entire Calcutta University in Physics Honours. It was a rare academic achievement.

The Govt. of Bihar and Orissa awarded him the state scholarship for higher studies in England. Shyam Chandra Babu got it and went to London to take admission into M.Sc. in Physics and Mathematics in September 1915 in the Cambridge University. He passed in both the papers in 1916 and 1918 and undertook research works.

He returned to India in 1919 and became the Head Master of the Ravenshaw Collegiate School—Cuttack in 1920, January 29th. After one year, he joined as the Head of the Physics Dept. of Ravenshaw College. He passed the Indian Education Service. Shyam Babu was appointed as the Superintendent of the East Hostel and Dr. Pranakrishna Parija was appointed as the Superintendent of the West Hostel. As a Lecturer, he taught Physics in such a manner that he kept the students spell-bound.

He then went to London twice with the Maharaja Purna Chandra Bhanj of Mayur Bhanj. Both of them were very intimate and friendly like Sri Krishna and Sudama. And it was because of Shyam Chandra's intimacy that Maharaja Puma Chandra Bhanj donated 1 lakh of rupees for the installment of Power Plant to supply electricity to Ravenshaw College, Laboratories and Class Rooms and Staff Quarters in 1925. Even Cuttack Municipality supplied the electrical power to the town from the 1st December 1930 initially 20 (50 Candle Power) and 180 (25 Candle Power), but the Maharaja's magnanimity lighted the fortune of Ravenshaw College in 1925.

In 1930, Shyam Chandra Tripathy got appointment as the Deputy Director of Public Instructions of Bihar and Orissa state on 1=4-1930. He stayed in Patna and spent nearly 6 years.

Then on 17th, January, 1936, Shyam Babu joined as the Principal of Ravenshaw College, Cuttack—the first Oriya and Indian to become the Principal of the Premier College of India. He stayed in this post for two years and during this period he rendered commendable services to the college.

On 1st April 1936, Orissa became a separate state. He was appointed as the D.P.I, of Orissa. He spent nearly 10 years as D.P.I of Orissa. When the proposal to establish a University in Orissa was discussed in the Cabinet of Maharaja Krishna Chandra Gajapati as the Prime Minister and Godavarish Misra as the Education Minister, Mr. Shyam chandra Tripathy played the key role in drafting the acts of the University. Maharaja Krishna Chandra Gajapati placed the entire responsibility of the proposed Utkal University upon Sri Shyam Chandra Tripathy. And he did all. Finally, the Utkal University came into existence on 27th November 1943. Thanks to the tireless efforts of Sri Shyam Chandra Tripathy for the setting up of the Utkal University.

In 1948, he retired from the Govt. job at 55. Then again he was appointed as the member of the Federal Public Service Commission in Delhi. One year after in 1949, he became the Chairman of the Rajastan Public Service Commission and stayed in Jaipur.

He stayed there hardly two years as the Head of the Public Service Commission, but the destiny inflicted a cruel blow upon him. He died of heart attack on 18th August 1951. A man who has dazzled the destiny of Orissa by his glittering personality and constructive activities, suddenly disappeared from the arena.

PRAFULLA KAR

The melodious tone of Sri Prafulla Kar is echoed in the rythm of "Kamal deshara Raja Kumar Mu hatare Indradhanu". Like wise many of his Oriya songs are hits through decades. Prafulla Kar is one of memorable Singers and Music directors in Orissa.

This celebrated singer is born on 2nd February 1939 at Markendeswar lane of Puri Town. His father was Baidyanath Kar and mother was Sushilamani Kar. Born and brought up in the family of Artists, Prafulla Babu also establishes himself as a towering singer of Oriya songs and Oriya films. He studied in the Gandharva University of classical music in Bomaby.

Mr. Prafulla Babu graduated himself from S.C.S. College, Puri and completed his L.L.B Degree from M.S. law college, Cuttack. But he did not devote himself in practicing law-rather keeping aside it, he embraced the performing art of singing the songs.

Prafulla Babu did not only amuse and entertain the mammoth audience by his melodious songs, but he also directed the music in many of the Oriya films like Mamata, Sesha Srabana, Hisab Nikash, Pooja, Balidan, Sindura Bindu, Pooja Phool, Ram Rahim, Mana Mandir, School Master and Naga Jyoti and many others. These films are the monuments of his name and fame, which will immortalise his life.

Because of his outstanding contributions to the Oriya film music, Prafulla Babu has been awarded the covetuous "State Award" several times in 1975 for Mamata, Sesha Srabana

(1976), Bandhu Mohanty (1977) Sati Anusuya (1978), Tapasya (1980), School Master (1985).

He sings too Bhajan, Gazal, Kawali in different colorful music functions. He has gone abroad several times—Russia, Australia, America and London and spell bounded the unlimited audience.

Prafulla Kar is a versatile genius in the world of music.

MANOJ DAS

Born in an aristocratic family of Balasore district in 1934, Manoj Das occupies a distinctive position in the world of creative writings both in English and Oriya. He is superlative in coining new Oriya words—in style and presentation of sequences before the readers.

After his Post Graduate Degree in English, he is engaged in teaching English as a lecturer in Christ College, Cuttack from 1959 to 1963.

He was uncompromising as a student leader and revolted against the injustice for which he was arrested in 1955.

In recognition of his leadership as a student, he was selected to participate in the Afro-Asian Bandung Conference in 1955.

He edited one of the leading Oriya magazines—"DIGANTA" (1959-1963) and ultimately the publication of it was closed.

Leaving aside all his engagements in Cuttack, Manoj Babu went to Pondichery, Sri Aurobinda Ashram where he taught English. He became a devout disciple of Sri Aurobinda and settled there till to day. But that does not mean that he had forgotten Orissa and its culture. His link with the Oriyas and Oriya literature becomes stronger and intimate than before.

The pursuit of Knowledge does not end—Manoj Babu makes writing of stories and books in such a manner that he keeps the readers in English and Oriya in India and abroad mesmerized. He is proficient in English and Oriya.

From Pondichery, he edited the English monthly "The Heritage" (1985-1989) published from Madras sponsored by V. Nagi Reddy—the Proprietor of Chandamama. The Heritage was halcyon and messenger of Indian culture.

As an analyst and interpreter of the human life and philosophy Manoj Babu excels in delivering speeches all over India. His literary creations are superb-difficult to give a list of his books in Oriya and English.

In recognition of his outstanding literary creativity, the Central Sahitya Academy has awarded him the award in 1972—got the Sarala literary award in 1980.

In 2001 AD the Central Govt. has .conferred on him the "Padmasri civilian title and the "Saraswati Award".

Manoj Babu himself is a jewel, a glittering star in the literary sky. He needs no ornaments. Readers bestow affection, appreciations and respect on him wherever he is.

KALU CHARAN MAHAPATRA

Kelu Charan Mahapatro is 'the undisputed master of Odissi dance in India. He earned an immortal fame as the greatest Protagonist of the performing art of Odissi dance. He elevated the position of the Odissi dance as the classical dance form to the highest level of international arena.

This fortunate Guru Sj. Kelu Charan Mahapatra is born on 8th February, 1926 at Raghurajpur in the district of Puri. His father was Chintamani Mohapatra and mother was Siridevi. His father was a great artist. Having been inspired by his father, Kelu Babu learnt dance, songs, and beating of

"Pokhauja". In 1944, he joined the "Orissa Theatres" at Cuttack managed by Kabichandra Kali Charan Patnaik.

But he left the theatres and came to Puri to join as the dance master in Annapurna "B" Theatre. Here itself, he acquired a great skill as a dance artist of Odissi.

He did not like to confine himself as a dance master at Puri. He left for Cuttack to join as the Guru to teach Odissi to different aspirants at Kala Vikash Kendra of Cuttack Town. From among the great Odissi dancers of Orissa who have dazzled the spectators of the world by their spectacular enacting Odissi dance are Smt.Sanjukta Panigrahy, Minati Das, Priyambada Mohanty, Kumkum Das and they are the obedient students who learnt different mudras, tactics of Odissi from Kelu Charan Mohapatra. All these students with Kelu Babu gave a new dimension and style to Odissi dance.

Due to the tireless efforts, dedication and devotion of Kelu Babu, Guru Pankaj Das, Guru Deba Prasada Das, Singers—Balakrishna Das, Bhubaneswar Misra, Dhiren Patnaik and Kali Charan Patnaik, the Odissi dance earned a position as one of the classical dance forms in India.

Kelu Babu not only made Odissi as the most popular classical dance in India but he made extensive tours under the Govt. of India cultural banner to London, America, Russia, Japan, France and organized innumerable dance recitals there. The audience of the world was hypnotised by the splendid cultural show of Odissi dance.

He organised an independent Odissi Workshop "Srujana" with his beloved son and wife to impart and execute Odissi dance to countless learners of Orissa, India and abroad. Till the last day of his breath, Kelu Babu will devote his energy and time to the cause of Odissi dance.

In recognition of his exceptional merit as a great dancer of India, the Govt. of India have conferred on him the great civilian award, Padma Sri and Padma Bibhusana in 1974 and 2-000 respectively. Besides he has got countless titles and Awards from the M.P Govt, Maharastra Govt, and Madras Govt.

Kelu Babu has projected a brilliant image of Odissi dance from the iconography of different Hindu temples of Puri, Konark Bhubaneswar and Khajuraho of M.P.

His achievements will outlive him.

SANJUKTA PANIGRAHY

Sanjukta Panigrahy was considered to be the greatest exponent of Odissi dance. It seemed that she symbolised Odissi dance and the Odissi dance lived in herself. She raised the position of Odissi dance to the pinnacle of undying glory in the world.

She was born to a parent of Abhiram Misra and Shakuntala Misra on 24th August, 1944. Her father was an Engineer. It was highly an objectionable trait to a lady who was born in a most conservative Brahmin family to learn dance. But her mother who was the daughter of Kailash Pati of Baripada in the district of Mayur Bhanj was a great patron of Chhou dance and Oriya music. She set aside all the social criticism encouraged Sanjukta to learn Odissi dance.

During her student days in 1953, she learnt Odissi from the great Master Kelu Charan Mohapatra at Cuttack and represented her school in Calcutta as a child artist. At the age of 9 only, she kept the Calcutta audience spell-bound by her dance recital with melodious songs and "Pakhauja". It was a spectacular feat. This was the beginning of the great forward march in the techniques of Odissi dance. She got a scholarship to learn Bharatnatyam at Madras. She learnt Bharatnatyam from Rukmini Devi Arundale and spent nearly more than 6 years there in learning the dance. Then she presented innumerable dance programmes in Coornol, Madras, Bombay, Hyderabad, Delhi, and Calcutta and in all the cities of India.

In 1960, she got married with Raghunath Panighray of Gunupur in Ganjam who too was a versatile as a classical singer of Orissa and India. Indian songs and dances find a common platform in Sanjukta and Raghunath.

Odissi dance was not only a means to earn her livelihood, but it became the life of Sanjukta. She made Odissi and Bharatnatyam the most performing art and popular in India and all over the world. She staged countless colorful dance shows in America, Philippines, Japan, Hungary, Rumania, Yugoslovia, Czechoslovakia, Nepal, Sikkim, France, London, Denmark, Switzerland, Norway, Netherland, West Germany, Sweden, Holland, Australia, Belgium, Canada, Indonesia, Singapore, South America, Israel, Iran and Russia. No dance of any part of the world has covered such continental countries in the world as Odissi dance. And it was made possible exclusively by Sanjukta Panigrahy and her husband Raghunath Panigrahy. They made Oriya culture international—most widespread in the entire globe.

Sanjukta ultimately established an Odissi Dance Academy at Bhubaneswar to teach Odissi dance to the interested girls and boys. She also undertook further research works on Odissi dance. Many girls of Orissa, India and foreign countries are greatly benefitted by her.

As an exceptional dance Artiste, the Govt. of India conferred on her the "Padmasri" in 1975. The Dance Academy of Delhi and Bhubaneswar also honoured her by awarding prizes and Certificates. The Govt. of foreign countries also showered glorious momentoes, certificates, prestige on her. But she was not destined to enjoy them for a longer period of time. She died an unexpected death on 24th June, 1997 at Bhubaneswar.

Odissi dance is the life and legacy of Sanjukta Panighrahy.

DR. PRAFULLA KUMAR PATI

He is one of the eminent teachers in English in Orissa state. Himself is a genius, and as a lecturer produced countless jewels of students who have occupied important positions in the state and Indian administration.

This celebrated professor-Dr. Prafulla Kumar Pati was born at Rampela in the district of Sambalpur in 1921. His father was Mrutyunjay Pati and mother was Satyabati Pati.

He passed matriculation from Sambalpur Zilla School and took admission into Ravenshaw College. He passed B.A. with Honours in English. Then he obtained his M.A. Degree in English from the Patna University.

Immediately after Post Graduate, he was appointed as a lecturer in English in Ravenshaw College, Cuttack in 1944 where he taught up to 1957.

In 1960, he went to Minisetta University—U.S.A. for his Doctorate Degree and returned to India after three years. He became the Professar of English in Ravenshaw College, Cuttack and later on in the P.G. Dept. of English, Sambalpur University. He also discharged his duties as the Principal of Keonjhar College and Khallikote College, Berhampur in 1968.

He was appointed as a member of Orissa Public Service Commission in 1979 and satisfactorily worked up to 1983.

As an Educationist, the Govt. of Orissa honoured him by appointing Dr. Pati as the Vice-Chancellor of Sambalpur University for 3 years—1983 to 1986.

After his retirement, he has devoted himself for the upliftment of Western Orissa.

VARAHA GIRI VENKAT GIRI

The man who adorned the highest position of the Indian Republic as the President in July, 1969 was Varaha Giri Venkat Giri. He belonged to Berhampur Town in the district of Ganjam, Orissa.

He was born on 10 August 1894 at Berhampur. His father was V.V. Jogia Panthulu—a leading advocate of Berhampur Town. The grand father of V.V. Giri was Ramiah Panthulu, he was also an advocate of Berhampur.

V.V.Giri read in the local High School and completed his B.A. in the Khallikote College, Berhampur Town. There after he went to read L.L.B in Ireland at Dublin University. After completing his barrister course, he practiced law at Berhampur.

He was a man of integrity and singular independence. Having been influenced by the freedom movement of the Irish against the British, he too participated in the Freedom movement of India. He participated in the deliberations of the Annual Session of Indian National Congress at Lucknow in 1921.

V.V. Giri was basically a leader of the common men—the labour classes of the society. He fought against the exploitations of rich men—the Capitalists and gave social and economic justice to the down-troddens. He was the President of the Trade Unions.

He was also a great organizer of the Congress Party in India. In 1934, he was elected to the Council of the Central Govt. from Vishakhapatna Constituency under the Madras Presidency. Two years after, he was elected to the Madras Council. He was fortunate to work under the Prime Minister of Madras C. Rajgopalachari, as the Minister of Industry, Co-operation, Commerce and the development of Harijan.

After Independence, V.V. Giri was appointed as the High Commissioner of India to Ceylon. But later on Jawaharlal

Nehru brought him to the Central Cabinet as the Minister of Employment and labour.

Later on, he was appointed as the Governor of Kerala, Karnatak and Uttar Pradesh. In 1967, Mrs. Indira Gandhi selected him to contest for the post of Vice-President of India. And he was elected as Vice President when Dr. Zakir Hussain was the President after the expiry of Dr. S. Radha Krishna's term as the President of India in 1967.

Dr. Zakir Hussain passed away in the early part of 1969 while in office. V.V. Giri took oath as the President of India. But according to the Constitutional Provisions, a new President would be elected. Mean while the Congress Party was split into two major groups. One group was led by Mrs. Indira Gandhi—called "Ruling Congress" and the other group was called the "Organisation Congress" led by Nijalingappa. Originally, two Presidential candidates were proposed Sanjiv Reddy and C.D. Deshmukh, But Mrs. Indira Gandhi did not like them. V.V. Giri was also aspirant for the post. It so happened ultimately Mrs. Indira Gandhi set V. V. Giri as the third candidate for the post of President. A triangular contest began. The preferential votes were divided. In the last counting, V V Giri was declared as the successful candidate in July, 1969 and took oath. He continued to serve completely for a full-term of 5 years up to 1974.

This period of 5 years (1969-1974) was marked by the serious and spectacular national events. In the wake of the Bangladesh war in March, 1971, India whole-heartedly supported the Bangladesh freedom fighters and extended immense military help to them. The Indian soldiers directly fought against the Pakistani Soldiers. Bangladesh became independent.

He gave consent for the abolition of the Privy Purses to the Kings and Maharajas of India in December 1971.

The Central Govt. nationalized 14 Banks by ordinance in 1969.

And the most sensational and proud event was the explosion of the nuclear test at Pokhoran in Rajasthan on May 18th of 1974. This incident enthralled the whole world and the Diplomats of all corners of the world.

DR. HAREKRISHNA MEHTAB (1899-1987)

A man who dominated the politics of Orissa for more than 60 years (1921-1987) was the celebrated Dr. Harekrishna Mahtab who was born on 21.11.1899 at Agarapada near Bhadrak.

After his graduation from Ravenshaw College Cuttack, he devoted his life, energy, wealth and wisdom to Indian Politics, Oriya History, Oriya literature and Prajatantra-the newspaper. He was also an indefatigable freedom fighter who left his deep footprints upon the sands of Time. Till the last breath, Politics and Oriya literature remained as an integral part of his life.

He first started his career as a Freedom Fighter in 1921. After his return from the Nagpur session of Indian National Congress, the Non-cooperation Movement was launched in Orissa, Gopabandhu Das, H.K. Mahtab and Niranjan Patnaik were the pioneers of the Movement in Orissa. To a great extent, they have materialized the objectives of the Non-Co-operation Movement in Orissa.

Harekrishna Mahtab was elected to the Balasore District Board in 1926 and become the Chairman of the Board.

Mahtab took active role in organizing the Civil Disobedience Movement of 1930 and the Quit India movement in 1942. And he was courted imprisonment in 1943 and was kept in Ahmed Nagar Jail of Maharastra with Jawaharlal Nehru 'and other national leaders.

He became the Chief Minister of Orissa in 1946. In 1950, he joined the Central Cabinet as a Minister. He was the Secretary of the Congress Parliamentary Party in 1952. As a great Congress leader, he was appointed as the Governor of Maharastra in 1955-56.

He was elected to the Loksabha in 1961-1967 as a member.

In 1975-76, Dr. Mahtab protested against the emergency declared by Indira Gandhi and was imprisoned at Bhanjanagar Jail.

He was a shrewd Politician, an able administrator and a clever diplomat.

His contributions to Orissa history and Oriya literature were immense and unforgettable. He not only published Prajatantra as a daily newspaper in Orissa but through this paper, he spread the constructive messages to the nook and corner of the Orissa villages. "Gan Majlis" was his unique column through which he broadcast the messages of work and wisdom.

"Jhankar" as a monthly Oriya literary magazine is the legacy and life work of Dr. Mahtab. He enlivened and spread the Oriya literature in the form of poems, research articles, literary criticism, short stories to all the lovers of Oriya language.

Besides, the people of Orissa would remember him for his outstanding writings of different books on Orissa. The two volumes of "Orissa History", "Beginning of the End", "Sadhanar Pathe" (autobiography in Oriya), "Palasi Abasane", and many political and historical novels are the jewels for the scholars to refer.

His role to shift the capital from Cuttack to Bhubaneswar, to buildup the Barbati Stadium, Rabindra Mandap, Museum, Orissa Sahitya Academy, Orissa Sangit Natak Academy and

Lalitakala Academy was highly praiseworthy and unique. There was nothing in Orissa, which has not been touched and rejuvenated by Dr. Mahtab.

He was a multi-faceted personality with the widest foresight and intuitive understanding of the problems and solutions. He was really a maker of modern Orissa. He passed away on 2nd January, 1987.

1. Dr. Prana Krishna Parija: Born on 1st April 1891 at Ichhapur (Balikuda) in the district of Cuttack. Father—Biswanath Parija. After finishing his early education at village, he took admission in to Ravenshaw Collegiate School—Cuttack. Then he read in Ravenshaw College, took admission in to Presidency College, Calcutta and passed B.Sc. with Math. Hons in 1913.

He went to London in 1914, became a student in Cambridge University, passed M.Sc and Ph.D. and returned to India in 1921.

Joined as the Professor of Botany in Ravenshaw College and became Principal of the same College from 1938 to 1943.

He was the Vice-chancellor of Utkal University from 1943 to 1948 andbecame the Pro-Chancellor of the Banaras Hindu University in 1948. Again became the Vice-Chancellor of Utkal University from 1955 to 1966.

Secretary of the All India Science Congress and Ultimately became the President of it.

In 1955, the Govt. of India awarded him the "Padma Bibhusana". He died on 2nd June 1978.

2. Godabarish Mahapatro: He was born on October-1898 at Banapur in the district of Puri. He founded and edited the most firebrand monthly Oriya magazine "Niankhunta" from 1938 where he vehemently criticised the corruption, irregularity and unlawful activities of the Govt. of Orissa, Minister, M.L.As, I.A.S, O.A.S officers and anybody under the sun. He was a terror to the Govt. He died in September 1965.

3. Kali Charan Patnaik: Born on 23rd December 1897 at Badamba in the district of Cuttack. Father—Durga Charan Patnaik, Mother—Radhamali Devi. His father was a great patron of songs. He was inspired by his parents to learn the classical music.

He was a great dramatist. In 1940, he stared a Theatre Movement at Cuttack and established the "Orissa Theatres'. With Aswini Kumar Ghose, he staged many of their plays—Kalicharan Parnaik composed several songs and wrote many Oriya dramas like Pratisodh, Girl school, Kamala, Jaydev, Bhat, Chakri, Abhijan, Raktamati.

In recognition of his merit, the Gajapati King of Puri awarded the title "Kabi Chandra" in 1927. He got the Kendra Sahitya Academy Award and died on July 1978.

4. Ram Chandra Mardaraj: Born in a royal family of Khallikote in the district of Ganjam on 13-1-1900. His father was the most Public Spirited man-Sri Harihar Mardaraj who died in 1907. He was also a student of a Royal College in Madras.

He was coronated as the Maharaja of Khallikote in 1921 and wielded all the powers. He was the President of the Ganjam District Board in 1936. He was also elected as the member of the Madras Legislative Council. He devoted his time, wealth and energy for the unification of Orissa State. He accompanied M.K.C.Gajapati to London to participate in the Second Round Table Conference.

After Independence, he was elected to Orissa legislative Assembly. He died on 23rd January 1963.

5. Radhanath Rath: Born on 8-12-1896 at Athagarh, Cuttack district. He passed Matriculation in 1916 from Ravenshaw Collegiate School. Due to his miserable financial condition, he could not undertake higher studies and joined as the manager of the Satyabadi Press of Gopabandhu Das at Sakhi Gopal for weekly "SAMAJ". In 1927 July, the Samaj Press was shifted to Cuttack. On June 17, 1928, Gopabandhu Das passed away. On 6th April 1930—"SAMAJ" became a daily newspaper. He became the Editor of SAMAJ in 1946 April. He wrote many constructive articles under "Jhitipiti Kahe" in Samaj.

He was the legislator of Orissa Assembly in 1946 and become the Minister. He died on 11 February 1998.

6. Sachi Routroy: Born in 1913 in Khurda, passed B.A from Ravenshaw College, Cuttack. He took active part in the Freedom Movement of India—Praja Mandal Movement, Students and farmers Movements and courted imprisonment twice.

Later on, he became a revolutionary poet with progressive ideas. He condemned the fascism, imperialism and the economic exploitation of the Kings and the British Govt.

The monumental poems are Pandulipi, Baji Rout, Pallisri and Abhijan. In recognition of his immense contributions to the Oriya and Indian literature, the Govt. of India awarded the 'Padmasri' title and Kendra Sahitya Academy in 1962. He is the poet of the Proletariats. The greatest achievement of his lifetime is the award of Gyana Pitha Prize in 1986 for his creative writings.

He has travelled America, France, Italy. Germany, Egypt, England, Australia, New Zealand, Japan, Thailand, Russia, Poland, Czechoslovakia and Bangladesh.

He is still active and enthusiastic as an octogenarian.

7. Gopinath Mohanty: Born in 1914, passed M.A in English literature in 1936 from Patna University. Joined in Orissa Administrative Service.

He is more an eminent Novelist in Oriya literature than an administrator. As a Novelist, he will live in the heart and mind of the countless Oriya readers. The monumental creations are: Paraja, Amrutar Santan, Sapan Mati, Danapani, Mati Matal, Pahanta, Kulae Pani, Harijan etc.

In 1955, he got the Kendra Sahitya Award. In 1974, he got the Jyanapitha Prize for his outstanding novel—"Mati Matala". The Govt. of India conferred on him the "Padma Bhusan" in 1981.

The great Oriya laureate died in August 1991.

8. Dr. Trilochan Pradhan: Born at Khandapara in Puri district in 1929, passed B.Sc from Ravenshaw College, Cuttack and went to Banaras Hindu University. He passed M.Sc in Physics occupying the Ist position in the University in 1951.

He did Ph.D in Chicago University, U.S. A and joined as a lecturer in Ravenshaw College. Then he went to join as the Professor of Physics in the Shah Institute of Theoretical Physics in Calcutta where he served from 1962 to 1974. Then he returned to Orissa to join as the Director of Regional Research Institute of Physics at Bhubaneswar.

He became the Vice-Chancellor of Utkal University in 1991.

The Govt. of India awarded him with the title of "Padma Bhusan" in 1990.

9. Samuel Sahu (Babi): He was born at Cuttack in a Christian family in 1918. He passed Diploma from the Orissa school of Engineering and joined in service at Chakradharpur—Bihar, but he was not satisfied.

He returned to Cuttack and joined as a Stage Actor in Orissa theatre in 1940 managed and founded by Kali Charan Patnaik at the salary of Rs.8/-per month. He requested to enhance the salary due to inflation during the Second World War, but Kali Babu did not do it, for which Babi left Orissa Theatre to join in the Annapurna 'B' Group. Here he made his histrionic talent professional and artistic. He directed more than 150 Oriya dramas and enacted different lead roles. They made the Annapurna 'B' Group as the Center of cultural activity in Orissa. And this period of Babi from 1945 to 1975 was the culminating point of his superb histrionic acumen.

Then he jumped in to Oriya films and played the lead roles in "Bhai Bhai", "Sri Lokanath", "Lakhmi", "Manika Jodi", "Sadhana", "Suryamukhi", "Jeevan Sathi", "Bhai Bhauja", "Abhinetri", "Kia Kahar", "Adina Megha", "Jajabar", "Suna Sansar", "Maa O' Mamata". "Hakim Babu", "Abhimaan" etc. and left a deep impression in the minds of the cine-goers of Orissa. He made Oriya drama and Cinema most popular in Orissa and became an integral part of it.

In 1961. he got Kendra Natak Academy Award and Orissa Natak Academy Award in 1971 and many institutional prizes.

He is an immortal figure in the history of Oriya drama in Orissa. But physically he died on 19th, November 2000.

10. Kanhu Charan Mohanty: Born in 1906, original native of Nagabali village of Cuttack district but was born at Sonepur, passed B. A, from Ravenshaw College—Cuttack in 1929. He joined in Orissa Administrative service in 1940. He served at different places as the ADM and in different posts. During his tenure, he gathered variety of experiences regarding the lives of the Tribal and Kings of the state. And basing on his personal experiences, he wrote as many as 36 novels from 1924 to 1994.

The outstanding novels he wrote are: "Tathastu", "Baliraja", "Aruna", "Palatak", "Nispati", "Ha'Anna", "Parakiya", "Parichaya", "Adekha Haat", "Tunda Baida", "Shasti", "Abhinetri", "Paani", "Jhanja", "Sharbari", "Kaa", "Bajrabahu", "Tamasa Tire", "Apa", "Namati Taar Champa", "Tapasi", "Pabani Kahibaku Laaj", "Satyabati", "Mamatar Maya" etc.

In 1959 he got the Kendra Sahitya Academy Award and Orissa Sahilya Academy Award in 1966.

Kanhu Charan Mohanty is the pillar of the Oriya Novels and enriched the Oriya literature by his immense contributions.

11. Radha Mahan Godanayak: Born at Kaindapaal near Anugul in the district of Dhenkanal on 25th August 1911. He passed matriculation but could not continue till B.A.

His educational qualifications are limited. But his imagination and creativity are spectacular. He composed inspiring and thought-provoking poems. His literary achievements are—"Mousmni", "Dhusara Bhumika", "Shamukar Swapna", "Omar Khayaam". He translated Gita Govind of Jaydev. He contributed valuable articles to several Oriya magazines like Sahakar, Utkal Sahitya, Mukura.

He was awarded Kendra Sahitya Academy prize in 1975 for his book—Surya O' Andhakar". He also got the Orissa Sahitya Academy Award in 1997.

He is a poet of the people. He died on 21St, February 2000.

12. Dr. Bhabani Charan Roy: Born on the Janmastami of 1921 in Puri district, Jagdalpur in a Zamindar family.

He passed B.A. in 1945 from Ravenshaw College, Cuttack and M.A. in Histoiy from Allahabad University in 1947, He joined in the Govt. College as a lecturer in History and served in G.M College, Sambalpur, Bolangir College, SCS College, Puri and Ravenshaw College, Cuttack

He got his Ph.D. Degree from London University in 1957. He went as the visiting Professor to America in 1961, Harvard University. In 1976, he went to Jagglellorian University of Poland. He has visited many countries in the World: England, France, Switzerland, Greece, Italy, Hungary, Czechoslovakia, U.S.A. Japan, Poland, Thailand and Hong Kong.

Professor Roy left the Utkal University and joined as the Professor of History, P.G Dept of Berhampur University in 1973.

He has written the outstanding and rare books on Orissa History.

1. Foundation of British Rule in Orissa.
2. Maratha Rule in Orissa.
3. Orissa under the Mughols.
4. Buxi Jagabandhu the Path, finder of the Freedom Movement in India.

Besides this, he has written so many Oriya books on the History of Orissa.

After his retirement, he has founded "The Centre for Advanced studies in History and Culture" at Bhubaneswar and is the founder President of it. To keep the spirit for reading History alive, he organises regular seminars under this banner.

Under his able guidance, nearly 15 scholars have got Doctorate Degrees from different Universities.

13. Sitadevi Khadanga (1905-1983): Born at Aska, Ganjam. She is famous for her two literary works "Mandir Prabes" (Drama) and "Posyaputra" (a novel).

14. Sriharsa Misra (1916-1984): was born at Chhamunda near Polsara on 16-6-1917. Editor—Samaj, Prajatantra, and Dainika Asha.

He was a free lence journalist, a dedicated freedom fighter and a great literary genius. He has written very important books "Paschima Diganta" Bipula Cha Prithvii", British Sasanar Chakra Tale Acharya Kripalint"

He died at Berhampur on 8th, April 1984.

15. Surendra Dwevedy: A freedom fighter, wrote many important books "Mo Niza Kahani", "August Biplab", "Mo Jeevan Sangram" (Autobiography) Governor of Arunachal Pradesh

16. Gopal Chhotroy: Born at Purunagada, Jagatsinghpur, Cuttack. A reputed-play writer in Oriya—"Ghatak", "Nasta Urvasi", "Sadhana", "Pheria", "Parakalam", "Bharasa", almost 33 dramabooks.

17. Jayanta Mohapatro: A well-known poet and has earned a great reputation in England and America. His poems are "A Rain of Rites", "The False Start", "Life Signs", "Temples" etc. In 1981, he received the Kendra Sahitya Academy Award. He is a man of Physics but a poet in English Literature.

18. Hrudananda Roy: Born at Gobinda Tota, Cuttack. A Philosopher teacher in life and profession. An eloquent orator on Bhanja literature. His books are "Bhanja Bhagabat", "Naba Jatak", "Vedanta" etc.

19. Debi Prasanna Patnaik: Born at Tigiria, Cuttack—a versatile linguist Director of linguist Study in Mysore. His books are — "Kabilipi", "Sahitya Dikhya", "Odia Bhasa" and "Odia Bhasa O' Bhasa Bigyan".

20. Pandit Gadavarish Misra (1886-1956): Born at Banapur a reputed poet and politician. He had immensely contributed to the Oriya literature by his writing of ballad, drama and fiction — "Alekhika" and his autobiography "Ardha satabdira Odisa O' Tahinre Mo Sthan a". Education Minister in 1943, introduced the Utkal University Bill in June 1943 in the Orissa Assembly.

21. Janaki Ballav Patnaik: Born 1927 at Rameswar, Puri, M.A (Sanskrit) Utkal University, M.A.(Pol.Sc) Bananas Hindu University; Author—Goutam Buddha, translated the book of Bhatru Hari—"Niti Satak"

Chief Minister of Orissa—(1980-1985), (1985-1990) and (1995-1998).

Deputy Minister of Defence in the Central Cabinet from 1973-1975.

Visited U.K. West Germany, UAR, Japan, Vietnam, Thailand, Cambodia, Burma, USSR, France and Italy.

Editor—Daily Prajatantra and Pouruso.

22. Mrs, Nandini Satapathy: Born 1931. She is the daughter of the great Oriya novelist, Padma Bhusan Kalindi Charan Panigarhy, born at Pithapur, Cuttack Town.

She is a good writer of short stories and composed poems. He the Editor of the newspaper in Oriya—"Dharitri"

She was the Chief Minister of Orissa during the Emergency in India-1975-1977. She became the Deputy Minister for Information and Broadcasting in 1970 at the Centre.

She had travelled U.K., U.S.A, France. USSR and held many important positions in Orissa and India.

She translated the Bengali version of "Lajja" of Tashlima—the author of Bangladesh.

23. Raghunath Mohanty: Born on 18th July 1910 at Bada Bhuin in the district of Puri. His father was Natabar Mohanty and Mother was Labanya Devi.

24. Dibakar Parida: Born on 30th November 1911 at Gadabani Killo. His father was Harihar Parida and Mother was Tara Devi.

Both Raghunath Mohanty and Dibakar Parida were very intimate from their childhood. Natabar Mohanty, the father of Raghunath Mohanty, has taught them in the village school. They were intimate and affectionate. They read up to the 10th class and then discontinued. Dibakar Parida worked in the "Samaj" office for sometime. He was a prolific writer who wrote Arteswar Janana, Jatakalankar and Khandayat Darpan in Oriya. He also knew the art of astrology forecasts the destiny of his own that death would come on the ground of patriotism. So he avoided his marriage.

In 1939, the Praja Mandal Movement gained momentum. The people revolted against their traditional Kings in Nilagiri, Talcher, Ranapur, Dhenkanal for their atrocities upon the people. The people of Ranapur also organised the movement against their King, Krishna Chandra and his dewan Jagannath Mohanty and Chandi Mishra, under the dynamic leadership of Raghunath and Dibakar. The visit of P. Sitaramaya to Orissa did not relieve the subjects in 1939. As in other estates, the people of Ranapur also gathered in thousands in front of the royal palace of the king. The King apprehended danger from the people and immediately called Mr. Bazellgate who was staying in the neighbouring feudatory state of Nayagarh. Mr. Bazellgate was the political Agent of the British Govt.

Bazellgate rushed to Ranapur with the contigent of forces. The people erected barricades on the roads by the trunks of the trees. Mr. Bazellgate was stunned to see huge crowd of people. To disperse the crowd he started the blank firing by his revolver but one of the firing hit the satyagrahi, Arjun Rout who was shot dead on the spot. This incident flared up the situation. Raghu and Dibakar inspired the people. The mob was unruly, indisciplined and aggressive who ultimately beat the political Agent by the bamboo sticks and killed Bazellgate on 5th, January 1939. This inhumane assassination of Bazellgate in Orissa created havoc in India and England.

Raghu *and* Dibakar and several other leaders were arrested. Police set fire all the houses of this locality and villages. The King was taken into police custody. More British soldiers rushed to Ranapur. Hare Krishna Mahtab reached Ranapur who advised the people to fly away to distant places otherwise the police would start atrocities.

Their cases were tried. Some of them like Agadhu Baral,Bansidhar Patnaik and Bhagaban Sahu were sentenced for life-long imprisonment. Raghu and Dibakar though they were not directly involved in Killing of Bazellgate, they were given the capital punishment. They were detained in the Ranapur Jail and then they were taken to the Bhagalpur jail in Bihar. Their appeal was dismissed by the sessions Judge, Mr. G.G. Sierre of Gaya.

On the 4 of April 1941 at 4 A.M., Raghunath Mohanty and Dibakar Parida were hanged in the premises of Bhagalpur Jail. Their dead bodies were not handed over to the parents of Raghu and Dibakar. The execution of Raghu and Dibakar was more a criminal activity of the British than the killing of Bazellgate at Ranapur.

25. Kanta kabi Lakhmikant Mahapatro: He was born in 1888 at Talapada in the district of Balasore. He was famous in Oriya literature for his lucid style of lyrics, poems, ballads, Bhajans and dramas. He had started the publication of a famous Oriya monthly—"DAGAR". He was the author of "Kanamamu", "Kaliya Dalan", "Desabandana" etc.

26. Lakhmi Narayan Sahu (1890-1960): He was a great social reformer written many books in Oriya.

27. Bijoy Misra: By Profession, he was an Engineer but has a tremendous weakness for Oriya dramas like "Janani",

"Suryasnan", "Saba Bahak Mane" etc. Besides he is the writer of the dialogues of many Oriya films and Oriya serials.

28. Nitya Nanda Mohapatro (1912): He was born in 1912 at Bhadrak, son of Kantakabi Mahapatro. He has also enriched the Oriya literature by his beautiful writings of poetry, Panchajanya, Jianta Manisa, Bhul Sukhar Sandhane, Patra O' Pratima, Gharadiha. He was awarded the Oriya Sahitya Academy prize in 1987.

29. Prasanna Kumar Das (1919): He was born at Bangriposi, but in due course of time, he migrated to Betanoti of Mayur Bhanj.

He was elected to the Orissa Assembly in 1980 from Betanati Constituency but before hand he was a member of Orissa Assembly in 1952, 1957, 1967, 1971, 1977.

He was the Speaker of Orissa Assembly—an honest and sincere worker of the society.

30. Pandit Raghunath Murmu: He was born at Dandbosh under the post office of Tamal Bandh (Rairangpur P.S.) in the Bamanghati subdivision of Mayur Bhanj.

He was the first man among the Santal Community who invented the "Olchiki" language for the entire Santal population of India. He made alphabets and arranged in a more scientific manner. Many books and dramas like "Bidu Chandan" are written. He was regarded as the "Guru Gomke" of all the Santals.

31. Lakhman Nayak: A native of Koraput district, he displayed unusual courage and sense of nationalism in his activities as a freedom fighter of India. He was a rare specimen of a martyr in India History. He was hanged to death in Berhampur Jail on 29th march, 1943 by the British.

32. Biswanath Das: was born at Polsara in the district of

Ganjam. He discharged his multifarious activities as a freedom fighter, as the Prime Minister (1937-1939) and Chief Minister of Orissa from 1971-1972.

He joined the Non-Co-Operation Movement of Gandhiji in 1921 and gave up practice as an Advocate.

As a legislator, he was elected to the Madras Legislature Assembly. He was a trusted Congress leader. He was appointed as the Governor of Uttar Pradesh in 1966.

33. Rajendra Narayan Singh Beo (1912-1975): As a prince, he took admission into the Mayo College, Ajmer. After his education, he took over the administration of Patna State as a King and devoted his wealth and attention for the development of Patna in the fields of education, employment, health and roads.

He signed the instrument of merger with India in 1948. He was the President of Utkal Sammilani in 1953 and of the Ganatantra *and,* Swatantra Political Party of Orissa.

He was elected several times to Orissa Assembly and Lok Sabha. Ultimately he became the Chief Minister of Orissa in 1969 to 1971. He was a dedicated King, a good orator and an able administrator of Patna and Orissa

34. Akshay Mohanty: Born on October 12, 1936 at Cuttack Akshay Babu after graduation worked as an employee in the Orissa Secretariat, left the job and devoted his entire attention to music.

He learnt the techniques of singing songs, composition and lyrics of the songs. He dominated the world of Oriya music for several years as a successful singer. He directed the music of nearly more than 100 Oriya films. He was a lyricist, a short story writer and wrote a book on foreign travel to U.S.A.

He has made Oriya songs popular in America and many states of India.

35. Dr. Manmath Nath Das: A renowned historian of Orissa. He was the Professor of History in the P.G. Dept. of Utkal University for several years. He ultimately became the Vice Chancellor of University.

He is an author of outstanding creativity. Other than his books on History, he has written many Oriya and English novels. "Keep the story secret" is his wonderful novel.

He is a much-travelled man to England, Russia Germany, Italy and France

Now he is the member of the Rajya Sabha on Congress ticket.

36. Ranganath Misra: He is the son of the famous Godavarish Misra of Banapur, who was a great literary genius, an able education Minister and a successful teacher.

Ranganath Misra became the Judge of Orissa High court and later on the Chief Justice of the High Court. He was promoted and transferred to Supreme Court as the Judge. He was ultimately appointed as the Chief Justice of the Supreme Court.

After his retirement he was appointed as the Chairman of the Human Rights Commission of India.

At present, he is the member of the Rajya Sabha on Congress ticket.

37. Dr. Bansidhar Panda: A renowned Metallurgist of Orissa who dreamt to establish the plant to produce the silicon Metal and Silicon Carbide at Therubali in Koraput dist. Under the banner of IMFA (Indian Metals and Ferro Alloys Ltd.) He did so on 3, May 1967 in technical collaboration with Elken Spigerverket A/S OSLO, Norway and exported the products to USA and other European countries.

38. Baishnab Pani (1882-1956): Born in Cuttack dist. He was the immortal dramatist of Oriya Gitinatya who made Oriya literature and mythological characters popular in Orissa.

39. Artaballav Mohanty (1887-1963): a great scholar in Sanskrit and Oriya literature. He edited the old writing of Madala Panji. He has also given an analytical study to Sarala Mahabharat.

40. Rama Devl (1899-1985): She was the daughter of Gopal Ballav Das, the brother of Madhu Sudan Das. She devoted her life, energy and time to the Freedom Movement of India and became an undisputed woman leader in Orissa.

41. Sarala Devi: a noted social worker freedom fighter and an eminent writer of Oriya literature. Her literary creations are "Bira Ramani", "Rabindra Puja", "Pancha Pradip", "Sati Dharma" etc.

42. Baikoli Mahapatro: Born at Khallikote, a famous astrologer, who wrote very important books on astrology like "Bharatiya Jyotisara Itihas," "Jyotisar Ramavali", Chandi Puran", "Odia Andolanar Itihas" etc.

43. Dr. Prabodh Kumar Misra: He hailed from Baripada—a brilliant student who ultimately retired as a Professor of History, P.O. Dept of Sambalpur University. For sometime, he was also the Vice Chancellor of North Orissa University, Baripada

He is a reputed historian. The outstanding books of Mr. Misra are: "Political History of Orissa", "Madhu Sudan Das and his speeches", "Evolution of Orissa and her culture", "Historians and Historiography in Orissa" etc.

44. Sribatsa Panda (1870-1943): Born at Netanga, a village near Bhanjanagar. He was a great social worker and reformer. He has written "Sarikala Parinaya", "Mamata", "Arogya Vidhan", "Mo Matrubhasa" and "Aryadharma" etc.

45. Sashibhusana Rath (1885-1943): A man of Saroda. He was the most public-spirited man who founded and edited the Asha—a weekly newspaper on 13.4.1913. He was also the member of the Madras Legislative Council. He wrote many books like "Gandhinka Bhagabat Gita", "Swasthya Sapan" etc. He died on 20, March 1943.

46. Paramananda Acharya: He was born in Baripada, who became a great Archeologist of Orissa. He has got to his credit many books on Orissan History, Archaeology and culture.

47. Kabiraj Krishana Chandra Tripathy (1914-): Born at Gunthapada near Aska. He founded the Pharmaceutical Company at Aska and produced Ayurvedic medicines. His products are most popular in Orissa.

He is not only a good dramatist, but under the banner of Chalachitra Pratisthan he produced many Oriya films like "Dasyu Ratnakar" "Mahalakhmi Puja" and "Parinam".

48. Dr. Bhunabeswar Behera: Originally he was an Engineer,but became a reputed author of Oriya literature.

He became the Vice-Chancellor of Sambalpur University in 1972 and was the member of the Union Public Service Commission, New Delhi.

49. Mahapatro Nilamani Sahu: A man of Niali, but a great writer and Novelist of Oriya literature. Many of his noted books are "Abhisapta Gandharva", "Sumitrar Hasa", "Akash Patal", "Tamasi Radha".

50. Acharya Tarini Charan Patro: He was born on June 3, 1901 at Pitola in Ganjam district and died on March 4, 1979.

He was a great scholar in Sanskrit and Oriya Songs, an eminent poet, a dramatist, actor and expert in Violin, Tabla, Pakhauja etc. He wrote many valuable books as ""Orissa Sangita Prakash" "Sangita Tatwo" etc.

51. Nemai Charan Harichandan: Born on July 1, 1901 and died on 20 July 1983.

He was a very emotional singer of Jagannath Bhajan, Chhanda, Champu and kept the Oriya people spell-bound by his melodious voice for a number of years. In 1943, he was awarded the title of "Banikantha" by the HMV Company, the Padmasri by the Govt. of India in 1976, Kendra Sahitya Academy in 1954 and Oriya Sangita Academy Award in 1979.

52 Sarat Pujari: An eminent educationist in Economics. He was the Principal of Laramba College, Sambalpur for a considerable period of time. But he is known to the Orissa Public as a versatile actor in Oriya films since 1960-61. He has acted nearly 40 Oriya films like "Dasyu Ratnakar", "Jeevan Sathi", "Arundhati", "Kla kahar" etc.

53. Dr. Krushna Chandra Panigrahy: Born at Khiching of Mayur Bhanj district, he was an eminent historian and Archeologist of India. He has served as an Archaeologist of the Archeological Survey of India. Then he left the job and joined as the lecturer in History. He was the professor of P.G. Dept. of History, Berhampur University.

As a great scholar in History, he has written some outstanding books on history like "Archeological remains at Bhubaneswar", "History of Orissa", "Legend and History".

He has been awarded Orissa Sahitya Academy for bis book "Mo Samayar Orissa", an autobiography.

54 Sinhari Shyam Sundar Kar: He was born on March 4,1908. He was a popular singer and Guru of Odissi songs,

Janana, Champu, Chhanda and Oriya songs more lively and enchanting. He has been awarded by the Orissa Sangeeta Academy is 1973. He died on 16 March 1975.

55. Basant Kumar Panigrahy: Originally he hails from Manjusa of Andhra Pradesh, but permanently settled at Berhampur Town of Ganjam district.

By profession he is an Advocate, but has associated himself with the Oriya drama and Oriya literature. Above all he is the President of the Utkal Sammelani. He travels far and wide to Andhra, Bihar and West Bengal states to champion the cause of Oriyas who are living there since 1936.

56. Balakrishna Dash: An immortal 'figure in the domain of Oriya songs in Orissa. He was born in 1923.

He has left his indelible marks in the Oriya films as the eminent Music Director in All India Radio, Cuttack, in Gramophone and Television. He was a rare genius in Orissa as a singer, who made Oriya classical songs and "Laghu" songs more popular and emotional. He has achieved unique distinction and laurels from the Orissa Sangeet Natak Academy in 1976, Kendra Sangeet Natak Academy in 1985 and Jayadev prize.

He passed away in 1996.

57. Satya Narayan Rajguru: Born on 19th, August 1903 at Parlakhemundi. Although he did not obtain any University degree, but he excelled many educated experts in reading and interpreting different archives and inscriptions. He published many research articles in different historical journals of India.

In 1950, he joined as a Curator in the Orissa Museum and later on became an Epigraphist He got published many books such as "Inscriptions of Orissa" in 8 volumes, "History of the Gangas", "Inscriptions of the Temple of Puri and

"Origin of Sri Purusottam Jagannath", "The Cultural History of Orissa". The progress of Oriya language and his autobiography named "My struggle of life" (Oriya).

He was awarded many prizes. The Central Sahitya Academy, Orissa Sahitya Academy, Padmasri in 1974 and the Berhampur University conferred on him the honorary D. Lit. in 1975.

He died on 19th August 1997.

58. Nilakantha Das: Born on 5th August 1884 and died in November 1967 at Ramachandrapur near Sakhi Gopal of Puri. After passing matriculation from Puri Zilla School, he took admission in to Ravenshaw College, Cuttack in 1905. He passed M.A. from Calcutta University in 1911. There after he became a teacher in the Banabidyalaya at Sakhigopal.

He was a versatile genius. He was not only a great Oriya poet and an Essayist, but also a great leader with political foresight. He jumped in to the main stream Non-co-operation Movement, Civil-Disobedience Movement and Quit India Movement and was arrested several times. He was also social reformer, who denounced the Caste system and Untouchability.

He guarded the Oriya literature, culture and public interests of Orissa and left the indelible marks in Orissa History.

59. Nrusingh Guru: He was born in 1902 and died in January 1984. Gurupalli in the district of Sambalpur was his birthplace. His education was scanty, but his activities as a freedom fighter and journalist were far-reaching in Orissa.

He was with Gandhiji at Sambalpur in December 1928 for a few moments, but this association left deep impact upon him for which he dressed himself just like Gandhi nothing more than a knee-clad dhoti and a cloth, jacket with bare foot.

As an active revolutionary, he was arrested several times in 1932 and 1942 during the freedom Movement.

He was true to his conscience—honest, sincere and firm in his decisions. As a true nationalist, he served the cause of Indian war of Independence.

He chose journalism as his mission of life. He became the Editor of "Jagaran" in 1937 and a member of Press Trust of India.

60. Gopal Chandra Praharaj (1972-1945): He was born on 27-9-1874 at Siddheswarpur in Cuttack district. Father was Narasingh Choudhury.

After matriculation, he took admission in to the Ravenshaw College, Cuttack and passed B.A in 1898 and LL.B in 1900. He worked as an Assistant of Madhu Sudan Das. As an Advocate, he earned a fabulous wealth but spent the entire earning in preparing the "Purn Chandra Bhasakosh" an extraordinary dictionary in the World. No dictionary in any language has been so prepared. He acquired and collected Lakhs of words in Oriya, Bengali, Hindi and English and spent his valuable time in writing this unprecedented dictionary. The meaning of an Oriya word has been interpreted in four languages of Hindi, Oriya, Bengali and English. This is the speciality of the dictionary. He took 27 years to complete the process of the dictionary.

He asked for financial help from the educationists, Govt. of Orissa Zamidars, Kings and Maharajas. It was Pratap Chadra Bhanja, the Maharaja of Mayur Bhanj, who paid huge amount of money of Rs. 13000/ for publication for which the "Bhasakosh" was dedicated and named as the "Purna Chandra Bhasakosh" in the fond memory of Maharaja Purna Chandra Bhanj the elder brother of Pratap Chandra Bhanj.

The total pages of the 7th volumes of dictionary are 9503. The Oriya race salute Gopal Chandra Praharaj for building such a literary monument as Konark Sun Temple and pay tributes to his good soul.

Besides this, he has written different other Oriya books as "Utkal Kahani", "Nananka Panji", "Bai Mahanty Panji", "Bhagabat Tungire Sandhya", "Nananka Bastani" and "Aam Gharara Halchal" etc.

He died on 16, May 1945.

61. Dr. Prahallad Pradhan (1910-April-17, 1981): He was born at Antapalli near Bargarh in Sambalpur district in August 1910.

He read Sanskrit at Puri and passed Achraya in 1929, then he passed B.A. from Patna University in 1937 and M.A. in Sanskrit in 1939.

He got a Govt. job as a lecturer in Ravenshaw College in 1943. In 1949, he was sent to China by the Govt. of India as the Professor of Sanskrit where he spent two years. During his stay, he also learnt Chinese language. After his return to India, he served as a faculty teacher in Sanskrit in Ravenshaw College, G.M. College, F.M College, Balasore and later on in 1958, he became the Professor of Sanskrit in the P.G. Dept. of Utkal University, Bhubaneswar. He retired in 1970 and produced different Ph.D Scholars.

He was a great linguist who had a commanding knowledge in Sanskrit, Oriya, Hindi, Pali, Bengali and China language—a versatile genius.

He was the first Vice-Chancellor of the Jagannath Sanskrit University of Puri in 1981. He died on 17.4.1981.

62. Dr.Mayadhar Mansingh (1905-1973): Born on 13 November 1905 at Puri district.

He passed matriculation from Khurda High school in

1926 and took admission in Ravenshaw College, Cuttack "Morning shows the day likewise, Mayadhar Babu began to write Oriya poems from the School and College days as a student and established himself as a great Oriya poet.

He passed B.A. (English Hons) from Ravenshaw College and M.A. (English) from Patna University in 1932. He did Ph.D Degree in London. He served in different Colleges as Lecturer and Principal in G.M College, Ravenshaw College, Khallikote College, Berhampur and retired from the service.

As a prolific Oriya poet, he was unchallenged. His poems were "Dhoopa", "Premasarya", "Konark", "Jeevan Chita", "Sindhu and Bindu", "Jema", "Sadhab Jhia" etc.

And as a prose writer, he has written books like "Jeevan Path", "History of Oriya literature", "Sarala Das", "Fakir Mohan", "Paschima Pathika", his autobiography etc.

He was also noted as an outstanding author of "The Saga of the land of Jagannath" History of Oriya literature, Kalidas and Shakespeare, Fakir Mohan Senapati etc.

Dr. Mayhadhar Mansingh had enriched and diversified the Oriya literature by his influential and forceful writing and would remain as an immortal figure in the history of Oriya literature. He died on 11-11-1973.

63. Sri Lalitendu Mansingh (I.A.S.): Lalitendu is the illustrious son of an illustrious father—Dr. Mayadhar Mansingh, a doyen of Oriya literature.

Lalitendu after his M.A. in Political Science from Allahabad University appeared the I.A.S. Exams, in 1964 and topped the list among all. He opted for I.F.S. (Indian Foreign Service) and was appointed in the Dept. of Foreign Affairs, Govt. of India.

He has served as the first I.F.S officer in the United Arab

Emeritus. He served in the Indian Embassy in U.S.A and England in 1999.

In 1999, Atal Behari Bajpayee appointed him as the Secretary of the Foreign Affairs, Govt. of India in New Delhi. Then he was appointed as the High Commissioner in England. Now he is continuing as the Indian Ambassador in the United States

64. Annupurna Maharana (1917): She was the daughter of Gopabandhu Choudhury and Rama Devi. As both the parent are inspired by the Indian nationalism and idealism of Mahatma Gandhi, Annapurna from the childhood developed the same sense of dedication ad social service.

It is astonishing that she was courted arrest in 1932 when she was only 15 years old. She was closely associated with Gandhiji and later on with the Bhoodan Movement of Binoba and Total Revolution of Jaya Prakash Naryan.

She got married with Sri Sarat Maharana of Bari in Cuttack district. Sarat Babu was a highly qualified man who passed M.A. and M.Ed, and was an employee of the British Govt. But later on he left the Job.

Annapurna is a good author who has written many Oriya books on Bhoodan Movement and on the idealism of Gandiji.

She is alive and still devotes her valuable time for the upliftment of the downtrodden people of the society.

65. Dr. Sadasiba Misra: A student of Sakhigopal Banavidyalaya, Dr. Misra was an eminent teacher in Economics. He became the Principal of Ravenshaw College, DPI of Higher Education and Ultimately retired as the Vice-Chancellor of Utkal University.

He was a man with oceanic knowledge in Economics and a proficient orator who could keep the audience spell-bound by his eloquent speeches.

66. Hrushikesh.Panda: Born in Balasore, and a student of Bhadrak College, Mr. Panda Secured the 1st position among all the I.A.S. candidates in India in 1978. He is a strong disciplinarian as an I.A.S officer wherever he is posted. The Govt. of Orissa took a negative attitude towards him during his early phase of service.

67. Dr. Beni Madhab Padhy: A renowned writer on Oriya Literature. His monumental book "DARU DEVATA" reflects the Lord Jagananth and his miracles.

68. Dr. Sudarshan Acharya: He has retired as the Professor of Oriya—P.G. Department—Berhampur Universities. He has written many books on Oriya literatures criticisms and research articles.

69. Dr. Krushna Chandra Jena: Retired as the Professor of P.G. Department of History, Berhampur University. He has obtained many doctorate degress in History and Economics and written a good number of books on history.

LANDMARKS OF ORISSA

UTKAL UNIVERSITY

Along with the creation of Orissa as a separate state, there must have been the provisions for a High Court and a University in the state but no step was taken to establish a University till 1943.

In consequence of the resignation of Mr. Biswanath Das as the Prime Minister of Orissa on 4th, November, 1939, the Governor Mr. Austin Hubback put Orissa under his direct administration till 23rd, November. 1941. Meanwhile Mr. Hubback retired from the post and he was succeeded by Sir William Hawthorne Lewis on 1st, April, 1941. He allowed the King Maharaja Krishna Chandra Gajapati to form the Ministry and he took oath as the Prime Minister of Orissa for the

Second time on 24th, November, 1941. Two other Ministers of his Cabinet were Godavarish Misra as the Education Minister and Moulovi Sobhan Khan as the Law Minister.

The entire draft works of the Provisions of the University were prepared by an eminent educationist of MayurBhanj—Dr. Shyama Chandra Tripathy—the first Oriya Principal of Ravenshaw College in January 1936. And it was during the Assembly Sessions in June-1943 that Godavarish Misra presented the Utkal University Bill and it was accepted by all the members on 30th June, 1943. Godavarish Misra considered this day as the Red-letter day in the history of Orissa Province. Accordingly the new University named as the Utkal University was inaugurated on 27 November, 1943. It was one of the crowning achievements of Maharaja Krishna Chandra Gajapati and Godavarish Misra in Orissa history. This University started functioning in Ravenshaw College-Cuttack.

As there was only one University in the state, the Utkal University has the jurisdiction over the entire state and the feudatory states. And the foundation of new site where the present University is set up was laid down by the then President of India, Dr. Rajendra Prasad on 1-1-1958 and was inaugurated by Dr. S. Radhakiishnan. Dr. Prana Krishna Parija ws the Vice-Chancellor. Utkal University was shifted to Vani Vihar, Bhubaneswar during 1962.

The University started with limited faculties of Arts, Science, Commerce, Medicine, Education and Law only. The University has got the P.G Depts. Of 20 subjects—History, Political Science, Sanskrit, Applied Economics, M.Com, Logic and Philosophy, Psychology, Oriya, Anthropology, Geography, English, Physics, Botany, Zoology, Chemistry, Sociology, Labour Welfare, Geology, Statistics, Mathematics, Economics, In an age of science, MBA, MCA, Information and Technology, and various other subjects are opened.

This University has produced a galaxy of I.A.S., I.P.S.,

I.F.S., O.A.S officers, scientists, professors, Advocates, political leaders and what not. But to day the University has been corrupted to the extreme for which Mr. M.Rajendran the Governor and Chancellor of the University has appointed a senior I.A.S. Officer Mr. Hrushikesh Panda the topper of I.A.S in 1978 of this University as the investigating officer. A shame to the Priemer University

SAMBALPUR UNIVERSITY

Due to the rapid growth of student population and to lessen the burden of the Utkal University, Sambalpur University was established on 1st, January, 1967. It was formerly inaugurated by the President of India™ Dr. Zakir Hussain on 4th, January, 1967.

It has got the jurisdiction over the districts of Sambalpur, Sundargarh, Balangir, Kalahandi, Athamalik Subdivision of Dhenkanal and Boudha Subdivision of Boudh—Kandhamal district.

The University has got seven faculties—Arts, Science, Commerce, Engineering, Medicine, Law and Education. This University has got two famous Engineering Colleges of Burla and Regional Engineering College of Rourkela. The University has got the P.G. Depts. of History, Political Science, Oriya, Mathematics, English, Chemistry, Physics, Biological Science and many other modern subjects of Electronics (Computers), Information and Technology, Internet etc.

The University authority instituted the Gangadhar Meher Award of Rs. 25000/- to be given to the Poets of outstanding contributions to Indian literature.

BERHAMPUR UNIVERSITY

Until 1966, December, there was no University in South Orissa. All the Colleges were tagged with the Utkal University the only University in the State. Due to the growing number of

Colleges in different parts of Orissa and the overburden of works on the Utkal University the establishment of two more Universities was felt urgent by the people and the Govt. of Orissa. So two Universities at Sambalpur and Berhampur were set up—Sambalpur University on 1st, January, 1967 and Berhampur University on 2nd January, 1967 under the Orissa University

The location of the University is really beautiful. The Gopalpur-on-sea is only 5 kms away from the Berhampur University. The Campus of the University is named after Upendra Bhanj—the doyen of Oriya "Riti Kavya". Initially the teaching of 'different subjects started at Komapalli near the present Jagannath Temple (Goilundi). Later on Administrative building of the University was inaugurated by the President of India, Mr. V.V. Giri on 4th, March, 1972. V.V. Giri was also a student of Khallikote College, Berhampur and the son of the Soil.

All the Colleges of Ganjam, Koraput and Phulbani are affiliated to this University. There are as many as 18 Departments in the University-History, Economics, Political Science, English, Oriya, Physics, Chemistry, Botany, Zoology, Mathematics, Commerce, Marine Science, IRPM, MBA, Journalism etc.

The University has produced a record number of research scholars (Ph.D.) in the state.

JAGANNATH SANSKRIT UNIVERSITY

As Puri is the abode of Lord Jagannath, Balabhadra and Subhadra and famous in history for its historic Car Festival, the Govt. of Orissa thought it inevitable to set up the Sanskrit University in Puri. Puri has attracted thousand of tourists, Pilgrims, and devotees. It has also attracted the great social and religious reformers like Shankaracharya, Guru Nanak, Sri Chaitanya, Jesus Christ (if true), Salabeg, Ramanuja,

Ramananda, Kabir, Aurobindo, Sivananda and Chidananda through the Centuries. It is not only the temple of the Lord Universe—but is the spiritual abode of the countless enlightened Sadhus. It is the place of Salvation of life for men.

As Puri is the Centre of the Sanskrit learning and one of the "Four Dhams" in India, the Sanskrit University was founded on 7.7.1981 to revive the Sanskrit culture in Orissa. Sanskrit is never a dead language, we have made it defunct and dead for our commercial and selfish attitude. Sanskrit was the language of the Gods and the ancient people, Kings of India.

It was the regime of Mr. Janaki Ballav Patnaik who was voted to power in 1980 and formed the Ministry under the Congress banner. He became the Chief Minister. Mr. Janaki Ballav Patnaik is a versatile genius who has got deep knowledge in Politics, Oriya literature and Sanskrit. He took the keen initiative and interests to establish a Sanskrit University and it was set up on 7.7.1981 as the Jagannath Sanskrit University. The then Governor of Orissa Mr. C.M.Poonacha inaugurated this University and he became the first Chancellor of it.

The Vice-chancellors who adorned the Chair of this University were Professor Dr. Prahallad Pradhan the first Vice-Chancellor who was an eminent professor of Sanskrit in the P.G. Dept. of Utkal University in 1968, Prof. Trilochan Misra, Satyabrata Shastri, Dr. Sradhakar Supakar, Major Bata Krishna Mohanty, Profesor Dinabandhu Misra, Dr. Gouranga Charan Nayak, Dr. Tribikram Pati, Padmanav Samal, Dr. Krashna Chandra Acharya, Suresh Chandra Mahapatro, Bramhananda Rout, Dr. Chandra Sekhar Sadangi and Dr. Alekh Chandra Sadangi.

With the approval of the University Grants Commission, this University imparts education in Literature, Veda,

Grammar, Philosophy, Dharmashastra, Tantra, Nyaya and Astrology. The teaching is being done by a group of nearly 22 Acharyas or Lecturers. The other employees of the University are nearly 50.

The member of Colleges in Orissa where Sanskrit is taught is 165 and all the students appear examinations under this University. Out of 165 colleges, 135 Colleges are affiliated by the Govt. of Orissa.

Scholars from France, America, Australia, England, Japan, Canada, Switzerland, Andhra Pradesh, Gujrat, West Bengal, Madhya Pradesh, Rajastan, come to visit this University on different occasions and at different times.

NORTH ORISSA UNIVERSITY-BARIPADA

Mayur Bhanj was one of the largest feudatory states of Orissa, situated in the extreme northern part of Orissa state. Mayur Bhanj played a prominent role in making Orissa a separate Province from Bihar. Maharaja Sri Rama Chandra Bhanj (1870-1912) of Mayur Bhanj was the most brilliant and benevolent who has got the widest range of vision. His regime (1892-1912) was the golden age in the entire annals of Mayur Bhanj. He presided over the inaugural meeting of the Utkal Sammilani which was held on 30th December 1903 at Cuttack. Madhu Sudan Das was the Secretary. Mayur Bhanj has got a galaxy of enlightened rulers-Maharaja Krishna Ch. Bhanj, Sri Ram Chandra Bhanj (1870-1912), Sri Purna Chandra Bhanj (1920-1928) and Sri Pratap Chandra Bhanj (1928-1948).

The people of a particular area claim their identity in every sphere, which brings clashes and conflicts with the people of other areas and with the Govt. When the proposal for establishing a University at Balasore was looming large, the people of Mayur Bhanj also claimed a University Simultaneously, the movements, rallies and demonstrations started at Baripada and Balasore, The Janaki Ballav Govt.

failed to materialize the demands for separate University at Baripada and Balasore. He awfully lingered the matters. But unfortunately he had to step down from the position and powers on the issue of the Anjana Mishra Case in January, 1999.

Sri Giridhar Gomango, who was the sitting member of Parliament was sent as the Chief Minister of Orissa. In the Govt. of Orissa notification dated the 3rd, July, 1999, the North Orissa University was founded. Sri Giridhar Gomango, the Chief Minister of Orissa inaugurated this University on 11th July, 1999 at Takatpur, Baripada.

This University covers an area of entire Mayur Bhanj and Keonjhar districts having nearly more than 50 Colleges.

FAKIR MOMAN UNIVERSITY-BALASORE

Balasore as a town figured more prominently during the early occupation of the British in the year 1633 when they founded a factory in Balasore town. Shah Jahan was the Emperor of Delhi in 1633. The local Governor allowed the British to trade at Balasore.

In 1803, the British Govt. took possession of Balasore from the Marathas. The British also did not develop Balasore into a flourishing town except establishing a municipality on 1st April, 1877. And the Bengal, Nagpur Railway line penetrated into the heart of the Balasore district and was opened to traffic in October, 1899.

Since the establishment of Utkal University on 27th November, 1943, the Balasore District was tagged with it and remained under this University up to 10th July, 1999. Under the Chief Ministership of Sri Giridhar Gomango in Orissa, he passed a Bill in state legislature to establish two Universities—one at Baripada and other at Balasore Town. And in the Govt. of Orissa Notificaton dated the 3rd July, 1999, a new University known as the Fakir Mohan University was founded at Balasore. This new University was inaugurated by the Chief Minister, Dr Giridhar Gomango on the 11th July, 1999 at Vyasa Vihar. This University has justified its name by giving it as "Fakir Mohan University". Fakir Mohan Senapati did not only belong to Balasore, but he was the Savour of the language and culture of the entire Oriya race. The defender of the Oriya language against the onslaughts of the Bengalis.

This University has got the jurisdiction of the entire Balasore and Bhadrak districts having nearly 59 Colleges.

ORISSA UNIVERSITY OF AGRICULTURE *AND* TECHNOLOGY

This College of Agriculture was established in 1954. By an Act in the Orissa Assembly in 1961 the University was established and it began to function during the academic session of 1962-63.

There are three dimensional faculties of Agriculture—Veterinary Science, Animal Husbandary and Agricultural Engineering and Technology. The OUAT is the only College of this nature and no affiliated Colleges in Orissa. Faculty of Agriculture, Engineering and Technology was started in 1966. And the College of Veterinary Science and Animal Husbandry was started on 24 August, 1963.

These Colleges produce a huge number of successful candidates every year-but the Govt. of Orissa does not utilize their valuable services for developmental works of agriculture. All Agricultural Graduates Post-Graduates students are now unemployed.

SRI RAMA CHANDRA BHANJ MEDICAL COLLEGE, CUTTACK

It is said that the Present Medical College at Cuttack was functioning as a Pilgrim's Dispensary during the Marathas.

In the year —1875, it was proposed by Dr. Steward the Civil Surgeon of Cuttack to convert the Dispensary into a Medical school. The establishment of the earliest dispensary at Cuttack was dateless. By the strenuous efforts of Dr. Steward and the Orissa Commissioner, Mr. T.E. Ravenshaw, the Proposal for the establishment of a Medical school at Cuttack received the willing consent and support from Sir Richard Temple—the then Lt. Governor of Bengal Presidency.

Initially, the candidates were trained as the Licentiate Medical Practioners-(L.M.P) and during 1916-17, the Orissa Medical School was affiliated to the Bihar and Orissa Medical Board which awarded the L.M.P. Diplomas.

It was during the glorious period (24-11-1941 to 29-6-1944) of Maharaja Krishna Chandra Gajapati as the Prime Minister of Orissa that some milestones were erected on the road of educational progress in Orissa. The first was the establishment of the Utkal University on 27-11 = 1943 and the second was the conversion of the Orissa Medical school of Cuttack into a Medical College in 1944. The third outstanding achievement was the establishment of the Central Rice Research Institute at Bidyadharpur-Cuttack.

Major A.T. Anderson—the Principal of the Medical school who was also the Civil Surgeon of Cuttack proposed to raise the standard of Medical School into a Medical College, Lt. Col. Mr. A.N. Chopra who was the Director of Health and I.G. of Orissa Prisons gladly accepted the suggestion. And the Medical College at Cuttack was born in 1944. The Maharaja of Mayur Bhanj, Sri Pratap Chandra Bhanj and Vikram Dev of Jeypore Koraput generously contributed donations to the Medical College. Mr. Anderson went back to his Parent Post and Major R.T Hicks became the first Acting Principal of the New Medical College of Cuttack.

In 1951, the Medical College was renamed as the Sri Ram

Chandra Bhanj Medical College in recognition of the huge amount of donations by the Maharaja of Mayur Bhanja.

The Medical College was affiliated to Utkal University in 1944 and the first batch of MBBS students came out in 1948. It was also recognized by the Indian Medical Council in 1952. During the long course of its history, the SCB Medical College has got subjects of all branches in Surgery, Medicine, Orthopaedics, Opthalmogy, Pharmacology, Obstrs and Gynoaecology, Anasthesialogy, Bio-Chemistry, ENT, Radiology etc. Due to the advanced Medical studies, many new Depts. are opened.

During the tenure of Srimati Basanta Manjari Devi—the Rajamata of Ranapur as the Health Minister of Orissa Govt. the Medical College fast expanded and got also abundant financial assistance to improve.

The SCB Medical College is one of the pioneer institutions in India, 13th position in India.

VEER SURENDRA SAI MEDICAL COLLEGE

The Medical College at Burla in the district of Sambalpur is named after the great freedom fighter of the mid-19th century of Orissa-Surendra Sai (Feb. 1808 to 1884). The Govt. of Orissa founded this Medical College in 1959 to produce the medical officers. As there was only one medical college at Cuttack and the number of medical graduates produced every year was not sufficient to provide medical facilities to the people of the nook and corner of Orissa. So the Govt. of Orissa decided to establish the second Medical College in the state.

Initially the College started in 1959 only with 41 students and 9 girls. Gradually the students are multiplied. The College imparts lessons on Medicine, Surgery, Physiology, Anatomy, Pharmacology, Forensic, Toxicology, Pathology, Obstetrics and Gynaecology, Opthalomogy, E.N.T., SPM, Radiology and

Anasthesiology. With the advancement of medical science, different Depts. were opened. Even P.G. Depts. were also opened.

The students live in hostels. The Govt. of Orissa introduced the entrance exams for the admission into the 1st year of MBBS course in which rampart corruption is being practised as a result of which the best students of the University are not selected. Except the few top students in the merit list, the rest seats are given to the highest bidders.

ENGINEERING COLLEGE OF BURLA

For the diffusion of the engineering knowledge, the Utkal University established an Engineering College at Burla in June, 1959. This Engineering College functioned under the Utkal University till 31st Dec, 1966 and produced the Engineers for the construction works of the Public buildings, bridges, stadium etc. but after the establishment of Sambalpur University, the College functioned under it on 1st, January, 1967.

This College produced engineers in Civil, Electrical and Mechanical branches. It was a four year integrated Course—but later on it was enhanced to 5 years in 1962-63.

MAHARAJA KRISHNA CHANDRA GAJAPATI MEDICAL COLLEGE, BERHAMPUR

This is the third Medical College in Orissa which was founded in 1962 by the Govt. of Orissa. It was named after the Maharaja of Paralakhemundi who ruled the Parlakhemundi state since 1913. He was the immortal son of the soil and was the dedicated and devoted leader of the Oriya race. Because of his tireless efforts that Ganjam, Koraput and Phulbani were annexed with Orissa on 1st April, 1936.

He was the Prime Minister of Orissa and during his

tenure of administration that the Utkal University was founded on 27th November, 1943.

This Medical College offers teaching in Surgery, Medicine, Phramacology, Bio-Chemistry, Pathology, Obstrics and Gynaecology, Radiology, Padeatrics, Optholomogy, E.N.T, S.P.M, Anasthesiology and many others.

In 1962, the College was started with only 75 students for M.B.B.S. Course. But in 1971-72, Post-graduate classes were started in major medical courses. The College worked under Utkal University till 1st January, 1967 and then it was affiliated to Berhampur University on 2nd January, 1967.

There are 6 MBBS and P.G. students Hostels in the vast campus of the Medical College at Berharmpur. Most of the Medical Professors, Readers live in the Govt. Quarters of the Campus.

New P.G. Depts. are also started. Indoor and outdoor patients are being treated.

The All India Medical Council also recognized this College.

There is also a Staff Nursing College within the campus where hundreds of girls read. There is a multi-storeyed building of having sufficient accommodation for the nursing students.

RAVENSHAW COLLEGE-CUTTACK

Ravenshaw College is the pioneer in the arena of Higher Education in Orissa. It has been radiating knowledge and wisdom to the hundreds and thousands of students since 1868.

The Calcutta University was founded in 1858. More-Bengali students of Orissa and Calcutta appeared the University Examinations there. As there was no College in

Orissa for higher education, Mr. H.L. Harrison, Inspector of Schools in 1864 wrote a letter to the Govt. of Bengal to upgrade the Cuttack Zilla School into a College. Mr. W.W. Hunter—the Inspector of Schools who succeeded Mr. Harrison also equally represented the case for higher education during his tenure in 1866 to Bengal Govt.

The DPI agreed to the proposal after a survey of the Cuttack Zilla School. It was sent to the Lt. Governor Sir Cecil Beadon of Bengal for final approval. In February 1867, the proposal was accepted and money was also recommended. In January 1868, the Cuttack Zilla School was converted into a Collegiate School. The College started functioning up to 1875 in a school. In 1876, Mr. T.E. Ravenshaw separated the College classes into a separate building. The Govt. of Bengal fixed up the ratio of finance—fifty per cent would be paid by the Govt. of Bengal and the fifty per cent would be collected by the Orissa Commissioner. The proposal was also accepted by Mr. Ravenshaw. It was a herculean task for Mr. Ravenshaw to collect such a huge amount of money. But there were some persons who acted as the Saviour—God in adversity. Such God-like man was Sri Krishna Chandra Bhanj the Maharaja of Mayur Bhanj Estate who donated Rs. 27000/- in 1877 and suggested to name the new College as Ravenshaw College in commemoration of Ravenshaw's valuable services to Orissa during his tenure as the Commissioner of Orissa (1865-1877).

In 1921, this new gigantic building was built and all classes were held here since then. In 1906, the total number of students enrolled in the College was only 188 which is now more than 8000 students. Many more Colleges are gradually established in Cuttack town. So naturally, the student population of Ravenshaw College is reduced.

His Majesty, Purna Chandra Bhanj (1920-1928), Maharaja of Mayur Bhanj and the son of Sri Rama Chandra Bhanj paid

Rs. 1 lakh to Ravenshaw College in 1925 to set up a Power-Plant to supply electricity to the College and Staff Quarters.

It is a co-education College where boys and girls read together. It imparts lessons in all subjects of Science, Humanities and Commerce from the Intermediate to Post-graduate classes. M.Phil. and IGNOU classes are also held. Morning and day classes are regularly held. More than 300 eminent Lecturers, Readers and Professors are engaged in teaching and research works. Ph.D., D.Litt. and D.Sc. degree holders are the teachers who guide the scholars for their academic distinction.

Till 1935, there was always an Englishman as the Principal of the Ravenshaw College but in January, 1936, Dr. Shyama Chandra Tripathy, an eminent and enlightened Oriya educationist of Mayur Bhanj became the first Oriya Principal of the College.

Ravenshaw College is the greatest alma mater of the great personalities of Orissa history. The College has produced a galaxy of gems and jewels of Orissa who have glorified the pages of Orissa history by their splendid and spectacular achievements. They are: Gopabandhu Das, Harihar Das, Nilakantha Das, Godavarish Misra, Nilamani Senapati, Biswanath Das, Harekrishna Mahatab, Shyam Chandra Tripathy, Pranakrishna Parija, Nityananda Kanuango, Biju Patnaik and many others difficult to mention.

Ravenshaw College is the lighthouse of the thousands of sea-farer students through ages. Let us salute the lengthening shadow of the great man—Ravenshaw who has built it.

KHALIKOTE COLLEGE, BERHAMPUR

This College was the second oldest College in Orissa next to Ravenshaw College of Cuttack. This College was founded in 1878 as native intermediate College at Berhampur town under the Madras University. But in 1893, the Raja of Khallikote, Sri Harihar Mardaraja donated an amount of Rs.1 Lakh to this College on the condition that the College would be named after his Khallikote Zamindari. And accordingly, the College was named as the Khallikote College of Berhampur since that year.

Orissa became a separate state on 1st April, 1936 and Ganjam, Koraput and Phulbani were amalgamated with Orissa. But still as there was no University in Orissa, the Khallikote College was functioning under Madas University. The Utkal University was established on 27th, November, 1943 and the College was affiliated to Utkal University. In the next phase, the Khallikote College was again brought under the Berhampur University on 2nd January 1967.

The B.A. classes were held in 1944 and B.Sc. and B.Com. were from 1945 and 1954 respectively. In 1963, the P.G. classes in Economics and Mathematics started. And gradually the other P.G. classes in History, Anthropology, English, Botany, Zoology, Geology, Physics, Chemistry and Commerce were started.

In 1989, the Khallikote College became an autonomous College. The syllabus, the exams and the evaluation works are being done by the College independently but the students obtain their degrees from the Berhampur University.

LINGARAJ TEMPLE, BHUBANESWAR

The Lingaraj Temple was the first and the greatest in the architectural structure of Orissan art which was built during the period from 1030 A.D. to 1065 A.D. It was during the reign of the Somavamsi or Keshari Kings in Orissa that Jayati Keshari and Lalateedu Keshari had built. It is said that Jayati Keshari II had originally begun the construction of such a gigantic foundation of the great Lingaraj Temple and finished by Lalatendu Keshari.

The height of the Temple was nearly one hundred and eighty feet and was so dominating in structure that people of nearly 10 miles radius were able to see the temple structure in those days. It occupies in a great compound of smaller temples of different gods and goddesses measuring five hundred and twenty feet length and four hundred and sixty five feet breadth in Bhubaneswar (Dr. K.C.Panigrahy, History of Orissa, p. 400).

Like the other architectural temple designs, the Lingaraj temple has got also three frontal projections as Jagamohan, Natamandir and Bhogamandap. The iconographic pictures are the great Ganesh and Katikeya Statues set upon the wall by the polished and magnified black stone. Besides the pictures of processions of soldiers, war elephants, horses with spears and drums are engraved. Different trees, Naga snakes, betalas, birds are also hewn in the stone on the walls of the temple.

As the Lingaraj is the Saiva Pitha, hundreds and thousands of pilgrims throughout the year throng round the temple. Abhada meals and Prasada are supplied to them on payment of a minor charge. But during the Sivaratri in March every year, the pilgrims are multiplied into lakhs. Thousands of 'deepa' are lit and the devotees spend the entire night sleepless.

JAGANNATH TEMPLE AT PURI

The origin of all the Gods 'and Goddesses on earth is undated and mixed with legends. The mystery of the deity is still not deciphered. The undiluted belief of a man to a particular God or Goddess depends upon the celestial blessings of beneficiary he has achieved. Either the man has got rid of from a dreadful disaster or got completely cured from a dreadful disease. Likewise through the centuries of generations, in the corridor of time, man has been attributing some mysterious super natural activities to a God or Goddess. Thereby the belief to the deities is fortified, strengthened and immortalized.

We believe in the legendary tale of Sabar Biswavasu worshipping the Lord NeelaMadhav in the unknown cave of a mountain. Raja Indradyumna deputed Bidyapati in search of God-NeelaMadhav.

Bidyapati took the long way in searching of the God and reached the vicinity of the cottage of Viswavasu. Viswavasu had a daughter named Lalita. Lalita was playing the game of hide or seek by temporarily blinding her eyes and trying to catch her companions. In course of game, Bidyapati suddenly appeared in the spot and Lalita by mistake caught Vidyapati. She opened her eyes and was surprised to see a young man *in* front of her. There was a custom in the Savara Community that if the daughter touches any unknown man he would marry the girl. Having been bound by the prevailing custom of marriage, Vidyapati stayed at the cottage of Viswavasu. Viswavasu also accepted this marriage with reluctance.

During his stay, Vidyapati one day asked Lalita where does your father go at the dawn. Lalita in reply told he is going to worship the God—Neela Madhav but she does not know the exact geographical location of the place.

After repeated requests, Viswavasu agreed to take Vidyapati to the place of NeelaMadhav on the condition that his eyes would be bound by a piece of cloth and he can not see the path. Lalita after hearing this gave a bag of mustard seeds to Vidyapati and advised her to sow the seeds all along the way to Neelamadhav. Vidyapati did so. And during the rainy season, the seedling started and the mustard flowers blossomed. Taking the help of these mustard flowers, Vidyapati one day secretly went and located the NeelaMadhav in the cave. Vidyapati could not tolerate to see the glittering image of the God-NeelaMadhav. He returned to Indradyumna and explained the entire episode of locating the God. In a dream, Indradyumna saw that the God NeelaMadhav would appear in the form of DaruBrahma in the seashore. A few days after,

Indradyumna brought this huge trunk of tree to the temple. An old carpenter— Biswakarma was employed to make the statues. He shut the doors and advised Indradyumna not to open before 21 days. The King heard the knocking sounds of chisel on the trunk incessantly for 14 days. After that the sound was not audible. The Queen Gundicha insisted on the King to open the door. The old carpenter might have died. The King did not abide. But the Queen forced the King. The King reluctantly opened the doors of the temple. They all were flabbergasted to see that there was no carpenter and the statues were incomplete without any palm or hands. The King, Queen and the Councilors repented. The God was consecrated. The incident of installation of NeelaMadhav was undated.

But the present temple of Lord Jagannath at Puri was built during 1137 to 1147 AD by the renowned King, Chodaganga of Ganga dynasty. Chodaganga ruled Orissa from 1078 to 1147 AD. The height of the temple was 215 feet. It is said that Chodaganga Deva had built the main temple and the Jogamohan was built by Anangavima Dev III.

According to the norms of the Ganga architecture, the Jagannath temple has three other frontal structures as Jogamohan, Natamandir and Bhogamandap. In the main sanctum or Ratna-Singhasana are seated Jagannath, Balabhadra and Subhadra. Around the main Vimana of Lord Jagannath within the boundary, there are Lakhmi, Surya, Vimala, Durga, Narayan and various other gods and goddesses.

On the main entrance of Puri temple there is a "Aruna Stambha" (Sun-Pillar) which was brought from the Sun temple of Konark installed there. Thereafter the "Baisi Pahacha" the significance of Pahacha is that they will help you to overcome the passions difficulties of life.

So many festivals are observed in connection with the Lord Jagannath throughout the year, but the most attractive is the Ratha festival during the month of June or July every year. Rathayatra has been being celebrated from the 15th century AD during the reign of Kapilendra Dev.

KONARK—THE EPITOME OF ORIYA SCULPTURE

Having been mesmerized by the enchanting and elegant beauty of Konark iconography. Sir John Marshal—One time the Director of Indian Archaeology comments: "There is no monument of Hinduism—I think, that is at once so stupendous and so perfectly proportioned and none which leaves so deep an impression on the memory".

This spectacular celestial Sun Temple does not only invokes admiration from the countless art critics and anxious spectators, but it leaves an indelible mark in the Cheek of eternity.

In the scintillating golden beach of the Kalinga Sagar (Bay of Bengal) at Chandrabhaga, this temple occupies a superb position in the entire annals of Orissan history and glorifies the land and people of Orissa. The idea of building such a monumental specimen of temple stuck to the mind of the magnanimous Ganga King Narasingh who placed the architectural artistic style and excellence of Orissa on the culminating point of perfection.

This greatest and grandest Sun temple of Konark was built by Narasingh Deva I of the Ganga dynasty during the period 1245-1260. Narasingh Deva ruled Orissa from 1238 to 1264 A.D. According to the Orissa style—the King was named as the Langula Narasingh. It took 16 years to complete and 1200 masons had worked day and night. Nearly 40 crores of rupees have been spent for the construction of this gigantic Sun temple.

The height of the main temple (it was presumed) was 230 feet and it was completely destroyed. The main temple of

Jagmohan was constructed into a Rath or Chariot of the Sun God. There were twenty-four huge wheels and well-set seven horses drew the Chariot.

The main temple of Sanctum and Jagmohan were demolished either by unusual flood, cyclone or earthquake. The total destruction of the Sun temple by the renegade, Kalapahar in 1568 AD has not been accepted because much of the temple was collapsed due to the structural design or due to the sandy foundation or saline wind.

Through the corridor of time facing its vicissitudes and ravages, only the basework of Natamandir survives till to day. The figures of Naga and Naguni, the erratic pictures of the couple, drums, horses, elephants, the human and celestial forms are exquisitely engraved in the walls. It creates wonder in the mind of the spectators. Sun Konark is the pride of Oriya culture.

HIRAKUD DAM

The proposal of Hirakud Dam project was unanimously adopted by the Orissa Legislative Assembly during the tenure of Harekrishna Mahtab as Chief Minister of Orissa on 28th August 1947. Proposals were drafted by Engineer Ajodhya Nath Khosla—the Chairman of Central Waterways of Irrigation of India. The original idea of constructing the Dam on this site was given by the Bharat Ratna, Sir Bisweswariya. The foundation of the Project was laid by the then Prime Minister of India Jawaharlal Nehru on 12 April, 1948 and it was also inaugurated by Nehru after completion on 13th January 1957 and by a tribal woman.

Hirakud Dam is situated at a distance of 6 miles from Sambalpur town. It has a reservoir of 6.6 million acre-feet with irrigation potential for 6.72 lakh acres of land.

It is a multi-purpose project and is the largest dam in the world. Stretching 3 miles across the riverbank, the main dam is a composite dam of earth, masonary and concrete. Nearly 13 miles long earth dyke has been built on either side to close the gap in the surrounding Hills. The dam has the maximum height of 200 feet at the Power house site and the earth dam is 190 feet high at the deep Channel station. It generates 270 Mw electricity. It irrigated 38,300 acres of land in Khariff and 2570000 acres of land in Rabi.

The Dam has got the capacity of 6.6 million acre-feet of water. It also controls the flood during the rainy season.

The town has got the population of 8593 in 1961. It has a Police station, a high school and Notified Area Council.

It has got India Aluminium Company and Industry here.

Annexure

ORISSA AT A GLANCE-1991

1. Total Area—155707 sq. kms. (1991)
2. Gross Cropped area - (1990-91) - 96422 (in thousand hectares, including fruits)
3. Irrigation potential created (Kharif and Rabi) in thousand hectares 29.35.
4. Total Area Under Forests - (in thousand hectares) 1991-92-5482 hectares.
5. Net Area Sown - (in one thousand hectares) - 1990-91-63 37
6. Total population - (1991- census) - 31659736, Male - 16064146 Female - 15595590
7. Density of population - (per sq. kms) - 203 (1991)
8. Total population (urban area) (1991) - 4234983, Male - 2269191 Female - 1965792
9. Total Rural population - 27424753, Male - 13794955, 13692798.
10. Total scheduled caste population - 5129332 and Percentage to total population (1991) - 16% .
11. Total Scheduled Tribe population - 7032352 and percentage to total population (1991)- 22%.
12. Total number of villages in Orissa in 1991—50972.
13. Number of districts - 30.
14. Number of subdivisions -58.
15. Number of Tahasils- 147.
16. Number of Gram Panchayats - 5263.
17. Number of Blocks - 314.

18. Number of Municipalities -31.
19. Number of NAC- 70.
20. Total literacy - (1991) - 12945917.

GOVERNORS OF ORISSA

01-04-1936 to 31-03-1941	Sir John Austin Hubback
11-08-1938 to 07-12-1938	G.T. Bag as Hubback was on leave
01-04. 1941 to 31-03-1946	Sir Hawthorne Lewis
01.04. 1946 to 14-08-1947	Sir Chandulal Trivedi
15-08-1947 to 20-06-1948	Dr. Kailash Nath Katju
21-06-1948 to 06-06-1952	M. Asaf Ali
07-05-1951 to 17-05-1951	V D.Menon as Asaf Ali was on leave
07-06-1952 to 09-02-1954	Sayed Fazal Ali
10-02-1954 to 11.09. 1956	P.S. Kumar Swami Raja
12-09-1956 to 31.07.1957	Bhimsen Sachar
31-7-1957 to 15-9-1962	Y.N. Suktankar
16-9-1962 to 31-1-1968	Ajodhyanath Khosla
5-8-1966-1 1-9-1966	Khalil Ahmed as Khosla was on leave
31-l-1968 to 20-9-1971	Dr. S.S. Ansari
21-9-1971 to 30-6-1972	Sardar Jogendra Singh as Ansari was leave
1-7-1972 to 8-11-1972	Sri Gati Krishna Misra
8-11-1972 to 20-8-1974	Banappa Dasappa Jatti

21-8-1974 to 25-10-1974	Sri Gati Krishna Misra
25-10-1974 to 17-4-1976	Akbar Ali
17-4-1976 to 7-2-1977	Siva Narayan Shankar
7-2-1977 to 22-9-1977	H.S. Brar
23-9-1977 to 30-4-1980	Bhagabat Dayal Sharma
30-4-1980 to 30-9-1980	C.M. Poonacha
1-10-1980 to 3-11-1980	S.K. Roy as Poonacha was on leave
4-1l-1980 to 24-6-1982	C.M. Poonacha
25-6-1982 to 31-8-1982	Ranganth Misra as Poonacha was on leave
l-9-1982 to 17-8-1983	C.M. Poonacha
17-8-1983 to 28-2-1989	Dr. Biswambarnath Pandey
1-3-1989 to 6-2-1990	Prof. Nurul Hussain
7-2-1990 to 31-1-1993	Yangyanadatta Sharma
1-2-1993 to 31-5-1993	Prof.Nurul Hussain
l-6-1993 to 17-6-1995	Satya Narayan Reddy
18-6-1995 to 1997	Gopal Ramunujam
1997 to 1999	Sri C. Ranganathan
1997 to 1999	Sri C. Ranganathan.
10-1999	M.M. Rajendran (continuing)

PRIME MINISTERS AND CHIEF MINESTERS OF ORISSA IN THE CORRIDOR OF TIME

	Period of Time	*Name of the Person*
1.	1-4-1936 to 31-3-1937	Ruled by Hubback
2.	1-4-1937 to 19-7-1937	Maharaja Krishna Chandra Gajapati (P.M.)
3.	19-7-1937 to 4-11-1939	Biswanath Das (P.M.)
4.	4-11-1939 to 24-11-1941	Governor's Rule
5.	24-11-1941 to 29-6-1944	Maharaja Krishna Chandra Gajapati (P.M.)
6.	29-6-1944 To 22-4-1946	Governor's Rule
7.	23-4-1946 to 11-5-1950	Hare Krishna Mahtab (PM)
8.	12-5-1950 to 18-10-1956	Nabakrisina Choudhury
10.	18-10-1956 to 24-2-1961	H.K Mahtab (First Coalition with RN Singhdeo
11.	25-2-1961 to 23-6-1961	President Rule
12.	23-6-1961 to 2-10-1963	Biju Patnaik
13.	3-10-1963 to 21-2-1965	Biren Mitra
14.	21-2-1965 to 8-3-1967	Sadasiva Tripathy
15.	8-3-1967 to 9-1-1971	Rajendra Narayan Singhdeo
16.	10-1-1971 to 3-4-1971	President Rule
17.	3-4-1971 to 13-6-1972	Biswanath Das
18.	14-6-1972 to 3-3-1973	Smt. Nandini Satpathy
19.	3-3-1973 to 6-3-1974	President Rule
20.	6-3-1974 to 16-12-1976	Smt. Nandini Satpathy

21.	29-12-1976 to 30-4-1977	Binayak Acharya
22.	30-4-1977 to 25-6-1977	President Rule
23.	26-6-1977 to 17-2-1980	Nilamani Routray
24.	17-2-1980 to 9-6-1980	President Rule
25.	9-6-1980 to 9-3-1985	Janaki Ballav Patnaik
26.	10-3-1985 to 7-12-1989	J.B. Patnaik
27.	7-12-1989 to 4-3-1990	Hemananda Biswal
28.	5-3-1990 to 15-3-1995	Biju Patnaik
29.	15-3-1995 to 16-2-1999	Janaki Ballav Patnaik
30.	17-2-1999 to 5-12-1999	Giridhar Gamango
31.	6-12-1999 to 4-3-2000	Hemananda Biswal
32.	5-3-2000-Continuing	Naveen Patnaik

GOVT OF ORISSA COUNCIL OF MINISTERS—1984

Dr. B.N. Pandey-Governor

1. Sri Janaki Ballav Patnaik - Chief Minister, General Administration Information and Public Relations, Planning, Rural Development
2. Upendra Dixit - Revenue and -Transport
3. Basudev Mohapatro - Agriculture and Co-Operatives
4. Gangadhar Mohapatro - Education and Youth Services.
5. Dayanidhi Nayak - Commerce
6. Raghunath Patnaik - Finance and Law
7. Rama Chandra Ulaka - Harijan and Tribal welfare

MINISTER OF STATE

1. Harihar Karan—Forest, Fisheries and
2. Jugal Kishore Patnaik—Labour, Employment, Tourism, Sports, Culture
3. Bhajaman Behera—Community Development and Rural Reconstruction
4. Niranjan Patnaik—Irrigation
5. Basant Kumar Biswal—Works, Housing and Urban Development,
6. Habibulla Khan—Excise
7. Kishore Chandra Patel—Industries, Food and Civil Supplies

DEPUTY MINISTERS

1. Smt. Saraswati Hembram—Community Development, Rural Reconstruction

SPEAKER

Somanath Rath

DEPUTY SEPAKER

Humanshu Sekhar Pady

GOVT. CHIEF WHIP

Gurupada Nanda

CHIEF JUSTICE -ORISSA HIGH COURT

Dambarudhar Pathak

CHIEF SECRETARY

Sri Gyan Chand, I.A.S.

ORISSA MINISTRY IN 1998

Cabinet Ministers **Prot folio**

1. J.B. Patnaik — CM - General Adm. Home, Energy, Steel, Mines, Games, Youth Services, Agriculture, Co-operatives, Women *and* Children welfare
2. Basant Biswal D.C.M. — Finance, Water Resources, Parliamentry Affairs.
3. Hemananda Biswal, Panchayati Raj, Housing - general complaints Pension.
4. Kanhu Charan Lenka — Transport
5. Jagannath Patnaik — Revenue
6. Ramachandra Ulaka — Developments
7. Niranjan Patnaik — Industry, Weaving and Cottage Industry
8. Prasanna Kr. Das — Environments, Science and Technologies
9. Bhagabat Pr. Mohanty — Planning and Coordination - Higher Education
10. Bhupinder Singh — Tourism and Culture
11. Shaikh Matlub Ali — Rural Development
12. Raghunath Patnaik — Law.
13. Habibuliah Khan — Food *and* Consumers Development
14. Harihar Swain — Construction
15. K.C. Patel — Forest *and* General Industry
16. Durga Shankar Patnaik — Labour and Appointment

RASTRA MINISTERS

1. Amarnath Pradhan — Urban Development (Ind.)
2. Jagannath Rout — Health and Family (Ind.)
3. Netrananda Mallick — Public Relations and Information (Ind.)

4. Prakash Ch. Debata — Fisheries and Animal husbandary (Ind.)
5. N.C. Narayan Das — Panchayati Raj
6. Smt. Bijoy Laxmi Sahu — Women and Children welfare
7. Rabindra Kr. Sethi — Co-operatives
8. Suresh Kr. Routroy — Octroi (Ind.)
9. Nagarjun Pradhan — Commerce (Ind.)
10. Jayadev Jena — School and Mass Education (Ind.)
11. Gadadhar Majhi — Sports and Youth welfare
12. Haladhar Karjee — Planning and Co-ordination
13. Ramakanta Misra — Agriculture.

ELECTIONS IN ORISSA ASSEMBLY

1.	1st Election	— January 1937
2.	2nd Election	— April 1946
3.	3rd Election	— 20-12-1951-15-1-1952
4.	4th Election	— 24-2-1957-14-3-1957
5.	Mid term Election	— June 1961
6.	5th Election	— 21-2-1967
7.	6th Election	— March 3-1971
8.	Mid term Election	— 22-24 February, 1974
9.	Mid term Election	— 10-6-1977
10.	7th Election	— 31-5-1980
11.	8th Election	— March 1985
12.	9th Election	— February 1990
13.	10th Election	— February 1995
14.	11th Election	— February 2000

IMPORTANT RIVERS

1. Budhabalanga — Mayur Bhanja and Balasore (175 kms.)
2. Salandi — Balasore and Bhadrak (144 kms)

3. Khadakei — Mayur Bhanj
4. Suvamarekha — Balasore (433 kms)
5. Bramhani — Cuttack, Sundargarh (799 kms), Keonjhar, Dhenkanal
6. Baitarani — Kendhujhar,Cuttack (365Kms)
7. Mahanadi — Cuttack, Sambalpur (857 kms)
8. Rusikulya — Ganjam, Aska (165 Kms)
9. Bahuda — Ganjam, Gajapati (73 fas)
10. Vansadhara — Koraput, Kalahandi (230 kms)
11. Nagavali — Koraput (210 kms)
12. Indravati — Kalahandi (530 tanas)
13. Kolab — Koraput
14. Mahendratanaya — Gajapati district

Springs - Nirmaljhar, Taptapam (Ganjam)
Jatni — Puri
Atri — Cutack

Water falls - Bareipani, Similipal Mayur Bhanj
Badaghara
Duduma — Koraput
Khandadhar - Sundargarh

Lakes - Chilika (Puri) 780 x 71 kmas.
Ansupa - Banki (Cuttack) 3 x 1.5 Sq. kms.

Bibliography

Reference Books and Magazines

1. *Feudatory States of Orissa -1982,* Ramsey-Cobden, Firma KLM Private Ltd.
2. *Feudatory States of Orissa, 1988,* Vol. I and II, Dr. Jagannath Patnaik, Vohra Publisher and Distributor, Allahabad.
3. *Netaji Subhas Chandra Bose,* 2001, Dr. Sisir Kr. Bose, NBT, New Delhi.
4. *Story of INA,* S.A. Ayer, 1997, NBT, New Delhi.
5. *Local Self-Govt. in British Orissa,* Dr. K. C.Rout (1869-1935) 1988, Daya Publishing House, New Delhi.
6. *History of Oriya Literature,* 1962 (English) Dr. Mayadhar Mansingh, Sahitya Akademi, New Delhi.
7. *Orissa State Gazetteers* by Govt. of Orissa, Vol. 1 (1990), Vol -II (1991) and Vol-III (1992), Bhubaneswar.
8. *Orissa Rajanitira Gupata Katha* (Oriya) June-2001, Basanta Das, Anusandhan Publications-A/17 Bhoumanagar Unit IV, BBSR-1.
9. *Reference Orissa,* 1999, Ed. A.N. Tiwari and A. P. Padhi and others Printed at Raj Press, New Delhi-110012.
10. *History of Oriya Literature (Oriya),* 1998 By Dr. Bauri Bandhu Kar, Friends Publisher, Cuttack-2.
11. *History of Orissa* (1986)- Dr.K.C. Panigrahi, Cuttack-753003.

12. *Odisara Swadhinata Sangram* (Oriya) Dr. J.N. Patnaik, January-2001 Vidyapuri, Cuttack.

13. *NALCO Diary*, 2001.

14. *History of Orissa,* Dr. N.K. Sahu, Dr. P.K. Misra and Dr. J. Sahu.

15. *Orissa in Turmoil,* Sunit Gosh (1979).

16. *History of Orissa,* R.D. Banerjee.

17. *District Gazetteers of Orissa,* By Govt. of Orissa: 1) Puri-(1977); 2) Cuttack-(1996); 3) Ganjam(1995) 4) Sambalpur (1971); 5) Bolangir (1968); 6) Kendujhar (1986); 7) Dhenkanal (1972); 8) Mayur Bhanj (1967); 9) Sundargarh(1975); 10) Baleswar (1992); 11) Kalahandi (1980); 12) Boudh Kandhamal (1983); 13) Koraput.

18. *Oriya Sahityara Kramavikash* (Oriya), Surendra Mohanty.

20. *Orissa (Oriya),* Sri Basant Das (Editor), June 2000, Anusandhan Publications, BBSR.

21. *Foundation of British Rule in Orissa,* Dr. B.C. Ray.

22. *An Advanced History of Orissa,* Dr. K.M. Patro.

23. *Satabdi Puruso Krishna Chandra Gajapati* By Padmalochan Sahu Berhampur, Ganjam.

24. *Maratha Administration in Orissa,* Dr. B.C. Ray.

25. *IMFA Literature.*

26. *Jhankar* - (Oriya) Sept and Oct., 1979, Dr. K.C. Rout.

27. *SCB Medical College Magazine,* Cuttack 1969.

28. *Govt. of Orissa Diary* - 1984 and 1998.

29. *Utkal Prasanga (Oriya),* Govt. of Orissa Publications, BBSR.

30, Special Issue on the death of Dr. H.K. Mahtab, *Prajatantra* , January 1987.

31. Special Issue on the death of Biju Patnaik, April 1997 *Anupam Bharat*, Industrial Estate, Berhampur.

32. *Anupam Bharat* (Oriya Daily), Berhampur.

33. Weekly *"Samaj", "Samay" and "Prajatantra"*

34. *"Samaj"* (Oriya daily), Gopabandhu Bhavan, Cuttack.

35. *Annual Issue of Fakir Mohan University*, Balasore - 2001.

Index

❑❑❑

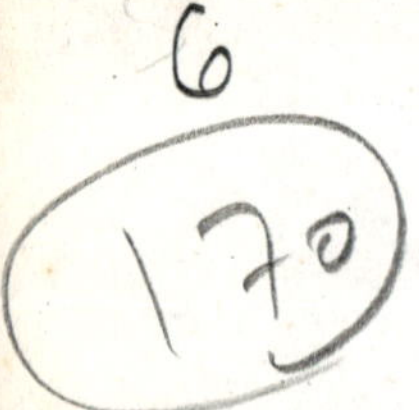